D0968477

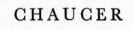

CHAUCER

CAROLE IN THE ROSE GARDEN

MS Harley 4425 f. 14ᵛ British Museum: *Le Roman de la Rose*

RAYMOND PRESTON

# CHAUCER

GREENWOOD PRESS, PUBLISHERS
NEW YORK

1952

TO THE MEMORY OF

# KENNETH SCOTT DIMMER

1920–1944

KILLED IN ACTION IN WEST EUROPE

LANDOR, on declining to contribute to a volume called *The Poems of Geoffrey Chaucer Modernized*—

'I like even his *language*.'


'And I saw that things are good, which yet are corrupted; neither if they were supremely good, nor unless they were good, could they be corrupted: for if supremely good, they were incorruptible; if not good at all, they had nothing to corrupt.'

ST. AUGUSTINE: *Confessions VII xii*

# ACKNOWLEDGEMENTS

My greatest debt is to the *Complete Works of Geoffrey Chaucer*, edited by F. N. Robinson (Harvard, 1933), and to Walter Skeat's Oxford edition, in which I first read Chaucer. Other obligations, I hope, will be recorded in the following pages. Bibliographies are already available for those who require them, and I have therefore not attempted to list all the books on the subject, but rather to draw attention to neglected chapters. In choosing editions of text or translation outside Chaucer I am not perfect or even consistent, and claim only to have quoted the best that I could obtain. This has sometimes meant accepting slightly modernized publications of fourteenth-century prose which was not accessible to me in manuscript. And I am grateful to unnamed editors of standard volumes. Authoritative texts of Walter Hilton's *Scale of Perfection* and of the *Revelations* of Julian of Norwich are still lacking; but Professor John Lawlor, who helped me also by encouragement and discussion at a moment of inertia, kindly supplied for my last chapter transcriptions of the British Museum MS Sloane 2499. Dr. C. S. Lewis and Professor Eugène Vinaver and Mr. Nevill Coghill generously gave time to report on my typescript, and for various assistance in preparing the book for the press I must thank Mr. K. H. M. Curtis, Dr. Erna Dannemann, Mr. A. I. Doyle, Dr. D. J. Enright, Mr. H. W. Heckstall-Smith, Fr. Martin Jarrett-Kerr, C.R., and Dr. Audrey le Lièvre.

# CONTENTS

# ILLUSTRATIONS

# PREFACE

IN THIS BOOK I SHALL TRY TO INTERPRET THE WORK OF CHAUCER to the reader of today. I do not propose to record historical memories, or to write about medieval astrology, or the private life of Dan Geoffrey. Yet one must have *some* historical curiosity in order to follow Chaucer at all. It is a question of making a way between on the one hand pure archæology and on the other pure ignorance. A twentieth-century reader cannot, except in fantasy, become a fourteenth-century reader; but he may read a fourteenth-century book. And it is the task of the critic who would encourage him, to see that the twentieth-century reading is a development, not a contradiction, of the fourteenth-century reading, and to see whether it may be a development that has some significance for the twentieth century. This does not mean bringing Chaucer up to date; it means meeting him more than half way. It is an effort to understand (without expectation of getting back to the middle ages) something which seems at first a little remote, and is at the same time too valuable to lose.

Laughter assists understanding, and we can still laugh at Chaucer; it is not yet necessary to explain all the jokes and thus to explain them away. I shall have a few things to say about the Wife of Bath, but I do not feel called to demonstrate why she was funny. She still is. Let us reflect, too, that Chaucer's is a 'poetry of crisis', and laugh at that. It is a poetry outside crisis, written in an age of ecclesiastical schism, political disunity, protracted war, internal revolution, and calamitous plague. And if demoralization had proceeded less far than one might expect from these disasters, that is perhaps because it was difficult to destroy or corrupt an order of the mind. Chaucer, though not the most profound, is the sanest of our English poets.

And he is the greatest English writer of narrative verse, and a European; as Shakespeare is the greatest poetic dramatist of Europe, but an Englishman. It might therefore be good for England, and for Europe as well, if those of us who are prepared to attend to Shakespeare would all read Chaucer. His language is older, but is also very much more lucid, than Shakespeare's. And even if it is true that Chaucer is sometimes most difficult when he looks easiest, how many persons who visit the local cinema, or even the Stratford Memorial Theatre, know the meaning of the most familiar quotations from *Hamlet*? Or does *the smylere with the knyf under the cloke* sound so obscure beside a soliloquy of Macbeth, that we must say 'the smiler with the knife under the cloak'? Here I am contradicting G. K. Chesterton; but this is not the only point about Chaucer on which that excellent man was ill-informed. He can take that criticism, and more. For as a result of G. K. Chesterton's book the task of introducing Chaucer to readers who are not assumed to be capable of exposure to the poetry itself will be superfluous for some time to come. This I intend certainly not as an expression of scorn, but as a fact for which anyone setting out to write on Chaucer must be heartily thankful. And in my opinion Chesterton has produced the two or three most mature paragraphs of appreciation of Chaucer of the first half of this century. Mr. Pound, unfortunately, has not written paragraphs; yet anyone who can correct his inaccuracies, and look between his lines, should be indebted, as I am, to the refreshing phrases of *ABC of Reading*.

R. P.

St. Crispin's Day 1950

# DIALOGUE

*Chauciers,* faiseurs de chausses ou culottiers.

LACOMBE : *Dictionnaire du vieux langage françois*

*This preliminary conversation is not presented as hors d'œuvre. It is simply the most convenient way of exhibiting certain extremities of criticism, of allowing the eccentric to expose itself and point to the centre. The initials refer to no living persons, and discovery of the names they stand for is mere curiosity.*

# WESTMINSTER: ST. CRISPIN'S DAY: 1950

## MAKER. A. C-L. SIR FRANK.

*C-L.* Your partridges are fat, Sir Frank.
*A.* Temptation to gluttony.
*Maker.* Ruin to a frail digestion.
*Sir Frank.* Please take wine, all of you. And you, Maker, draw up your chair. We are to drink to Geoffrey Chaucer, and I have tried to give you a dinner worthy of the occasion. In spite of that, C-L is already poring over the volumes of *Five Hundred Years of Chaucer Criticism and Allusion*, which I purchased to decorate the side-table.
*C-L (reading)* '. . . the behaviour of a child rather than of a man': Thoreau, 1843.
*A.* '. . . childlike and loving genius': Leigh Hunt, 1835.
*C-L.* '. . . childlike . . . his tears and smiles': Elizabeth Barrett Browning, 1842.
*A.* 'You almost seem to hear the hot tears falling, and the simple, choking words sobbed out': Lowell's 'Philip', 1845.
*Maker.* 'Tender to tearfulness—childlike, and manly, and motherly': Meredith, 1851.
*C-L.* 'His worst characters have some little saving grace of good nature': 1846.
*A.* '. . . wide tolerance': 1874.
*C-L.* '. . . large-hearted toleration': 1894.
*Sir Frank.* Gentlemen. This sport is unseemly. Cease laughing at our great Victorians, and tell me what the twentieth century has to say.
*Maker.* It is not here.
*C-L.* But the Tudors are much more interesting.
*Sir Frank.* Let me see. I do not suppose I shall look at this tome again. What's this? 'Our vyces to clense . . . kindling our hartes, wyth the fiery beames of moral vertue'—Hawes, 1506. 'He never failes to hit every marke he levels at'—Beaumont, 1597. . . . 'Master of Satyr . . . severely lashing an ignorant and corrupt clergy'—Dart, 1721. 'The HOGARTH of his Age'—Bancks, 1738. 'Ses satyres si cruelles . . .' Yart, 1753—
*C-L.* I can see you raising scholarship, Sir Frank, to your judgement of vintage.
*Sir Frank.* Well, what are we to think of the old sinner now?
*A.* I BEG YOUR PARDON!
*C-L.* I think you have shocked a devout Chaucerian, Sir Frank.

3

While he is recovering, I may say that the evidence for or against our poet's personal morality is of the slightest. He is said, on not unreliable authority, to have beaten a Franciscan Friar in Fleet Street, but—

*A.* Gossip; repetition of second-hand report. As for the poetry, has Sir Frank read a piece called *An ABC*, that neglected address to the Blessed Virgin? Let me draw his attention to the letter V. Has he read the *Tale of the Man of Law* or the *Clerk's Tale* or the *Parson's Tale* or the translation of Boethius? We have had two heresies of critical opinion: Chaucer the Lashing Satirist, Geoffrey the Tender and Tolerant. Now if Sir Frank will have Geoffrey the Frivolous, I am for Chaucer the Improving. C-L. will give dates.

*C-L.* 1670–1760: Geoffrey Chaucer thought unworthy, except by a few, of serious reading: the idea perhaps survived in Matthew Arnold. 1540–1690: Geoffrey Chaucer considered a reformer and moralist: and again by Ruskin.

*Sir Frank.* I think I only meant that he was not a saint, but an ordinary respectable married man.

*A.* Then Sir Frank has certainly not read the *Second Nun's Tale*.

*Maker.* Perhaps he read it as the Second Nun's.

*A.* I should like to leave aside the squire, husband, diplomat, controller of custom, J.P., M.P., Clerk of the King's Works and surveyor of sewers, about whom we have information and no knowledge. Turn to the poet. I will put a question to you, Sir Frank. Who wrote that 'in our days there is but covetousness, treason and envy, poison, manslaughter and murder in many kinds'?

*Sir Frank.* Certainly not Chaucer. I guess Langland.

*C-L.* Before A crows in triumph, I must point out that the answer is neither. The question is a trap, a misleading paraphrase of a snippet of *The Former Age*. You can prove anything you like by taking lines out of their context and modernizing them.

*A.* The question remains. I suspect that Sir Frank imagines Chaucer as a comfortable vintner's son who might retire to keep an inn. I wish to persuade him that Chaucer was one of the most distinguished minds of Europe, a mind comparable on the one hand with Plato and on the other with Mozart. He had the intelligence to adapt Socratic irony to his own purpose. He could see courtly love as a refined game and at the same time let the churls speak out; he had to the last degree tact, *politesse*, and poise. He knew how to move his feet for a kick or a dance, which can both be done with style; and having the wit to realize he was not adapted for elevation, made comedy out of a flight with an Eagle.

*C-L.* You are shifting your ground a little, A.

*Sir Frank.* I am relieved. I was beginning to smell a Loller in the wind.

*Maker.* You have my sympathy, Sir Frank. And before A fires another salvo in the air, I should like to push him to a conclusion. Chaucer was really LE GRAND INDIFFÉRENT.

*A, Sir Frank.* WHAT?

*Maker.* Who was it who said that for us he is the father of the 'humanities'? He had the indifference (as well as the voracious appetite) of the professional scholar: but what is now all in the day's work was for Chaucer all out of it, and therefore more amusing. And the medieval poet was expected to produce a few novels, an encyclopedia, and if possible a little of the Higher Reviewing as well, while he was writing poetry: to practise his art on anything he could lay hands on or get sight of.

*C-L.* I think we have jumped from *politesse* to the bear-pit.

*A.* To Acheron, I think. But after all, Sir Frank would put Chaucer lower down.

*Maker.* I shall not 'put' him anywhere—though no doubt he would be content with Virgil just across the ferry. And I am content to leave the divine judgement of Dan Geoffrey out of the question.

*C-L.* Perhaps we should leave human judgement out of it too, and establish a few facts.

*Maker.* One needs judgement of some sort to do that. And may I continue? On the occasions when Chaucer finished a work, it was complete—that is to say, it was satisfying, it had spiritual zest, was *spirituel*, and yet was not an incitement to action or zeal or indignation. It was possible to enjoy the poetry without expecting an accession to fortitude.

*C-L.* Sir Frank has said very little—the two of you have not given him a chance.

*Maker.* But do we not know Sir Frank's point of view? You have adopted it yourself, C-L, in your lectures.

*C-L.* My dear Maker, you are much too acid to appreciate our poet aright.

*Maker.* *Your* poet, perhaps. *My* poet might have said with Socrates, 'I neither know nor think that I know'—and have said it, in particular, of the attempt to understand human beings on a pilgrimage or a tour. And that has nothing to do with geniality. It is intelligence advanced to wisdom. *O Socrates!*

*C-L.* Thus was Chaucer addressed by Eustache Deschamps; and Émile Legouis wrote in 1910 that Chaucer represents a progress of the intelligence marked on the one hand by a weakening of passion, and on the other by the pleasures of observation. It is difficult even for Maker to add anything new to Chaucer criticism.

*A.* I agree with you, Maker, and with Legouis. But where is the *indifference*?

*Maker.* It is not quite so easy to know what we mean when we speak of Chaucer: there are three of the name. One of the three observed, let us say, pardoners on the fourteenth-century highway. A second retained the observations to sift and combine. A third composed a portrait in the *Prologue*. The first probably experienced revulsion, the last was not concerned with emotion at all—was completely indifferent to it.

*Sir Frank.* Split personality. Rubbish.

*C-L.* I think that Maker is referring, in his own odd way, to the

5

mystery of creation—three persons, one poet: which A would call an ingenious blasphemy of a kind to turn the 'religion' of courtly love inside out.

*Maker.* I can assure Sir Frank that producing a masterpiece requires a process of multiplication rather than division.

*Sir Frank.* I am glad to hear it. After division your moderns would have nothing left. So now our honoured ghost is Dan Geoffrey, Chaucer, and G.C. The port must be better than I thought. I plump for Dan Geoffrey. The others (forgive me) are figments of your dusty imagination.

*C-L.* Sir Frank reminds me of a question I had meant to ask you, Maker. Do you think that our moderns can learn from Chaucer? The late Professor Walter Raleigh, at the beginning of this century, said that no generation since Chaucer's is better fitted to appreciate him than the present: I wonder whether that was true, and if so, whether it is still.

*Maker.* I think it unprofitable to debate your second question; but I am gratified, C-L, that you can show an interest in our poetry. There are two heresies of Chaucer criticism which we have not mentioned, one of which I shall call the Documentary: the view developed in the early nineteenth century, and still with us, that Chaucer is to be valued because he left a record of the surface of life and manners at a particular time and place. We do not regard Shakespeare because he tells us what it was customary to drink in an Elizabethan tavern, and how much you were expected to pay for a capon. And C-L gives me assurance that he has reasons of another kind for admiring Chaucer. I don't know what our young poets are capable of learning; we must wait and see. But the question whether Chaucer matters to a poet writing today is a question of importance. I think myself that for English poets of our time Chaucer is the best English master, and Shakespeare very nearly the worst. I think also that Chaucer is the only second to Shakespeare, among English poets. And we can learn most from him in matters of technique: how, in particular, to combine high complexity with the utmost lucidity of statement. We cannot of course attempt a return to his diction, to Middle English— and that brings me to the second heresy we have not yet named. It is that Chaucer, in a literal sense, remodelled the language, that he introduced a whole new vocabulary into English speech. I believe this notion was exploded long ago—

*C-L.* By Thomas Warton in 1778, if not by Tyrwhitt in 1775.

*Maker.* —but is also current. Chaucer the vintner's son, like Boccaccio the moneylender's, had to be careful to respect the conventions, including the spoken language, in order to gain an aristocratic audience; and it was not for him to suggest a large extension of the number of English words to be employed by his betters. He must be 'original', if that was his aim, in profounder ways. And in fact he is that remarkable rarity, a major technical innovator in a particular language who is also a great master. He turned away from the bard's memory, from the monotony of alliterative verse, from the singer's melodic line, to a new metric subtlety. That is why he was concerned for the correctness of his 'copy'. He introduced an altogether new *movement* of language, and probably his combination of French verse-patterns and an English beat was too difficult for his successors to imitate, certainly with his ease of variation of rhythm.

*C-L (reciting with emphasis)*

Whán that Ápril with his shóures sóote

—that is the English beat, in the opening of the *Canterbury Tales*. The French pattern, in the couplet that Chaucer presumably imported, is a verse of ten syllables, which in English becomes generally a line of five stresses. It appears that Chaucer expected a kind of 'double audition'—I think, Maker, that you would find Mr. C. S. Lewis's paper on 'The Fifteenth-Century Heroic Line', *Essays and Studies*, Volume XXIV, Oxford, 1939, pp. 28–41, coge it.

*Maker.* No doubt. I was about to suggest that the nearest in our century to a *grant translateur* (which is not the same as a *correct* translator —or, on the other hand, as a *great poet*) is Ezra Pound. And just as Pound's technical weakness is in the forming of a long poem, so on another plane was Chaucer's in comparison with Dante. You might say that in the end Chaucer learnt how to turn even this limitation to account, by the dramatic device of *interruption* in the *Canterbury Tales* . . . yet the series itself remains incomplete. The *grant translateur* must be able to re-create, or to adapt, poetry of another language in fresh poetry of his own; and Chaucer was a *grant translateur* of super-lative genius. He is also to be recommended to our authors as a supreme ironist, because irony is a way of getting a great deal under one's lines without complicating the surface. The essential is not extreme acuity, but delicate adjustment within a very wide range. What do you think, C-L?

*C-L.* I distinguish at least four types of irony in Chaucer.

*Sir Frank.* Are we to hear them all?

*Maker.* C-L is determined.

*C-L.* I suspect that Maker sees a number of innuendoes that Chaucer never meant; but let it amuse him. Since you have green fingers, Sir Frank, I shall talk gardening. If you speak of the beauty of the daisies on your neighbour's lawn, you are speaking ironically. And if you go on to remark about the untidiness of your own very healthy cabbage-patch, that is irony again—although the intended meaning is not precisely the opposite of the literal. Statements of this kind, not necessarily so naïve, would commonly be called ironical statements. If your potatoes are suddenly blighted, you have suffered a third kind of irony, which the Oxford Dictionary defines as 'a contradictory outcome of events as if in mockery of the promise and fitness of things'. You would illustrate a fourth kind—the Socratic— if, when you were sounding your neighbour on the subject of X's fertilizer and he praised it, you then asked him to account for the fact that a small dose of it nearly killed your tomatoes. The *range* of Chaucer's irony can be gauged from a single type, and a single word.

Consider the different uses of the term *worthy* in the Canterbury *Prologue*.

*A.* I think (if I may return to this conversation) that C-L's definition will be useful to bear in mind when we come to decide how far the term 'irony' is applicable at all to Chaucer. I have not yet accepted Maker's *Grand Indifférent*. Is Chaucer's *politesse* and urbanity and serenity purely a by-product, then, of composition?

*Maker.* Yes; but that does not mean that it is an accident. It is rather the priceless pearl produced by the action of his milieu upon him. Let me speak again in terms of 'Dan Geoffrey', 'Chaucer', and 'G.C.' It is not an attitude which G.C. deliberately set out to express, or the habitual manner of Dan Geoffrey at the office; but something in Chaucer which G.C. could not help expressing.

*A.* There is another way of looking at it. When in Chaucer's poetry English surpassed the best French literature of the time, a truer grace of civilization was achieved than our consciously civilized eighteenth century could manage. And the ultimate reason for the difference—you will not agree, Maker—is *theological*. There is no need to pick up Dante to reveal the shortcomings of a later age: we have more than enough in Chaucer to make the roots of the eighteenth century look dry, and the dry flowers taste bitter.

*C-L.* All this brings to my mind a serious objection to Maker's advocacy of Chaucer, and rejection of Shakespeare, as a model for our modern poets. Chaucer's audience appears to Professor Bronson, and myself, to have been more civilized than Shakespeare's ; and so we shall probably have to wait for the civilization before we can expect a brood of young Chaucers.

*Maker.* I do not anticipate the arrival of one, let alone a brood. I meant that of the great masters in English, Chaucer is the safest to follow and Shakespeare the most dangerous. And as long as the real Chaucer is alive in some minds today, we must not cease to hope that the civilization will come—I mean a civilization with comparable manners and mind. I agree that art of the refinement and range of Chaucer's is impossible except in certain circumstances, especially a strong tradition of satire. Chaucer had no need to bother with straightforward hard hitting; the preachers could do it, and Jean de Meun had done it before him.

*A.* I should like to go back to the eighteenth century, which thought itself superior both to Shakespeare and to Chaucer. What do you say, Maker, to Pope's narrow personal malice beside Chaucer's truth? (Notice I do not say 'indulgence'.) Put Sporus beside the Summoner: that is a fair comparison. Can we apply the one term 'satire' to things so different in kind?

*Maker.* When you speak of 'narrow personal malice', A, you are allowing your own old-fashioned and quite unfounded personal dislike of Alexander Pope the man to confuse the issue. If you compare the two verse-portraits without prejudice, I think you will discover that Pope (the poet) is not mud-slinging, but *expressing a negative emotion*. Chaucer on the other hand is observing in his mind's eye an object

8

which is grotesque yet still recognizably human. Chaucer writes about the man's appearance, about what he ate, what he drank, what he said, what he did. Pope combines images and manipulates verse to offer, not Lord Hervey, not 'Sporus', not a man; but a balance of sensation and of gesture, a poised thrust. I admit the superiority of Chaucer, but I do not therefore blacken Pope. And I will admit your doubts about calling Chaucer 'satirical'. At the same time you must remember that he could let others do the dirty work: in Kent, the preachers—in *Canterbury Tales*, his fellow-pilgrims.

*A.* And in the *Canterbury Tales* he cancels any animus of his own by playing off one pilgrim against another. We agree, then, that Chaucer is not satirical in the sense that Dryden and Pope were satirical, and yet there is no question of timidity or genial tolerance of vice. Some of the Reeve's lines about the parson of the town remind me of Dryden; but they tell as much about the choleric Reeve who says them as about his ecclesiastical butt.

*C-L.* I now incline to believe that Chaucer was not content to let sleeping dogs lie, and that his irony was not really conciliatory or 'diplomatic' or 'tolerant' as the nineteenth century thought. And, Maker, I beg of you not to refer to my lectures. The time has come to read the earlier critics in the light of modern scholarship.

*A.* The time has come to read Chaucer. And I suggest that Chaucer is very rarely, in the ordinary sense, ironical at all. And by the 'ordinary sense' I mean C-L's garden daisies.

*Maker.* If by an ironical statement we mean the exact opposite of the literal, I agree that Chaucer is rarely ironic. And yet he probably exhibits a finer range of irony than any other English author. You cannot read him in an algebraic fashion, by changing the sign of the bottom line and adding. What Chaucer has delicately balanced, the modern reader clumsily interprets by tipping the scales on the one side or the other. You were right, A, to warn us about the term 'satire'. I think of the artistry in placing a simple description so that it ceases to be descriptive and becomes expressive:

And al was conscience and tendre herte,

follows a remark about the Prioress's feelings for trapped mice and daintily fed dogs. I recall his different uses of the famous line from Guido Guinicelli, that *pitee renneth soone in gentil herte*. For the *gentil herte* is the Duke Theseus persuaded to reconsider a hasty death-sentence, and Alceste showing mercy to a poet who has offended the god of love, and Canacee recognizing the deserted falcon as a Good Woman in distress, and old January's pretty wife deciding to commit adultery. You have exactly the same words in different degrees or *nuances* of irony.

*Sir Frank.* You have all become very involved. I always thought there was no mystery in Chaucer, that it was all daylight, with no nonsense, and the King and Queen of fayerye turning up in January's back garden were pantomime, only very . . . *French*. But now—I

9

open the *Legend of Good Women* to find love-sick Dido tossing and turning when she ought to be asleep:

> As doon these lovers, as I have herd sayd

—and I have to stop to think how Maker's super-subtlety would account for that.

*C-L.* There is no compulsion, Sir Frank.

*Sir Frank.* But how much did Chaucer really know about women?

*Maker.* As much as any man will ever find out.

*A.* Surely he had enough mind to understand the *olde daunce* without taking part in it, enough wit to know that the spectator sees more of the game? And as the 'African' said in the *Parliament of Birds*, many a man that can't stand a pull likes to be in at the wrestling. Turn to the last page of your *Canterbury Tales*, and you see him confessing *many a lecherous lay*.

*Maker.* But Sir Frank has hit on a delightful line, and I do not think it so easily explained. Chaucer gives nothing away on a subject which he was under no obligation to advertise: that is, his private life. We smile because, however far he was outside the game, he had not been bred in strict enclosure from an early age. But the line also shows an impulse behind his *Troilus and Criseyde*, which would not have been written if there had been no tension in his mind between the rejection of vanity and the attraction of courtly love: a Chaucerian tension, and therefore carried easily, yet the sort of balance of forces that could still be found in a building or motet of the time. Chaucer knew the right answers from the start, as well as A ; the fact remains that the satisfaction of human desire is not so simple; which he knew also. *Troilus and Criseyde*, in fact, might have weaned many a courtly lover when a sermon would have sent him back to the breast. The case of Jerome *versus* Jovinian is to the point, as you are certainly aware, A. Perhaps you will address the company on the subject.

*A.* It is enough to say that Jovinian was an opponent of Christian asceticism who was condemned in the fourth century as a heretic.

*Maker.* I was hoping that you would be more communicative. The editors tell us that Chaucer made dramatic use of Jerome's debating points against wives—but was the Epistle just so much handy material for tales about marriage? It appears to me a treatment of the problem which must have interested the poet of courtly love who later wrote the *Canterbury Tales*.

*A.* And who later wrote the Retraction. The story of final repentance was believed in the fifteenth century, and I believe it now.

*Maker.* Of Dan Geoffrey we can only say that he was not an ascetic except just possibly at the very end of his life: we really know very little about the state of his soul, and it is not our business to know more. But his *works* embody the dilemma of Jerome *versus* Jovinian. The question was how far asceticism should go; and Chaucer's answer was to point through the polemical conflict to a centre of balance.

*A.* The centre of balance was already there in Jerome: the saint had more common sense than I think you allow him, Maker. 'How could virginity grow without the seed of marriage?' The Wife of Bath merely repeats Jerome's question. She fails to add his comment, that gold adorns not the miner but the wearer. No, it was not for Chaucer to discover the centre of balance, but to erect upon it an art of superior amusement—something like E. M. Forster in poetry, only greater, and Catholic.

*Maker.* Perhaps. And where Mr. Forster is sentimental, Chaucer is bookish.

*Sir Frank.* That reminds me of a saying I read yesterday—that in the Middle Ages people remembered too much and saw too little. Whatever the scholars tell me about Chaucer's reliance on books, what I enjoy is the way he sees things for himself. I enjoy them because he enjoys them, like the sight of the canon sweating at Boughton under Blee. The humour. None of you have mentioned it because it is not worth theorizing about. There is balance for you. The broad farce—what has become of it nowadays? Read George Orwell on picture postcards, and you will see. Today it would be censored, and the celluloid immoralities let through. Pass the brandy.

*C-L.* I confess I used to think, myself, that the father of English poetry was really a great-uncle.

*A.* C-L had better go into a corner and console Sir Frank. I wish to discuss the Problem of Evil.

*Maker.* Good God.

*A.* That, I believe, is the answer; but even Chaucer, with his advantages over a comedian of to-day, must not be expected to grasp it all at once. *The Former Age* concludes with a tone of despair about contemporary horrors—

*C-L.* —which are all in Ovid and Boethius and Jean de Meun. The poem is utterly conventional.

*Maker.* What exactly do you mean by 'conventional'? The line about the first miners grubbing up metal, *lurkinge in darknesse,* is quite freshly conceived, even if distantly suggested by *itum est in viscera terræ* of the *Metamorphoses.*

*A.* I had not quite finished. I was saying that the end of *The Former Age* is perceptibly more than an exercise in versification and copying. And so is the *Lak of Stedfastnesse,* in a line or two. They are poems of protest. And Chaucer's line about poison, manslaughter and murder has quite as much force as the whole of the *Age de plomb* of Deschamps. On the other side we can put *Fortune* (in which protest is comic) and *Truth,* the *balade de bon conseyl* which all of us on this side of the Atlantic must have heard at least once from a loudspeaker. Such minor poems suggest, briefly, how Chaucer came to an understanding of the problem of evil, came to realize—for everyone must work it out for himself—that 'Sin is Behovely'. *Tempest thee noght al croked to redresse* is Chaucerian advice to Chaucer, as well as to the sick cow he appears to be addressing.—Subdue yourself and do not be too eager to subdue others: *daunte thyself, that dauntest otheres dede.* You see, it requires an education of the will to begin to learn why evil is temporarily permitted by divine providence. A proof of its nonentity will not

11

subtract a toothache, except by special grace. And the time when we understand both ourselves and the problem of evil has probably to be found and lost and found again and again, before we can come to perfection beyond change.

*Maker.* I was afraid that A would fly off into theodicy before long. I have been reflecting, while he did so, that Chaucer lacked a classical or renaissance sense of Tragedy, which is an important qualification in the subject. There is no catharsis at the end of *Troilus and Criseyde* : and since Chaucer cannot laugh himself, he has to imagine the laughter of Troilus. There is no terror in the Monk's version of the Ugolino story.

*A.* That is because the medieval could fear for others without fearing for himself; and the response to what we call Tragedy always includes fear for oneself. Chaucer did not require Tragedy because he had the Mass, which contains and transcends the very sacrificial origin of Tragedy.

*Maker.* I believe that Dante also had the Mass, yet the *Divine Comedy* has Tragedy.

*A.* If so, it exceeds it. Tragedy may have been *possible* in the middle ages, but it was not necessary. And I am inclined to agree that by the late fourteenth century it was not even possible.

*Maker.* A civilization in which Tragedy has ceased to be possible is dying.

*A.* And Tragedy *becomes* possible at the death: for Tragedy, at its highest, is a means of new life.

*Sir Frank.* I wish you two would shake each other by the bills, and land.

*C-L.* And I was about to observe that it would do A good to listen to what Alexander Smith said in 1863. 'Chaucer was a Conservative in all his feelings; he liked to poke fun at the clergy, but was not of the stuff of which martyrs are made.'

*Maker.* Facetiousness.

*A.* I should like to confess, before we finish, that I do not believe Chaucer was granted any *exceptional* consciousness in spiritual matters, but he learnt to recognize and respect exceptional consciousness. That is a way of saying that he was not, in a special sense, a great religious poet, but he knew where great religious poetry was to be found. He depends on a Catholic civilization, which he accepts with gratitude and wisdom, but with no very manifest personal struggle to gain a truth out of reach. He is a kind of frail bridge between Dante and Shakespeare: able to bear a great deal of reality, but designed to carry one thing at a time. He is a third master.

*C-L.* I hesitate to pour cold water over A's pontifical pronouncements, but (like Maker) he has an engaging manner of repeating old truths as if he had just discovered them. Hazlitt said, in 1817—

*Maker.* To hell with Hazlitt.

*Sir Frank.* Gentlemen: it seems to me that if we had the opinions of all the pilgrims on Chaucer, we might arrive at a verdict. As it is, we have only the Host's, and perhaps it is fortunate, if I may say so . . . not too seriously . . . that we have not the Parson's.

*A.* That sounds like a closing speech, but again I have been interrupted; this time accidentally. I was thinking of Byron.

*Maker.* So was I.

*A.* Chaucer had learnt 'to care and not to care': Byron, who had to instruct himself—

*Maker.* —got as far as not caring a damn, which is quite an achievement under his own steam. I say *steam*, because Byron, as you can hear when you read him, wrote in an age which had invented the steam-engine.

*Sir Frank.* I hear that another poor innocent is about to write a book on Chaucer. What would you advise him to do?

*Maker.* Write a *critical study*, and not be afraid to distinguish. I will give him a rough stratification.

1. The richest humane narrative verse, which is not always separate from

2. The best work of the *grant translateur*, or from

3. Inferior stuff, shoddy adaptation, over-literal versions, worthless catalogues. It is the critic's business to make such distinctions firmly and delicately, and so to help the reader. Chaucer can stand it. We have more information and speculation about facts than anyone can digest; we could do with further criticism. When he has finished his book, he may leave to someone who knows more than he does the task of writing, say, a comparative study of Chaucer and Chaucer's Spanish contemporary Juan Ruiz. I think I interrupted C-L.

*C-L.* I recommend him to read these stout volumes of Miss Caroline Spurgeon's, which you have so prudently acquired; and ask himself whether he can add a third to the two most remarkable statements that have been made on the subject.

*Sir Frank.* And what are those?

*Maker.* Here is one: Shakespeare 'is equal to the greatest poets . . . except in a certain primeval intensity, such as Dante's and Chaucer's.' Leigh Hunt, 1844.

*A.* I remember another. 'Chaucer never thought about God if he could possibly help it.' Mr. Aldous Huxley, 1939.

*C-L.* Well, those are not what I had in mind, but they will do. They are difficult to beat.

*Sir Frank.* Our toast. To the memory of Geoffrey Chaucer, on the five hundred and fiftieth anniversary of the date upon his tomb.

*A.* And have you noticed its perfect fitness? On the feast of the patron saint of cordwainers our 'hose-or-breeches-maker' gave in his last. Pray for our *chauciers* on St. Crispin's Day.

# I

*El temps qe·l roissignol faz nausa,*
*Que de nueit ni de zor no pausa*
*Desotz la fuella de cantar,*
*Pel bel temps que vei refrescar,*
*Aven que Fin'Amors parlet*
*Ab sos baros en son rescet,*
*En son del puei de Parnasus;*
*Zoi e Solasz foron laisus,*
*E Ardimens e Cortezia,*
*Qe de flors l'en zonchon la via . . .*
*Lo cortes pueih, de l'autra part,*
*Del fuoch d'amor relusz e·s art:*
*E d'aqui mout tota le joza*

*Qu'Amors per mei lo mond'envoza.*
*E d'autra part son las floretas,*
*Las ruosas e las violetas,*
*Qi trameton lor gran douszor*
*Denant lo leit de Fin'Amor.*
*E d'autra part ha cent pulsellas,*
*Q'anc negus hom non vi plus bellas;*
*E chascuna ha son amador,*
*E son vestu d'una color,*
*E·s baison e·s braisson soven,*
*E mantenon pretz e joven . . .*
*Ez el mei loc ac un castel,*
*Q'anc negus om non vi plus bel . . .*

In the time that the nightingale lifts up her voice and ceases not to sing night and day beneath the leaf, in the fair time that I see bringing freshness, it happens that Pure Love speaks with her barons in her retreat, on the summit of Parnassus: Joy and Solace were there, and Ardour and Courtesy, who strewed the way with flowers . . . The court hill, moreover, shines and glows with the fire of love, and thence proceeds all the joy which Love sends throughout the world. There also are flowers, roses and violets that spread their great sweetness before the couch of Pure Love. There too are a hundred maidens, more beautiful were never seen; and each has her lover, and both are dressed in one colour, and often they kiss and embrace and are ever young and gallant . . . And in the midst of the place a castle, never was one more beautiful seen . . .

*Cour d'Amour* :  anonymous Provençal *romanz*
Cheltenham MS

# MANY A LECHEROUS LAY

LET US OPEN THE FIRST FRAGMENT OF THE FOURTEENTH-century English version of Guillaume de Lorris and Jean de Meun. Nobody can say that this was certainly written by Chaucer, but we may all suppose that this was how Chaucer began. So my chapter begins in the garden of the rose.

> Tho myghtist thou caroles seen
> And folk daunce and mery been,
> And make many a fair tournyng
> Upon the grene gras springyng.
> There myghtist thou see these flowtours,
> Mynstrales, and eke jogelours,
> That wel to synge dide her peyne:
> Somme songe songes of Loreyne;
> For in Loreyn her notes be
> Full swetter than in this contre.[1]

A whole essay might be written upon the life, the habit of thought, behind these lines. I shall try to keep to two subjects: music and the art of verse. They will then force me on to a third.

We start with a forgotten dance-song enjoyed by the courts of medieval Europe. Possibly it was an overrated diversion; but Dante, after all, could lift up the *carole* to paradise.[2] I choose it

---

[1] *Romaunt of the Rose* 759–68
*Flowtours* flute-players          *Her* their
   I mention, at an early opportunity, that the glosses in this book are to provide no more than explanatory first-aid for persons who require it. I shall sometimes try to supplement standard editorial comments, but I shall not attempt to replace them; and those who need less than I give may silently congratulate themselves. The new reader is recommended to discover as soon as possible approximately how Chaucer was *pronounced* (no one can tell him exactly). For the rest, he may gain courage from Coleridge:

> As to understanding his language, if you read twenty pages
> with a good glossary, you surely can find no further difficulty . . .
>                     *Table Talk*, March 15, 1834

This is not literally true, but one can go a long way, and with enjoyment, before discovering its falsehood.
[2] *Paradiso* XXIV 16

as a symbol, in the belief that it had more relation to the arts of the time than a fox-trot, and that on the other hand the most distinguished courtly composer or poet was there to provide superior amusement. I think of two courts, a century after the *Romance of the Rose* opens in Orléans; of Chaucer born for one, and Guillaume de Machaut alive in another. The art of the troubadours had arrived two hundred years before Dante, three hundred before Chaucer. There, in Provence, is a beginning. What Guillaume de Poitiers in the eleventh century, Bernart de Ventadour in the twelfth, and Guillaume de Machaut in the fourteenth had in common (though we know little about the composition of the first) was a practising interest in both music and poetry; and the *ballade*, which Guillaume de Machaut made a complex musical and poetic form, was at first a dance-song, like the *carole*.

Now it is possible that M. Max Meili, by *singing* the Provençal songs, has done more than anyone else in our time to demonstrate the extraordinary contained force of art which propelled so much of early poetry in France, Italy and elsewhere. For Guillaume de Machaut, on the other hand, we have to rely on the admirable edition of Friedrich Ludwig.[1] Of the great *ballades* I have not yet heard a single adequate performance. But anyone who examines *De toutes flours* for the first time will do so with amazement. This music is completely different from anything of Chaucer's. It expresses, with a technical mastery approaching Bach, an intense personal emotion which Chaucer would have preferred to keep at a polite distance and would certainly not, I believe, have tried to imitate. A line of the *Compleynt unto Pity*,

I fond hir ded, and buried in an herte

is the only suggestion to the contrary that I recall in the early poems; and anyone who had not heard that verse and who finds it striking will be disappointed by the whole poem. In the

---

[1] *Guillaume de Machaut: Musikalische Werke* (Leipzig: Breitkopf & Härtel, 1926). When this chapter was written the only recording available of the *ballades notées* was an interpretation of *Ploures, dames* at which the ladies might well weep. Further records have since been made, and Mr. Wilfrid Mellers assures me of their quality.

GUILLAUME DE MACHAUT
*De toutes flours*

Triplum

Contra-Tenor
Tenor

De
Ga -

*This part may have been vocal, or instrumental, or both

De  tou - tes    flours  n'a - - -
Ga- stes  e - stoit   li

- - - - voit et de tous  fruis   en  mon ver-
seur-plus et de - struis  par  For - tu -

gier   fors  u - ne  seu- le  ro - - - - - -
- - ne  qui  du-re-ment s'op- po -

Mais vraiement ymaginer ne puis
que la vertus, ou ma rose est enclose,
viengne par toy et par tes faus conduis,
ains est drois dons natureus; si suppose
    que tu n'avras ja vigour
d'amanrir son pris et sa valour.
Lay la moy donc, qu'ailleurs n'en mon vergier
autre apres li ja mais avoir ne quier.

He! Fortune, qui es gouffres et puis
pour engloutir tout homme qui croire ose,
ta fausse loy, ou riens de biens ne truis
ne de seür, trop est decevans chose;
    ton ris, ta joie, t'onnour
ne sont que plour, tristesse et deshonnour.
Se ty faus tour font ma rose sechier,
autre apres li ja mais avoir ne quier.

music and verse by GUILLAUME DE MACHAUT
(?1303 - 1377)

The authenticity of the *triplum*, preserved in a single manuscript and without Guillaume's
name, is not certain. This, like the vocal part of the first section, is for convenience transcribed an octave higher than it is sounded. No indications of tempo or dynamics are given:
the one safe direction, and the essential one, is *espressivo*.

*Compleynt of Mars* Chaucer is already a distinguished ironist. We can grant that he had at least as much musical accomplishment as the Squire of his Canterbury *Prologue*, but there is no evidence that he was interested in the essential Guillaume when, for his own purposes, he made use of Guillaume's verse. Guillaume de Machaut was a great musician, Chaucer a great poet: the separation of trouvère poet and composer had begun, and in spite of the opinion of Professor Manly[1] I doubt whether Chaucer ever seriously attempted to perform both functions. Guillaume's achievement in verse, as Dr. Pattison has observed, was a *tour de force*.[2] What Chaucer did, in relation to Guillaume de Machaut, was to make poetry of the poetics which, to Guillaume the composer also, only assisted the design. The whole pattern, in either case, is still 'music'. Poetry is not yet the 'second rhetoric' of the numerous *arts poétiques* of the fifteenth century, the century which embalmed Chaucer as a rhetorician. In the *Art de faire chansons* Eustache Deschamps, the French poet of his own age with whom Chaucer exchanged compliments, gave the name *musique naturele* to the 'music of poetry', the music of the speaking voice, in order to distinguish it from what he praised as the *musique artificiele* of the accompanied singer; and we can apply the first term of Deschamps to Chaucer. Taking hints, perhaps, from Deschamps' practice, he extended the range of tone of the *ballade* to a degree which would perplex a musician trying to set his words, and we may even think of the *envoys* to Scogan and Bukton as free developments of the form. The *Compleynt of Chaucer to his Empty Purse* is probably a last squib, incidentally parodying the fashionable love song; and half-recalling the days when he followed Guillaume de Lorris and tried to be always dying but never quite dead.

> I compleyned and sighed sore,
> And langwisshed evermore,
> For I durst not over go
> Unto the Rose I loved so.[3]

---

[1] *Canterbury Tales* ed. J. M. MANLY (New York, 1928) p. 503; more cautiously advanced in *Some New Light on Chaucer* (New York, 1926) pp. 278–9.
[2] BRUCE PATTISON, *Music and Poetry of the English Renaissance* (London: Methuen, 1948) p. 46
[3] *Romaunt of the Rose* 3485–8
  *Book of the Duchess* 588:
              Alway deynge and be not ded.

The opening of the *Compleynt of Mars* is certainly a long way from the *alba* of a troubadour, but is also a dawn-song: the *alba* of Troilus[1] is not a song at all. It is the fourteenth-century equivalent of the beginning of Donne's *Busy old foole, unruly Sunne* . . .

I am not saying that Chaucer abandoned music, that when he became a poet interested in the dramatic possibilities of narrative verse, he ceased to be a 'lyrical' poet. It is no mere curiosity that the Clerk's *envoy*, one of the most 'dramatic' episodes in all the comedy of the *Canterbury Tales*, has a musical form which was common in Provençal and unusual in English;[2] and (whether he wanted to or not) Chaucer handled a musical form every time he tried out a new arrangement of rhymes. For the arrangement of rhyme was still a matter of musical structure, of the pattern of melody which the troubadours used to hold copyright.[3] But there is also the question of inviting the composer (who may be the poet as well) to set to work, and from this point of view there are passages in Chaucer which musicians have overlooked. Nothing more *singable* has been written in English than the closing lines of the lay of the knight in black, from Chaucer's earliest long poem:

> I have of sorwe so gret won
> That joye gete I never non,
> Now that I see my lady bryght,
> Which I have loved with al my myght,
> Is fro me ded and ys agoon.
> Allas, deth, what ayleth thee,
> That thou noldest have taken me,
> Whan thou toke my lady swete,
> That was so fair, so fresh, so fre,
> So good, that men may wel see
> Of al goodnesse she had no mete.[4]

A composer could add a great deal to this, but on the other hand there are 'lyrical' passages of Chaucer to which he need add nothing. The great lament of Troilus sings itself. And in the later *Canterbury Tales* the *cantabile* line is in a larger context, but still to be found: Alison, who was *long as a mast and upright as a bolt*, was also lovelier *than is the newe pere-jonette tree*. The drama-

---

[1] *Troilus and Criseyde* III 1450–70
[2] H. J. CHAYTOR, *The Troubadours and England* (Cambridge, 1923) p. 103
[3] This does not of course mean that the relation between verse form and musical form was *invariable* (see, for example, JEAN BECK, *La Musique des Troubadours*, Paris, p. 80). Music, and metrical poetry, are impossible without discord.
[4] *Book of the Duchess* 475–86
*Won* abundance      *Fre* bounteous      *Mete* equal

tization of modernized Chaucer is not Chaucerian, because it is bound to destroy the superb flow of what I can only call *melodic speech* in which everything happens, even an interruption, in the best of this poetry; and which is as essential to Chaucer as the musical *sequence* to Bach.[1]

We began with the rhythm of the *carole*, and it comes again in the *Book of the Duchess*, expressing, after the knight's tedious lament, his remembered gladness of love.

> I saw hyr daunce so comlily,
> Carole and synge so swetely,
> Laughe and pleye so womanly,
> And loke so debonairly;
> So goodly speke and so frendly,
> That, certes, I trowe that evermor
> Nas seyn so blysful a tresor.[2]

The beat is surer here, but there was a beat before; an English rhythm. The French of Guillaume de Lorris has the movement of the *turn* of the dance:

> *Lors véissiés carole aler,*
> *Et gens mignotement baler,*
> *Et faire mainte bele tresche,*
> *Et maint biau tor sor l'erbe fresche* . . .[3]

Something of this particular swirl was possible in Chaucer's medium; in a line like

> Sprong up the sote grene gras[4]

the foot is only once on the ground, the rest is in the air. But if you translate the line into our modern language, its effect is completely lost. And I think there is a distinctively English relation to the dance that makes the passage at the beginning of this chapter the most interesting piece of translation in the whole of the *Romaunt of the Rose*. It is *English poetry*. The metre looks

---

[1] The whole subject of the last three paragraphs is pursued more closely in my article 'Chaucer and the *ballades notées* of Guillaume de Machaut', *Speculum*, October 1951.

[2] *Book of the Duchess* 848–54

[3] I am here using the convenient parallel text given in Skeat's edition of Chaucer (Oxford, 1894), I pp. 93–164. The lines correspond to my first quotation from the *Romaunt of the Rose*.

[4] *Romaunt of the Rose* 1425
*Sote* sweet
The final vowels of *sote* and *grene* are pronounced slightly, much as they are pronounced in *faire mainte bele* of Guillaume de Lorris.

the same, at first, as the French, but is not the same; and our admirable editor Walter Skeat was perhaps too disinclined to admit that Chaucer's own verse cannot always be measured according to a metric system.[1]

I am not denying that the *Romaunt* has pleasant lines elsewhere. Think of the opening of the dream, the May tune that Chaucer recalled in his *Book of the Duchess*—

> That it was May me thoughte tho
> (It is fyve yer or more ago)
> That it was May, thus dremed me,
> In tyme of love and jolite,
> That al thing gynneth waxen gay,
> For ther is neither busk nor hay
> In May, that it nyl shrouded ben . . .[2]

And as we read on, or (better) as we begin Chaucer's own dream, we observe a great advantage enjoyed by the English of the fourteenth century: they possessed the French word *clere*. A Frenchman might then cross the Channel and be aware of no increase in the density of the atmosphere, and Froissart at the English court was lucky. For the fogs descended soon afterwards, and are still here. England in the Hundred Years' War was closer to France than she has been ever since: by the next period of intellectual communication, the late seventeenth and the eighteenth centuries, the languages had grown apart. Even so, there was another difference between the language of Guillaume and the language of his translator, besides a metrical difference. French was, as it is now, the language of the adjective, which is more precise, or at least more explicit than the English.[3] The translator inclined to prune generally descriptive terms, and to add phrasing idiomatic in his own dialect.[4] Where the French is content with the quality, English wants the thing; and when

---

[1] Skeat shared the assumptions of Tyrwhitt (1775) and F. J. Child (1862), and it is impossible to believe that these scholars have not brought us nearer to a true reading. Without them, we should be in the dark. But more recent editions, particularly the work of F. N. Robinson, and more particularly *The Text of the Canterbury Tales* established by J. M. Manly and Edith Rickert (Chicago, 1940), suggest that editorial rectification had sometimes proceeded too far. The manuscripts support certain 'irregularities' of line for which 'in almost every case' write Manly and Rickert (III p. 423) 'a reader sensitive to rhythmic effects will find justification'. In my own quotations, where the doctors disagree, it is such a reader I have in mind.

[2] *Romaunt of the Rose* 49–55
*Busk* bush    *Hay* hedge    *Nyl* will not

[3] Compare lines 361–2, 494–5, 753–4, 1207–10, 1486, 1610 with the French.

[4] *e.g.*, 507–8, 531–2, 561, 677, 1031–2; 928, 1196, 1219, 1420.

the French gives it, is still not satisfied. So it must have a basin *scoured newe*, or dew on a flower, or a bride in her bower:

Ne she was derk ne broun, but bright,
And clere as the mone lyght,
Ageyn whom all the sterres semen
But smale candels, as we demen.
Hir flesh was tendre as dew of flour;
Hir chere was symple as byrde in bour;
As whyt as lylye or rose in rys
Hir face, gentyl and tretys . . .

*Tendre ot la char comme rousée,*
*Simple fu cum une espousée,*
*Et blanche comme flor de lis;*
*Si ot le vis cler et alis . . .*[1]

This is Beautee; and Beautee and Ydelnesse and Mirthe all reappear, in another form (one of them, at least, surprisingly disguised) among the Canterbury pilgrims or their tales; and we can see more in the late if we have first looked at the early. The *rose in rys*, which is added in the English, gives a double image that can be found in the anonymous English lyrics or popular romances, that goes back to the *plus fresca que rosa ne lis* of the Provençal. In the romances the tradition is debased; but even Beautee is not the finest art; and the translator, good as he can be, lapses into the rhythm as well as the diction of the bourgeois minstrelsy. *For the love of his lemman* is not quite a courtly translation of *pour s'amie*—

And for the love of his lemman
He caste doun many a doughty man . . .

The knight was fair and styf in stour,
And in armure a semely man,
And wel biloved of his lemman . . .[2]

—but is much less risible than the very beat of Chaucer's parody, *Sir Thopas* :

[1] *Romaunt of the Rose* 1009–16: I give the French of the last four lines.
*Chere* look          *Symple* modest          *Rys* spray          *Tretys* (Old French *tretis*)
graceful, well-proportioned          *Alis* smooth
[2] 1209–10, 1270–2
*Styf in stour* strong in battle
For the word *lemman*, consult the Manciple (*Canterbury Tales* H 212–20): if they are both unfaithful there is no difference, he says, between a wife of high degree and a poor wench—except that one is called a lady and the other a leman. In itself the word is of course entirely unexceptionable (it was in fact used in love lyrics addressed to Christ). I am only saying that the *Romaunt* does not always reflect Guillaume's diction of *amour courtois*.

23

For well wende he the forme see
Of a child of gret beautee.[1]

Yet these lines can be read (as long as *Thopas* is out of mind) simply as a reversion to the respectable native lyrical tradition. And the first fragment of the *Romaunt of the Rose* is on the whole discreet and accurate: a better poem, in English, would have been a less faithful translation. One can rarely say so much of translations of poetry, which are usually either very different from the original, or very much worse.

It is a pity that the Northern fragment which follows is not more readable, for it contains a short guide to *amour courtois*, to the obstacle dance of love and its psychology, together with a statement by Jean de Meun's Reason of the orthodox view of sex.[2] The only thing I find to suggest that the translator was also a poet is the lover's abstraction fit:

> . . . many tymes thou shalt be
> Styl as an ymage of tree,
> Dom as a ston, without steryng
> Of foot or hond, without spekyng . . .[3]

The third fragment, which seems nearer to Chaucer's language, has also landed, on one page, much further away.[4] If this was written by Chaucer he repented of it, and never elsewhere descended to the dreariest style of the morality.

But I shall return to the *Romaunt* (and the *Romance*) of the Rose later on. I began with music and the dance, to connect them with musical composition and the art of verse. Now in verse the possibilities of a particular form are only learnt by experience, fully learnt only by the experience of a master, and then learnt for one language only. For the first half of his career Chaucer experimented, in the troubadour manner, with many forms; and reached the utmost virtuosity in the *compleynt* of Anelida,[5] which in its sheer brilliance has something more than the technical

---

[1] *Romaunt of the Rose* 1521–2
*Wende* . . . supposed he could . . .
[2] I believe that anyone who reads the passage in Reason's discourse containing lines 4821–4 will suspect that the translator was elaborating his matter, and Professor F. N. Robinson points out that these lines are not in fact in the French texts we possess. Possibly lines 4875–6 were in the translator's original, though they have not survived in ours.
[3] 2407–10
[4] 6631–6660
[5] From *Anelida and Arcite*. Of this poem W. P. Ker, in *English Literature Medieval* (Oxford, 1912, 1945), pp. 174–5, 181, wrote a brief judgement which it would be difficult to improve.

exercise of *Womanly Noblesse*, of the *Compleynt to his Lady*, or the mistitled *Compleynt of Venus*. By the second half of his career he had found two forms that were most flexible and effective for what he wanted to do: the verse now named after him, and the couplet later hammered into new elegance by our Augustan age, hardened and re-polished and sharpened for clean decapitation and then worn out. In those whispers of dying allegory called the *Compleynt unto Pity*, we find what are probably our first 'Chaucerian' stanzas. They open a little uncertainly, and at least twice one can detect the torpid movement of Lydgate. But there is also a prolongation and levitation of the rhythm:

> A compleynt had I, writen, in myn hond,
> For to have put to Pitee as a bille;
> But when I al this companye ther fond,
> That rather wolden al my cause spille
> Then do me help, I held my pleynte stille;
> For to that folk, withouten any fayle,
> Withoute Pitee ther may no bille availe.[1]

The effect that I so portentously describe comes about through an arrangement of pausing and rhyme; the whole pattern of the verse moving without constraint, as one. The poem is imperfect, but it gives a hint that Chaucer's mind is turning towards narrative; and *St. Cecyle* (later the *Second Nun's Tale*), the *Compleynt to his Lady*, *Anelida and Arcite*, the *Compleynt of Mars*, all contain 'Chaucerian' stanzas at a similar point of development. Chaucer is never more consciously poetical than at the beginning of *Anelida*—

> Be favorable eke, thou Polymya,
> On Parnaso that with thy sustres glade,
> By Elycon, not fer from Cirrea,
> Singest with vois memorial in the shade . . .[2]

This makes out of memories of Dante something undeniably beautiful, and slightly more than Tennysonian. But there are awkward moments later on, before Anelida's *compleynt*. The best Chaucerian verse requires the greater *ease* that is forecast in the

---

[1] *Compleynt unto Pity* 43–9
*Bille* petition        *Spille* ruin        *Held . . . stille* withheld        *That folk* is the company of Beauty, Youth and the rest, that do not help the lover unless Pity is alive in the heart of the lady.
[2] *Anelida and Arcite* 15–8
*Polymya* Polyhymnia, a Muse—the *Polinnia* of Dante, *Paradiso* XXIII 56. *Cirrea* (Cirrha) is also mentioned in the *Paradiso* (I 36), apparently as a place associated with the god Apollo.

25

poem and story of the *Compleynt of Mars*: a calm air of understanding with the reader.

Then comes a poem called not the *Song*, but the *Parliament of Birds*; and in it, a new flexible arrangement of speech within the stanza, done with much greater assurance than in the *Second Nun's Tale*. This is the second stage, and the third is mastery, in *Troilus and Criseyde*. Here we can take a passage of dialogue and find a naturalness which it has required great labour to achieve. I open Book II—Pandarus has thrust a love-letter in the bosom of Criseyde,

And seyde hire, 'Now cast it awey anon,
That folk may seen and gauren on us tweye.'
Quod she, 'I kan abyde til they be gon;'
And gan to smyle, and seyde hym, 'Em, I preye,
Swich answere as you list youreself purveye,
For trewely I nyl no lettre write.'
'No? Than wol I,' quod he, 'so ye endite.'

Therwith she lough, and seyde, 'Go we dyne.'
And he gan at hymself to jape faste,
And seyde, 'Nece, I have so greet a pyne
For love, that every other day I faste—'
And gan his beste japes forth to caste,
And made hire so to laughe at his folye,
That she for laughter wende for to dye.

And whan that she was comen into halle,
'Now, em,' quod she, 'we wol go dyne anon;'
And gan some of hire wommen to hire calle,
And streght into hire chambre gan she gon.
But of hire besynesses this was on—
Amonges othere thynges, out of drede—
Ful pryvely this lettre for to rede.

Avysed word by word in every lyne,
And fond no lak, she thoughte he koude good;
And up it putte, and wente hire in to dyne.
But Pandarus, that in a study stood,
Er he was war, she took hym by the hood,
And seyde, 'Ye were caught er that ye wiste!'
'I vouche sauf,' quod he, 'do what you liste.'[1]

[1] *Troilus and Criseyde* II 1156–83
*Gauren* stare    *Em* uncle    *Swich answer as yow list* . . . give what answer you
will    *Endite* dictate    *Out of drede* no doubt    *Avysed* [when she had]
conside:ed [it]—the ellipsis conveying Criseyde's haste and secret excitement.
*Koude good* knew how to behave in the circumstances

As Professor Bronson has pointed out,[1] this is an arrangement of dialogue that could be enjoyed at a recital of the poem, by a *listening* audience. What is more remarkable is the rhythm sustained through a sequence of stanzas, in the great lament of Troilus of the fifth book. Chaucer, we may feel, had mastered the possibilities of this verse, and had no more to learn. So he went on learning. The little tale of the Prioress is a triumph in the most precarious situation.[2] The Canterbury pilgrims will not be squeezed into this chapter; but I believe we can say also that Chaucer's progress in handling the seven-line stanza is enough to make us doubt the very early date which Skeat proposed for the *Clerk's Tale*. A form had been found for medieval high comedy in English, and died fighting in Skelton's *Bouge of Court*.

The metre of five beats, in rhymed couplets, whether it was taken from the French or not, was found and brought to perfection for English verse in Chaucer's maturity. It occurs in the course of the stanza; but its regular employment demanded another fineness of rhythmic variation, and so was a new opportunity. The couplet, in Chaucer's English, is never sing-song, and never sings too operatically. It is the least opaque medium, in which everything is clearer (and *clerer*) than prose. It does not give accidental colour, as the stanza is inclined to do; it is neutral. And it will accommodate the Nun's Priest as well as the Summoner. The stanza prefers *heigh style*, is for the courtly, a *mirour of alle curteisye*. The couplet refracts all the world to those who will look.

But what was the meaning of the *carole* in Guillaume de Lorris? I have not even mentioned the meaning. So much more than Guillaume de Lorris comes in: all the cilia of courtly love. In good time, we should cut through them; but Chaucer teaches, effectively, that it is not wise to be in a hurry. To begin, there should perhaps be an invocation to Venus, though that is beyond my powers. I start with a matter of experience in everybody over the age of — but I do not even know what age. For Dante the age was nine; for others it may be earlier still. The sudden experience of love is equivocal, is expressed from ancient time in contradictions, is subsequently perverted, broken, or unified,

---

[1] 'Chaucer's Art in Relation to his Audience', *Five Studies in Literature*, ed. BERTRAND H. BRONSON (University of California Press and C.U.P., 1940).

[2] 'I do not see,' writes one reader, 'what is "precarious" about the *Prioress's Tale*'. But let us wait until we come to it.

according to the person and the civilization and the belief of the person. The lover does not know what to do—or, if he knows, has passed beyond the first experience, to lechery, or to marriage, or to divine contemplation. Upon what appears to be between two of these one hesitates to pronounce, and the critic must be conscious of the humour of his situation. So must the poet, though whether he has ambitions in comedy is another thing. The troubadour writes

> *Domna, metges e mezina,*
> *lectoaris et enguens,*
> *los nafratz de mort guirens;*[1]

Chaucer:

> For there is phisicien but oon
> That may me hele . . .[2]

And it would not be easy to trace all the mutations of love poetry through Provençal literature, through *amour courtois*, through *Frauendienst*, and the circle of Guinicelli alone; but to define exactly the possible steps between the two stages I have just quoted is a sufficiently delicate task. It is too hard to resist a generalization, to refrain from saying that the language of love, being human, is therefore ambiguous. With what memory April mixes desire, it has always been difficult to decide. The opening of the Canterbury *Prologue* has this doubleness: that the renewal of Spring and the mating of birds and the healing of sickness do not necessarily recall the veneration of the martyr, or that of the Queen of Heaven. All the singing and the saving Springs are to be found before Chaucer in an anonymous English love poetry which, as Mr. Chaytor has shown, comes of the Provençal manner. And if we consider the eleven pieces of Guillaume de Poitiers alone, or the account M. Jeanroy has given of the eleven pieces of Guillaume de Poitiers,[3] we can see plainly the contradictions of a great deal of later poetry. They include six specimens of *poésies jongleresques*, of which the third, we are told, 'defies even the most veiled analysis'. There are then four courtly love songs,

---

[1] Peire de Corbiac, quoted by H. J. Chaytor
'Lady, physician and medicine, lectuary and unguent, healing the death-stricken . . .
[2] *Book of the Duchess* 39–40
[3] ALFRED JEANROY, *La Poésie lyrique des Troubadours* (Toulouse and Paris, 1934) II p. 5 ff. There is also, in *Romania* LXVI pp. 145–237 (1940), an extremely interesting article on 'Guillaume IX et les origines de l'amour courtois' by Reto R. Bezzola.

'evidently for another public', perhaps in a manner already established. The last poem is a pious farewell to the world. Chaucer confessing 'many a lecherous lay' also thought, and with truer penitence, of salvation: at the end of a very different career, and in another century.

It would require a very intimate acquaintance with two languages to detect, in the later troubadours and early Italians, the exact moment at which a purified diction corresponds to a purified sensibility. The last, desperately chaste, movement of Provençal poetry required a Dante, says M. Jeanroy, to become a genuine renewal. And about Dante there is no doubt. Love poetry since the troubadours is like a series of transmigrations, in which some lives are better than others, and the *vita nuova* the best of all. Poetry is human; and even the *Divine Comedy* is never, except indirectly, divine. But no attempt to sublimate and order the emotions to one end could improve upon the *Divine Comedy*. And that is why Chaucer was interested in the critical mind of Jean de Meun. Chaucer moved towards the one end of Dante, towards paradise, by another way.

I believe there has even been an attempt to prove that Jean de Meun, who made the *Romance of the Rose* by Chaucer's time notorious, was really in the circle of courtly love. And it is easy to forget that the old seductress La Vieille first appears in Guillaume de Lorris, before Jean de Meun arrived to continue the story. Mr. C. S. Lewis has pointed out that courtly love 'protects itself against the laughter of the vulgar . . . by allowing laughter and cynicism their place *inside* the poem'.[1] Only the Pandarus who has twinges of conscience is outside the convention. And in Jean de Meun, it might be insisted, the god of love, the spirit of *amour courtois*, is not dismissed, but simply reinforced by the higher command of Venus and the propaganda of Nature. Jean de Meun will expose, in False-Seeming and his friend, the pretences of polite fornication; but the god is still left to say

---

[1] *The Allegory of Love* (Oxford, 1936, 1938) p. 172. Mr. Lewis's book contains the best short account of the *Romance of the Rose* that I have seen. *Chaucer and the Roman de la Rose* by Dean Spruill Fansler (New York: Columbia University Press, 1914) is of considerable editorial interest, though standards of accuracy in that branch of American scholarship must have improved a great deal since Dr. Fansler corrected his proofs. There is still a place for a critical study of the subject. The latest French bibliography at the time of printing may be found in the *Manuel bibliographique de la littérature française du moyen âge* by Robert Bossuat (Melun, 1951).

*Jamais, au meins par verité,*
*Ne seront preudome clamé*
*S'il n'aiment ou s'il n'ont amé.*[1]

But it would be absurd to press a single interpretation. Jean de Meun lived in the great century of medieval disputing, and knew how to handle Reason in his poem. We must not read literally those parts of it which are satirical. He is a poet who is also an encyclopedist; one could still go to him, in the fourteenth century, for ideas before they were dead; one would not apply to him for *beliefs*. Mr. Lewis remarked in his excellent book that Jean de Meun lacked the co-ordinating power of Dante, and this is quite true. But Jean de Meun no more aimed at the co-ordination of Dante than did Chaucer. There are one or two moments in Jean de Meun (and a moment in Jean de Meun always lasts five minutes) when we see Dante in the distance; there are the rivers of Fortune.[2] But the rest, even in intention, is a long way off. What Jean just failed to be was a great comedian of the schools; and where his age may have seen in his work argumentative discipline comically released, we find digression and disorder. Chaucer, though not (I think) consciously, transformed the stress of the medieval dispute into an art of comedy that is permanent.

*Troilus and Criseyde* and the *Canterbury Tales*, the great finished and unfinished masterpieces of Chaucer, are not simple, and we shall find them much less amusing if we pretend that they are. There is more to see in *Troilus and Criseyde* if we have looked into the garden of Guillaume de Lorris, and more in the *Canterbury Tales* if we know Jean de Meun to be somewhere behind the lines. The *Romance of the Rose* is like a game in which the player, believing himself to have reached the end, is suddenly whisked back to the beginning again; and this may have taught our poet what

---

[1] *Le Roman de la Rose*, edited by ERNEST LANGLOIS (Paris, 1914–23), 15840–2
I quote the translation by F. S. Ellis (London, Dent, 1900):

> No living man shall be acclaimed
> For noble, or as gentle named
> Who loveth not, or hath not been
> By damsel's loving eyes beseen.

Of the *Roman de la Rose* Professor Vinaver writes, privately: 'One is, of course, always suspicious of any reference to this work based on the existing edition, which, as I have recently found, is extremely unsatisfactory. In many places it distorts the manuscript tradition and it never really reproduces any particular manuscript or group of manuscripts . . . but I do not think that this affects the particular aspects of the work in which you are interested.'

[2] 5978ff. Yet the passage is translated from Alain de Lille.

in any case he learnt from other experience; it may have shown human nature unstable and human relations precarious.

Chaucer had a finer understanding than either Jean de Meun or Guillaume de Lorris of the problems that I have tried to display in the last few pages, and his understanding is always patient. So he proceeds to human complications through the language of birds.

# II

*It is not within the province of a musician to talk about the song of angels, unless he is a theologian or a prophet.*

JOHANNES DE GROCHEO: *Theoria* (c. 1300)

*Objection 1. It would seem that ecstasy is not an effect of love. For ecstasy seems to imply loss of reason. But love does not always result in loss of reason: for lovers are masters of themselves at times. Therefore love does not cause ecstasy.*

ST. THOMAS AQUINAS: *Summa Theologica II Q. xxviii a. 3*

*On Friday when they were all assembled, the King sent a messenger, Sir Raynalde Bukkeshill, praying them on the King's behalf that they consider his estate; for he was impatient for them to grant the petition and request that he had made the first day of the Parliament so that Parliament might be delivered as soon as possible, for he himself wished to be taking his pleasures elsewhere.*

Good Parliament 1376 : *Anonimalle Chronicle 1333–81*

# TO THE PARLIAMENT OF BIRDS REDUCED
# TO LOVE

CHAUCER LOOKS ROUND WITH THAT GLEAM OF THE EYE
which might mean tears of laughter or tears of distress;
and presents us with his problem. Art is long, life is short
—the subject seems to be the art of poetry, and turns out to be
the art of love.

> The lyf so short, the craft so long to lerne,
> Th' assay so hard, so sharp the conquerynge,
> The dredful joye, alwey that slit so yerne:
> Al this mene I by Love, that my felynge
> Astonyeth with his wonderful werkynge
> So sore iwis, that whan I on hym thynke,
> Nat wot I wel wher that I flete or synke.[1]

But if poetry is long, the art of poetry interpreting the art of
love is even longer. It is especially difficult—to continue this
unliteral report—if the poet himself is not a lover; yet one is as
anxious to be on the right side of the god of love as to be acquainted
with any gods who can tackle insomnia. One may experience
both together, and find love more troublesome than lack of sleep.

We begin, this time, with the art of poetry, which appears
especially 'long' in the *House of Fame*—and I am not referring
to the diffuseness of the poem but to the difficulties of the poet.
I believe the *House of Fame* was written during one of those periods
that every artist must endure, when he is working towards a new
direction or a new point of balance, when he has to try to resist
both despair and idleness, and to wait. Chaucer's way, at such a
time, was to occupy his leisure with translation. Perhaps he did
too much of it; but he never knew when a translation might not
turn into an original poem. How he avoided despair is a question
not to be answered in a sentence. It is a question sufficiently
important to postpone. A whole book might be written about it,

[1] *Parliament of Birds* 1–7: an opening *sententia* in the rhetorical manner
*Slit so yerne* passes so soon      *Wher that* whether      *Flete* float

35

to explore all the influences of the senses, the intellect and the spirit which were different in the fourteenth century from the influences to which a poet is now subject. And even the chronologist may experience a moment of joy at the thought that no one is very sure about dates. He may reflect that Chaucer was born when the Ely Octagon was nearing completion, or John de Grandison was building the Nave of Exeter, or the Choir of Gloucester had not long been finished. We look behind the expected fact when it is not, quite certainly, there. But we know, or think we know, that the *Book of the Duchess* was written towards the thirtieth year of his age. This poem has, in its way, the equilibrium that the artist desires; and so, at a maturer period, has the *Parliament of Birds*. The *story* of the *Compleynt of Mars*, which may be even later than the *Parliament of Birds*,[1] is no more (and no less) than a successful *jeu d'esprit*, an adroitly ironical sophistication of natural appetite, courtly love, and the movement of the sun and the other stars. The god wins Venus not simply through the ' grace ' of *amour courtois*, but

> As wel by hevenysh revolucioun
> As by desert . . .[2]

And one or two lively verses suggest that *Troilus and Criseyde* is not very far away. At the end of the tale, when at the approach of the Sun Venus departs abruptly from Mars and takes refuge with the god Mercury, the bird who is supposed to be singing the tale impertinently wishes every wight joy of his mate.

Whatever his exact age when he composed the *Book of the Duchess*, Chaucer was beyond adolescence. If we read it after the *Romaunt of the Rose*, it is easy to perceive an assured distinction of rhythm which is his first present to English poetry. This rhythm is certainly not sustained in every page; the poem is long. But consider, in a later passage not in itself remarkable, the development of the beat of the knight's lay that I quoted as words for music. It is polite speech grown to art:

> 'She had so stedfast countenaunce,
> So noble port and meyntenaunce—
> And Love, that had wel herd my boone,
> Had espyed me thus soone,

---

[1] I doubt whether the *compleynt* itself, at least, was written after 1380.
[2] *Compleynt of Mars* 30–1

That she ful soone, in my thoght,
As helpe me God, so was ykaught
So sodenly, that I ne tok
No maner counseyl but at hir lok
And at myn herte; for-why hir eyen
So gladly, I trow, myn herte seyen,
That purely tho myn owne thoght
Seyde hit were better serve hir for noght
Than with another to be wel.
And hyt was soth; for, everydel,
I wil anoon ryght telle thee why' . . .[1]

The remembered *carole* follows. This is how we appreciate the rhythm of a long poem of the first period: there is a tenuous relation between parts of the whole, and single lines cannot be given as samples. All the same, there are two or three verses which may surprise anyone who has not read the piece, or not read it recently. Here is a French and an English Spring together:

Ful thikke of gras, ful softe and swete
With floures fele, faire under fete . . .[2]

The goddess Fortune:

The dispitouse debonaire . . .
She is the monstres hed ywrien,
As fylthe over-ystrawed with floures . . .[3]

This is detail. If we can possibly discover Chaucer's poem in a couplet or two, it is in his urbane remark one sleepless night after picking up Ovid.

For I had never herd speke, or tho,
Of noo goddes that koude make
Men to slepe, ne for to wake;
For I ne knew never god but oon.[4]

In the whole piece there is already a developed manner of variation and inversion of a theme: so the theme of sleep, of the

---

[1] *Book of the Duchess* 833–47
*Port and meyntenaunce* demeanour      *Boone* prayer
[2] *Book of the Duchess* 399–400, recalling the *Romaunt of the Rose* 1417ff., as well as anonymous English lyrics.
*Fele* many
[3] 624ff.
*Dispitouse* scornful      *Ywrien* concealed
[4] 234–7
*Or tho* till then

introduction, is overturned when Chaucer's messenger approaches the god and blows a horn *ryght in here eere*.[1]

And Spenser did not equal this brief poetical variation in the Spenserian manner: on the wells that

> Came rennynge fro the clyffes adoun,
> That made a dedly slepynge soun . . .
>
> *Book of the Duchess*

> And more, to lulle him in his slumber soft,
> A trickling stream from high rock tumbling downe,
> And ever-drizling raine upon the loft,
> Mixt with a murmuring winde, much like the sowne
> Of swarming bees, did cast him in a swowne:
> No other noyse, nor peoples troublous cryes,
> As still are wont t'annoy the walled towne,
> Might there be heard: but carelesse Quiet lyes,
> Wrapt in eternall silence farre from enemyes.[2]
>
> *Faery Queen*

Spenser's stanzas remind me of a letter of Landor's to a friend: 'I found the *Faery Queen* the most delightful book to fall asleep upon by the seaside. Geoffrey Chaucer always kept me wide awake.'[3] But would Geoffrey Chaucer disturb the operations of nature? I doubt it. We need to be fresh if we are to attend to his handling of the lover's lament. The theme is again inverted, so that even the lover can see the opposite point of view from the one which obsesses him—can admit that Fortune plays a good game:

> Myself I wolde have do the same,
> Before God, hadde I ben as she;
> She oghte the more excused be . . .[4]

The dialogue is a re-creation of fine social *maners*, which are more than 'manners', and without which the poem would not have been written. It belongs to the time when a Frenchman at the court could praise gentlemen of England for courtesy and charm. A statement is made provisionally, to advance conversation, and with an awareness of another's attitude towards

---

[1] 182
Ovid's messenger is Iris: no such behaviour is expected of her.
[2] *Book of the Duchess* 161–2
*Faery Queen* I i. 41
[3] Quoted by C. F. E. Spurgeon under the date 1844.
[4] 676–8

it; the knight's tone is admired because it is pleasant, yielding, *resonable*; its opposite is that which is said once and for all. And the poet's part is the part of a Reason who, in spite of compassion, sleep and forgetfulness, cannot help thinking logically. This fictitious and intermittently lively person is Chaucer's, but not Chaucer—there is no 'disclosure', no 'personal statement', no 'spokesman'. The poet has expressed no final opinion upon the knight's love for the lady, or upon the affection of John of Gaunt or the death of John of Gaunt's first wife, which are supposed to be commemorated by the poem. In the end we have learnt that 'young' Chaucer could understand the joy of love, and could show that its contradictions are not necessarily absurd, even though, enumerated, they may be tedious. And from this time his work is a gracious poetic correction of *tout comprendre c'est tout pardonner*. It is not true that understanding always pardons. Nor is the reverse. In this poetry we shall have the pleasure of thinking that we see, now and again, in particular instances, the just point between the opposites.

The *Book of the Duchess* is, among Chaucer's works, rather more than a minor success; the *House of Fame* is nearly a major disaster, unfinished, but left off either too early or too late. It is unfortunate, one feels, that Dr. Johnson did not give the same critical attention to Chaucer's lists or catalogues that he bestowed upon the 'quibbles' of Shakespeare. No doubt he could have found a point of attack in the earlier poem, in the *kyrielle d'anti-thèses* that Sandras rightly called *un emprunt malheureux fait à Guillaume de Machaut*;[1] but he might have had a field-day later on, if Chaucer's own fame had not already grown unfamous. The catalogues of the *House of Fame*, I believe, give way to the poetry of the *Parliament of Birds*: but the dates, again, are uncertain. In the introductory discussion of dreams Chaucer not only recalls the most repetitive and digressive passage of the *Romance of the Rose*; he is wearisome himself. An air of amused casualness breathes infrequently upon the exhaustion of the verse, and the list of past fames is a prize-giving relieved by an occasional joke about a personage. Æolus is forced to prominence in the tame puppet-show that follows. The *rym ys lyght and lewed* indeed. Chaucer, for the time being, seems to have

---

[1] E. C. SANDRAS, *Étude sur G. Chaucer considéré comme Imitateur des Trouvères* (Paris, 1859), p. 292, referring to the *Book of the Duchess* 599–616. This is not to imply that I accept the judgement of Sandras on the whole poem.

lost interest in the refinement of language, and to be writing for another audience. The second book begins in the manner of a provincial bestseller of the fourteenth century:

> Now herkeneth, every maner man
> That Englissh understonde kan,
> And listeneth of my drem to lere . . .

It continues as first-rate comedy which my wettest detraction cannot blanket.

> O thought, that wrot al that I mette,
> And in the tresorye hyt shette
> Of my brayn!  Now shal men se
> Yf any vertu in thee be . . .
>
> This egle, of which I have yow told,
> That shon with fethres as of gold . . .
> Me, fleynge, in a swap he hente,
> And with hys sours agayn up wente,
> Me caryinge in his clawes starke
> As lyghtly as I were a larke,
> How high, I can not telle yow . . .
> And, for I shulde the bet abreyde,
> Me mette, 'Awak' to me he seyde,
> Ryght in the same vois and stevene
> That useth oon I koude nevene;
> And with that vois, soth for to seyn,
> My mynde cam to me agayn;
> For hyt was goodly seyd to me,
> So nas hyt never wont to be.
>    And here-withal I gan to stere,
> And he me in his feet to bere,
> Til that he felte that I had hete,
> And felte eke tho myn herte bete.
> And tho gan he me to disporte,
> And with wordes to comforte,
> And sayde twyes, 'Seynte Marye!
> Thou art noyous for to carye,
> And nothyng nedeth it, pardee!
> For, also wis God helpe me,
> As thou noon harm shalt have of this;
> And this caas that betyd thee is,
> Is for thy lore and for thy prow—
> Let see!  darst thou yet loke now?
> Be ful assured, boldely,

I am thy frend.'   And therwith I
Gan for to wondren in my mynde.
'O God,' thoughte I, 'that madest kynde,
Shal I noon other weyes dye?
Wher Joves wol me stellyfye,
Or what thing may this sygnifye?
I neyther am Ennok, ne Elye,
Ne Romulus, ne Ganymede . . .'[1]

The nearest to this in later English poetry is Swift's *Baucis and Philemon*, though Swift is inferior.  He has not the sheer imaginative elation of a poet portable to an Eagle, and afraid of turning to a star.  To enjoy Chaucer's allusiveness to Dante one need recall no more than a line or two of the original:

*O mente, che scrivesti ciò ch' io vidi . . .*

*Veramente quant' io del regno santo*
*nella mia mente potei far tesoro,*
*sara ora materia del mio canto.*[2]

The sparkle is still brighter if we place together Dante dreaming of a dangerous journey, Chaucer of an uncomfortable flight, and Mr. Eliot on Prufrock:

*Io non Enea, io non Paolo sono . . .*[3]

I neyther am Ennok, ne Elye . . .

No!   I am not Prince Hamlet, nor was meant to be . . .

*Now herkeneth, every maner man . . .* is now, after all this, almost a preparation for the author who told the tale of *Sir Thopas*, and who was so much more than a cultivated parodist.

I hope this author was dissatisfied with his 'digest' of the *Æneid*.  Even if he was not, he had seen what could be made of popular exposition in the bill of a fowl of Virgilian (or Dantesque) brood.  This bird should be appointed emblem of the British Broadcasting Corporation:

---

[1] *House of Fame* 523ff.
*Mette* dreamed          *Swap* swoop          *Sours* upspring          *Abreyde* recover
consciousness    *Nevene* name    *Stere* stir    *Noyous* troublesome    *Lore* instruction
*Prow* profit    *Kynde* nature          *Ennok*, who 'walked with God, and he was not;
for God took him' (*Gen.* v. 24).  'And Elijah (*Elye*) went up by a whirlwind into
heaven' (II *Kings* ii. 11).  Romulus, according to Ovid, was carried heavenward by
Mars, and Ganymede by Jupiter the Eagle.
[2] *Inferno* II 8: 'O mind, that wrote that which I saw'
   *Paradiso* I 10–2: 'Whatever of the Holy Realm I had power to treasure in my
memory, shall now indeed be matter of my song'
[3] *Inferno* II 32: 'I am not Aeneas, am not Paul'

'Telle me this now feythfully,
Have I not preved thus symply,
Withoute any subtilite
Of speche, or gret prolixite
Of termes of philosophie,
Of figures of poetrie,
Or colours of rethorike?
Pardee, hit oughte thee to lyke!
For hard langage and hard matere
Ys encombrous for to here
At ones; wost thou not wel this?'
And I answered and seyde, 'Yis.'
    'A ha!' quod he, 'lo, so I can
Lewedly to a lewed man
Speke, and shewe hym swyche skiles
That he may shake hem by the biles . . .'[1]

Here, if nowhere else, we can see a reason for Ben Jonson's interest in the poem.[2] With a diminutive and uneasy poet between his talons, the Eagle risks a theatrical gesture that in the circumstances even a distinguished Elizabethan might have remarked:

'Now turn upward,' quod he, 'thy face,
And behold this large space,
This air! . . .'[3]

The *House of Fame* is not a masterpiece, though it contains a masterly flight. Within his development, it is Chaucer's great *loosening*. It has a swifter verse-movement than before, and sometimes a new freshness of imagery; both of them perceived by Skelton. The poem is addressed not simply to another audience, but to more than one audience at once, and is thus a preparation for the Chaucer of the *Canterbury Tales*. If it is a search for stories,[4] what is discovered is not yet quite Chaucerian. It is written out of temporary depression, a poem of winter, dreaming (but ineffectually) of a waste land. The dreamer has been reading too much, and wants other experience. Then his

---

[1] 853–68
*Colours* . . . fine rhetorical phrases   The *lewed man* is what we now call the Plain or Ordinary Listener.   Chaucer knew his Light Programme, and had got beyond the Third, but was not in a position to argue—that is, to 'show his skills' in return.
[2] See the *Staple of News*, and the quotations in his English Grammar.
[3] 925–7
[4] Compare R. C. GOFFIN, 'Quiting by tidings in the *House of Fame*', *Medium Aevum* 1943.

spirits rise in the upper air, shaken by Jove's Eagle and elevated
by spiritual laughter; so that he can forget Venus, and wonder
at the Creation of God.

> Tho gan I loken under me
> And beheld the ayerissh bestes,
> Cloudes, mystes, and tempestes,
> Snowes, hayles, reynes, wyndes,
> And th'engendrynge in hir kyndes,
> All the wey through which I cam.
> 'O God', quod y, 'that made Adam,
> Moche ys thy myght and thy noblesse!' [1]

I find no uncertainty here. The volumes of love are left behind.
And when at the last page of the poem *a man of greet auctoritee*
is seen in the House of Rumour, Chaucer breaks off—as if the
proposed end of the journey, the communication of tidings of
love which has been so long delayed, was now an embarrassment. He could have found a way of alluding to some court
gossip or other,[2] but allusion to court gossip was not enough.
I do not think he had yet discovered a fresh handling of the
subject of love which satisfied him, and that is why all that he
saw fit to write of the poem lacks either balance or direction.
But even here there is a first sign of the new start:

> And, Lord, this hous in alle tymes,
> Was ful of shipmen and pilgrimes,
> With scrippes bret-ful of lesinges,
> Entremedled with tydinges,
> And eke allone be hemselve.
> O many a thousand tymes twelve
> Saugh I eke of these pardoners,
> Currours, and eke messagers,
> With boystes crammed ful of lyes
> As ever vessel was with lyes.
> And as I alther-fastest wente
> About, and dide al myn entente
> Me for to pleyen and for to lere,
> And eke a tydynge for to here,

---

[1] 964-71
*Ayerissh bestes* dæmons of the air, mentioned in Plato, Ovid, Apuleius, Augustine and
Alain de Lille.
[2] Professor Bronson's seems to me as good a guess as any about Chaucer's plans for
the end of the poem: 'Chaucer's *House of Fame*: Another Hypothesis', *University of
California Publications in English* 1934.

That I had herd of some contre
That shal not now be told for me—
For hit no nede is, redely;
Folk kan synge hit bet than I;
For al mot out, other late or rathe,
Alle the sheves in the lathe—
I herde a gret noyse withalle
In a corner of the halle,
Ther men of love-tydynges tolde . . . [1]

This has often been quoted as a 'backward tracing'. A slight shift or spring of the mind, and Chaucer could let his shipmen and pilgrims speak: courage came with mastery. For he found a supreme way of dealing with a mixed crowd, the way of the finest intelligence in comedy of medieval or modern English. A great art of comedy like Chaucer's can only arrive in certain circumstances, which will enable the most surprising encounters to take place with an explosion of silent laughter. One circumstance is that the language must have been worked, as it had been in the *Romaunt* and the *House of Fame* and through the traffic of fourteenth-century London, to a high degree of flexibility, and not left to harden; and when the right conditions are there, the poet must be ready.

There is the readiness in the *Parliament of Birds*. Without distorting his lucid diction, Chaucer has written with a complexity that makes the complication of most verse today appear a child's puzzle. Interpretations have therefore multiplied.[2] We are to look for an allegory of negotiations for a royal marriage, a debate for St. Valentine's day, a super-cultivated version of folktale, and an exposition of the nature of love. We have also heard, at different times, that the poem satirizes the lower classes, that it satirizes the upper classes, and that it advises them both to behave themselves. We are referred to actual proposals of marriage, including Chaucer's own; and, on the other hand, to the Peasants' Revolt. So there are two directions in which readers have walked, jumped, or plunged. And both are seen

---

[1] 2121-43
*Bret-ful of lesinges* brimful of lies    *Boystes* boxes    *Lyes* lies, lees
*Redely* truly    *Lathe* barn
[2] Details of the interpreters may be found in R. M. Lumiansky's very interesting article in the *Review of English Studies* of April 1948. Mr. Lumiansky's own conclusion is that the poem indicates an earlier and less decisive form of the attitude behind Chaucer's retraction of 'many a lecherous lay'.

44

in Chaucer's outline of the *Dream of Scipio* which he has taken down before bedtime.

When the younger Scipio arrived in Africa, says Chaucer, the elder appeared in his sleep and advised him of the life after death:

> Thanne asked he if folk that here been dede
> Han lyf and dwellynge in another place;
> And Affrican seyde, 'Ye, withouten drede',
> And that oure present worldes lyves space
> Nis but a maner deth, what wey we trace,
> And rightful folk shul gon, after they dye,
> To hevene; and shewede hym the Galaxye.[1]

This is better epitome than Virgil is accorded in the *House of Fame*. The neat last rhyme gives an amused tone of *quod erat demonstrandum*, as if to say 'you see, you may find assurance in the old Romans too'. But the conclusion is the important matter: and this has a very different emphasis from Burckhardt's description of a 'transfigured hereafter for great men'.[2]

It is also a more generous interpretation of Scipio, who admits the minute extent of worldly reputation. Chaucer's attitude to Fame is not what is called the Renaissance attitude: he knows her as a quite unreliable goddess, to whom no sane man would look for salvation. 'Master Chaucer' in Skelton's *Garland of Laurel* invites the self-crowned Poet Laureate to join him in a college above the stars, but that was an elevation Chaucer himself never presumed to expect. There is nothing here about 'historical greatness':

> Thanne preyede hym Scipion to telle hym al
> The wey to come into that hevene blisse.
> And he seyde, 'Know thyself first immortal,
> And loke ay besyly thow werche and wysse
> To commune profit, and thow shalt not mysse
> To comen swiftly to that place deere
> That ful of blysse is and of soules cleere.

---

[1] *Parliament of Birds* 50–6
*Affrican* the elder Africanus    *The Galaxye* the Milky Way, to heaven
[2] JACOB BURCKHARDT, *The Civilization of the Renaissance in Italy*, tr. S. G. C. Middlemore (London: Harrap, 1929), p. 513: with reference to the diffusion of the *Dream of Scipio* in the period of his study.

45

'But brekers of the lawe, soth to seyne,
And likerous folk, after that they ben dede,
Shul whirle aboute th'erthe alwey in peyne,
Tyl many a world be passed, out of drede,
And than, foryeven al hir wikked dede,
Than shul they come into this blysful place,
To which to comen God thee sende his grace.'[1]

Heaven is the reward of those who work for the common good.
Those who do not have first to be purified. So have the lecherous.
And these are two principal themes of Chaucer's poem: con-
cupiscence, and social disorder. And whether in the form of love
and war, or of marriage and domestic strife, they are to be the
themes of all Chaucer's major work.

> *Nam eorum animi qui se corporis voluptatibus dediderunt . . .
> corporibus elapsi circum terram ipsam volutantur; nec hunc in
> locum, nisi multis exagitati saeculis, revertuntur.*[2]

Cicero's *volutantur*, as Skeat saw, became the *voltando* of the second
circle of Dante's Hell:

> *La bufera infernal, che mai non resta,
> mena gli spirti con la sua rapina;
> voltando e percotendo li molesta . . .*

> *Intesi, che a così fatto tormento
> enno dannati i peccator carnali,
> che la ragion sommettono al talento.*[3]

And the original image recurs in *Measure for Measure* (III i):

> To be imprisoned in the viewless winds,
> And blown with restless violence round about
> The pendent world . . .

This returns us, from the Jacobean stage, to the *Parliament of
Birds*. Although the possibility of *eternal* torment does not
occur in his account of Cicero's dream, it can hardly have
escaped Chaucer's attention. In the very next lines he recalls

---

[1] *Parliament of Birds* 71–84
*Werche and wysse* do and teach     *Likerous* licentious
[2] CICERO, *Somnium Scipionis*: 'For the souls of those who have given themselves to
sensual pleasures . . . when they have left the body shall whirl about the earth itself;
nor return to this place until they have suffered torment for many ages'
[3] *Inferno* V 31ff.: 'The infernal hurricane, which never rests, leads the spirits in
its sweep; whirling and smiting it vexes them . . . I learnt that to such torment
carnal sinners are damned, who subject reason to desire'

the *Inferno*; and again, as even those who have not read Dante can perceive, at the beginning of his story.

Chaucer's dream represents at first an unresolved memory of Cicero and Dante, of Jean de Meun and Boccaccio. Africanus leads the new dreamer to a park; and two inscriptions on the gate, which announce the blessings and sorrows of love, suggest both the entrance to the *Inferno* and the healing Garden that Genius of the *Romance of the Rose* promises to all fruitful lovers. It is very perplexing indeed.

> 'Through me men gon into that blysful place
> Of hertes hele and dedly woundes cure;
> Through me men gon unto the welle of grace,
> There grene and lusty May shal evere endure.
> This is the wey to al good aventure.
> Be glad, thow redere, and thy sorwe of-caste;
> Al open am I—passe in, and sped thee faste!'

> 'Through me men gon,' than spak that other side,
> 'Unto the mortal strokes of the spere
> Of which Disdayn and Daunger is the gyde,
> Ther nevere tree shal fruyt ne leves bere.
> This streem yow ledeth to the sorweful were
> Ther as the fish in prysoun is al drye;
> Th'eschewing is only the remedye.'[1]

Chaucer, who has been standing, in his dream, like iron between two magnets, is now thrust in by the 'African' and told that since he is past loving he can safely count as a spectator—

> 'But natheles, although that thow be dul,
> Yit that thow canst not do yit mayst thow see.
> For many a man that may nat stonde a pul,
> It liketh hym at the wrastlyng for to be,
> And demeth yit wher he do bet or he . . .'[2]

This piece of comedy is the proper preface to the dreamer's attitude towards Venus. 'What you cannot do, yet you can see', he is told. So he enters the garden and looks in the well—

> That swymmen ful of smale fishes lighte,
> With fynnes rede and skales sylver-bryghte[3]

[1] *Parliament of Birds* 127–40
*Hele* ease, health      *Daunger* the haughtiness of the hesitant lady of romance
*Were* weir
[2] 162–6
[3] 188–9

—without fear of Guillaume's Rose. But he remembers Guillaume,[1] and even an image of Dante's Earthly Paradise, besides Boccaccio and Jean de Meun and Ovid's Priapus. Nothing, it seems, could be more confusing—so many different ideas of joy at once. And nobody could be less confused. I do not detect the slightest sign of embarrassment as Chaucer approaches Venus: it is all done in the gentle gait of sleep. He is a little more summary than Boccaccio, but Boccaccio is not censored. Chaucer even gives gold for her bed, and golden thread for her hair, and points out that she was resting only until sunset.

> And on a bed of gold she lay to reste,
> Til that the hote sonne gan to weste.[2]

*Thou of love hast lost thy tast, I gesse!* So thinks Africanus. And the game grows, when a list of many a lover inscribed in the temple of Venus is found to include the names of carnal sinners from the *Inferno*. The comedy of Chaucer is never afraid of becoming serious: for there is nothing that need be outside this comedy except the ultimate Cause. It can remain perfectly assured, at the very moment when it has come nearest to the bone.

Boccaccio's praise of Venus which Chaucer has omitted is now granted, in traditional terms, to Nature.

> *Il suo viso era tal che le più genti*
> *Hanno a rispetto bellezza nissuna*
> Teseide

> Whan I was come ayeyn into the place
> That I of spak, that was so sote and grene,
> Forth welk I tho myselven to solace.
> Tho was I war wher that ther sat a queene
> That, as of lyght the somer sonne shene
> Passeth the sterre, right so over mesure
> She fayrer was than any creature.

---

[1] F. N. Robinson notes the reminiscence in lines 190–6, which add Guillaume's squirrels to the *carissimi bestiuoli* of Boccaccio. We may also compare lines 186, 211, with lines 1433, 1578, 1456 in the *Romaunt*.
[2] 265–6
The details I mention are not in the passage of Boccaccio's *Teseide* which Chaucer is using.

And in a launde, upon an hil of floures,
Was set this noble goddesse Nature.¹˙
*Parliament of Birds*

This new game is played with compliments to Alain de Lille *doctor universalis*. And if only Nature's birds were less human, we feel, they would be entirely respectable. The noble goddess, after the cosmology of the distinguished divine, is *the vicaire of the almyghty Lord*, the executive of the Supreme Power. And as the dreamer walks from the temple of Venus to the open air and the *frosty feldefare*, there are other things to see besides a gallery of lovers, or a distant vision of whirling souls. Chaucer places more names on a list, and the garden is changed to Nature's world, and God's. There is *Venus sone* the sparrow; *Behest* and *Art* are in the speech of the royal eagle, and *Curteisye* and *Gentillesse* in

> The gentyl faucon, that with his feet distrayneth
> The kynges hand . . . ²

But there are also *the wedded turtil with hire herte trewe* and *the stork, the wrekere of avouterye*,³ which were not found in the cult of Venus. The comedy of the *Parliament of Birds* now broadens from a comedy of subtle literary allusion, and reaches further than the *House of Fame* towards the *Canterbury Tales*.

> The noyse of foules for to ben delyvered
> So loude rong—'Have don, and lat us wende!'—
> That wel wende I the wode hadde al to-shyvered.
> 'Com of!' they criede, 'allas, ye wol us shende!
> Whan shal youre cursede pledynge have an ende?
> How sholde a juge eyther parti leve,
> For ye or nay, withouten any preve?' . . .

> Nature, which that alwey hadde an ere
> To murmur of the lewednesse behynde,
> With facound voys seyde, 'Hold youre tonges there!

¹ BOCCACCIO, *Teseide* VII. 65: Venus. 'Her face was such that most people are in comparison utterly without beauty.'
*Parliament of Birds* 295–303
*Sote* sweet      *Launde* glade
² 337–8
*Distrayneth* grasps
³ 355, 361
The stork was supposed to destroy his mate if he found her unfaithful, and according to a story in Aelian put out the eyes of a servant who committed adultery with his master's wife.

And I shal sone, I hope, a conseyl fynde
Yow to delyvere, and fro this noyse unbynde:
I juge, of every folk men shul oon calle
To seyn the verdit for yow foules alle.' . . .

The water-foules han here hedes leid
Togedere and, of a short avysement,
Whan everych hadde his large golee seyd,
They seyden sothly, al by oon assent,
How that the goos, with her facounde gent,
'That so desyreth to pronounce oure nede,
Shal telle oure tale', and preyede 'God hire spede!'

And for these water-foules tho began
The goos to speke, and in hire kakelynge
She seyde, 'Pees! Now tak kep every man,
And herkeneth which a resoun I shal forth brynge!
My wit is sharp, I love no taryinge;
I seye I rede hym, though he were my brother,
But she wol love hym, lat hym love another!'

'Lo, here a parfit resoun of a goos!'
Quod the sperhauk . . .

The laughter arose of gentil foules alle
And right anon the seed-foul chosen hadde
The turtle trewe, and gonne her to hem calle . . .

'Wel bourded', quod the doke, 'by myn hat!
That men shulde loven alwey causeles,
Who can a resoun fynde or wit in that?
Daunseth he murye that is myrtheles? . . .'

'Now fy, cherl!' quod the gentil tercelet,
'Out of the donghil cam that word ful right!
Thow canst nat seen which thyng is wel beset!
Thow farest by love as oules don by lyght:
The day hem blent, ful wel they see by nyght.
Thy kynde is of so low a wrechednesse
That what love is, thow canst nat see ne gesse.'

Tho gan the kokkow putte hym forth in prees
For foul that eteth worm, and seyde blyve:
'So I', quod he, 'may have my make in pees,
I reche nat how longe that ye stryve.

50

Lat ech of hem be soleyn al here lyve!
This is my reed, syn they may nat acorde.
This shorte lessoun nedeth nat recorde.'

'Ye, have the glotoun fild inow his paunche,
Thanne are we wel!' seyde the merlioun;
'Thow morderere of the heysoge on the braunche
That broughte thee forth, thow . . . glotoun! . . .'

'Now pees,' quod Nature, 'I comaunde heer!
For I have herd al youre opynyoun,
And in effect yit be we nevere the neer . . .'[1]

This, in the words of the title of a manuscript of the poem in
the library of Trinity College, Cambridge, is the *Parlement of
Byrdes Reducyd to Love*. What is Love? That seems to be the
question at issue; for the elected representatives are manifestly
incompetent to settle the eagles' business. A turtle-dove speaks
for the few who, like the Ploughman on Canterbury way, are
true and good, and the humblest. But Chaucer is not answering
the question: he is giving, with his birds, the comic underside
of a human debate which has its relation to that very fine thirteenth-century English poem the *Owl and the Nightingale*, to the
procedure of medieval law, and even to the dialectic that taught
the schoolmen logical argument. His superior entertainment
would be impossible in a culture without the *sic et non* of disputation, without that delimited scepticism which is essential to the
thinker, and which is so finely expressed at the beginning of the
*Legend of Good Women*. When Dante and Boccaccio are unexpectedly brought together—or a goose, a turtle-dove and a
cuckoo become, as we have heard, articulate—we are given the
comedy of a poet of a civilization with a philosophy, and not
the comedy of the philosophy of a poet. In the 1370's or 1380's
these things, at least, were in the right order. And so it is not
at all improbable, though to guess dates is far from my intent,
that the poetry I have just been enjoying was written at a time of
revolution.

---

[1] 491ff.
*To ben delyvered*—the phrase used, as in the *Anonimalle Chronicle*, for the adjourning of
Parliament      *Shende* ruin      *Leve* believe      *Facound* eloquent
*Golee* 'mouthful'      *Facounde gent* (the goose's) exquisite fluency
*Rede* advise      *Seed-foul* birds living on seeds      *Wel bourded* very funny
*Tercelet* male falcon      *Blent* blinds      *Putte hym forth in prees* pushed forward
*Blyve* forthwith      *Soleyn* solitary      The *merlioun*, we were told earlier,
preys on small birds such as the lark      *Heysoge* hedge-sparrow

51

*Explicit tractatus de congregacione volucrum* . . . conclude three Bodleian manuscripts. And as we look into the clear mind of the dreamer, at his congress of only too human fowls, we see him more interested in the kind than the genus, and still more interested in the person. Chaucer could not have written the *Inferno*, and could not have attempted it without complicating the apparatus. He was finding, for himself, the old and hard truth that (like Criseyde) every human being is, and is not, the same in every moment.

# III

*E per questa cagione . . . quella gentilissima, la quale fu distruggitrice di tutti i vizii e regina delle virtù, passando per alcuna parte mi negò il suo dolcissimo salutare, nel quale stava tutta la mia beatitudine.*

And for this cause . . . that most gentle one who was destroyer of all vices and queen of virtues, as she passed a certain way denied me her most sweet salutation, in which lay all my beatitude.

DANTE: *Vita Nuova X*

TROILUS . . . *This is, and is not Cressid!*
*Within my soul there doth conduce a fight*
*Of this strange nature, that a thing inseparate*
*Divides more wider than the sky and earth;*
*And yet the spacious breadth of this division*
*Admits no orifex for a point as subtle*
*As Ariachne's broken woof to enter.*

SHAKESPEARE: *Troilus and Cressida V ii*

# THE POETRY OF THE BOOK OF TROILUS

H AVING SET DOWN 'POETRY', I SHALL BEGIN WITH NARRATIVE;
for the two are not separate, nor are my chapters. And
since we are thinking of a poem and a story of the fourteenth century, let us remember that the fourteenth century had
in the language of Scotus the Subtle Doctor an exact term to
describe their relation. They are *formalitates*.

Now what is the story of *Troilus and Criseyde*? There is only
one right answer, and that is a copy of the poem, together with
the previous poetry that its author had read on the matter of
Troy. In this sequence of literature the personality of a single
poet recedes, as Chaucer would wish. He does not hurry to
judge his characters; he arrives to give evidence to another court
of appeal, and the 'story' is the whole history of the case until a
final verdict. Judgement is not, directly, the poet's business.
All that he can do is to invoke Clio and Calliope, Venus and the
Furies, and get down to composition.

But if this notion of story is strange to those of us who are
nourished on the modern novel, our question returns, with so
much more insistence, in a different shape. What did Chaucer
make of the matter handed down to him? We may reply, here
and again, in a geological figure: *Troilus and Criseyde* has several
layers to its world. There is the day-to-day social life of Troy,
even now so actual that the first visit of Pandarus to Criseyde is
(whatever else it may be) as bright as a new film blessed by a
lady critic. There is the intrigue of Pandarus, complicated by
Deiphobus and Helen, Helen and Paris, the episode in which
for a thousand lines everything gives way to Chaucer's own comic
narrative. There is the pattern of courtly love, raised from
intrigue to the constancy of Troilus, to his short happiness, to
the poetry of Venus in the third book. There is the dialectic
to which the conversation tends, being written for an audience
of civilized minds that could digest without discomfort the
thoughts on predestination of a disappointed knight. And, on

55

one side, there is a rumour of fate and the city's doom. Add also that the story is about lovers' seasons and a variable female mind, and this is not all. In *Troilus and Criseyde*, above any other poem of love that I know, *finis coronat opus*. If we ask what in its world is, for a moment or a season, *believed*, the answers that we find are indifference, trivial excuse, or the suggestion that fear invented the gods; paganism, worldly wisdom or the nobility of man; or the theology of courtly love; until the eventual collapse which compels a conclusion. This, as far as I can sketch it, is Chaucer's story. And one thing which may be understood from a reading, is the meaning of scepticism in a society of developed religion: the scepticism which is neither unbelief nor frozen doubt, but that which makes possible a philosophical discussion, a disputation, or any conversation proceeding beyond the weather. Conclusions have a way of making an end of all these: and even a poet must be able at least to pretend not to know, in order to have the pleasure of finding out. For this delight Chaucer was granted an exceptional flexibility of mind, a gift that could be cultivated in the age that produced Decorated Gothic. It is a mind interested not only in those who live in glasshouses and throw stones, but in sad glasshouse-dwellers with a very good aim. It is a mind capable of spiritual laughter.

*Troilus and Criseyde* has already been read by several persons as a psychological novel, and by Professor Karl Young as *par excellence* a romance. Let us now look at it as a poem. We have admired on the one hand the virtuosity and directness of its verse dialogue, which is much of the essential action of the story; on the other, the lyrical grace which can hold up, in the stream of narrative or conversation, feelings of more than momentary point. And the author of a play called *Sir Gyles Goosecappe* paid his compliment to Chaucer's art of conversation in poetry by adapting a great deal of it for the Jacobean stage. But what is of greater interest today is the advantage of the poet over a novelist writing prose of comparable subtlety. There are certain things, such as the lyrical pattern, or the epic manner that Chaucer admired in Dante, which the novelist will not

ELY OCTAGON
*Photograph by courtesy of the National Buildings Record*

attempt; others, which Chaucer does with ease, he may try for laboriously. Dr. D. J. Enright has said that *Troilus and Criseyde* is laboured in comparison with the *Tristan und Ísolt* of Gottfried von Strassburg,[1] and on this I can only respect his opinion. But if he is right, where does the poor novelist come in? He does not. A Henry James will make himself richer by edging towards poetry:

> In her large countenance her dim little smile scarcely showed. It was a mere sketch of a smile, a kind of instalment, or payment on account; it seemed to say that she would smile more if she had time, but that you could see, without this, that she was gentle and easy to beguile.[2]

This is what the writer of prose must aim at if he wants anything like the Chaucerian delicacy. But I do not say that all novelists should have this ambition; or that *Troilus and Criseyde* itself will not appear intolerably wearisome if we approach it with the insensitiveness to language most novelists assume in their readers; or even that a few passages of the poem are not unrelieved tedium to any honest man. We must allow Chaucer to tell the story in his own time. He wrote for an audience prepared to listen to long stretches of verse, especially verse which is calmly, fluently confident of being understood, and which can smile without familiarity between two rhymes. This was the manner that allowed a cultivated bourgeois to carry his wisdom to the court. And let us remember that refinement was not a restriction but an extension of the possibilities of English in his age. For Chaucer's purpose Boccaccio's young gallant would not do, but Chaucer's down-to-earth Pandarus was essential:

> 'Nece, I have so greet a pyne
> For love, that every other day I faste'.[3]

Chaucer was using a courtly convention and a literary artifice; he was also writing English pure but not sterilized. He had mastered a form of verse as well as of narrative; and this means

---

[1] *Scrutiny* XII 302ff. (1944). I should also like to draw attention to Mr. John Speirs's brief and admirable suggestions on *Troilus and Criseyde* in an early issue of the same journal: II 296ff. (1933).
[2] *The Bostonians* I iv: Miss Birdseye
[3] *Troilus and Criseyde* II 1165–6

that he could give, with the utmost lucidity, a fine innuendo of a kind which would involve Henry James in contortions, and which no other English writer can quite achieve.

We do not discover how this is done until we can hear the poet striking his tone in nothing more than a deliberate rhyme:

> *Per caso avvenne che in fra la gente*
> *L' occhio suo vago giunse penetrando*
> *La dov' era Criseida piacente*
>
> Il Filostrato

> And upon cas bifel that thorugh a route
> His eye percede, and so depe it wente,
> Til on Criseyde it smot, and ther it stente.[1]
>
> *Troilus and Criseyde*

Chaucer has expanded Boccaccio's *penetrando* for his own comic emphasis. On the other hand we may find the rhyme of a lyrical tune that the musician would direct *dolce*—

> Criseyda gan al his chere aspien,
> And leet it so softe in hire herte synke,
> That to hireself she seyde, 'Who yaf me drynke?'[2]

The hero has just come home in triumph: let the heroine have this moment, says the poetry. And let the reader wait for the time when Troilus and Troy town *shall knotteles thorughout hire herte slide*.[3] Between these two quotations we might assemble the finest gradations of tone perceptible in rhyme. But there is also a means of expression which the writer of prose will employ, and which some novelists have used with less moderation than the poet Chaucer: and that is imagery. Look no further than the poem *Il Filostrato* which he was adapting, and Chaucer's reticence is admirable. He reduces the feverish phrases of Boccaccio, *il fuoco* and *l'ardenti fiamme amorose*, for the same reason that he omits Troilo's second attempt at suicide—he is not an Italian in love with Maria d'Aquino. Criseida is as transparent as the morning air she is said to resemble: Criseyde's mind interests

---

[1] BOCCACCIO: *Il Filostrato* I 26: 'It chanced that his wandering eyes, glancing through the crowd, lighted where stood the charming Criseida'
   *Troilus and Criseyde* I 271–3
   *Stente* stopped
[2] II 649–51
   *His chere* the appearance of Troilus
[3] V 769

Chaucer more than her complexion. And Troilus did not
suggest to him a rose, or even a lily. To Criseyde he was

a wal
Of steel . . .[1]

'Stolen waters', says Criseida, 'are sweeter far than wine in
plenty', and *l'acqua furtiva*[2] is the right phrase for the affair of
Troilo: Troilus and Criseyde are further from the coupling of
animals. I am not anxious to damn Boccaccio, or to suggest
that every adaptation of Chaucer's is an improvement. On the
contrary, I think we have to admit that at least at one point
Boccaccio is rubbed a little smooth:

> *E si come l' uccel di foglia in foglia*
> *Nel nuovo tempo prende dilettanza*
> *Del canto suo; così facean costoro,*
> *Di molte cose parlando fra loro.*
>
> Il Filostrato

> And as the briddes, whanne the sonne is shene,
> Deliten in hire song in leves grene,
> Right so the wordes that they spake yfeere
> Delited hem, and made hire hertes clere.[3]
>
> *Troilus and Criseyde*

These lines have the slightly uniform beauty of late Gothic
leaves in stone, and lack the definition of the Italian *di foglia in
foglia*. There is a more than compensating allurement in the
whole of the English design. Chaucer complicates the intrigue,
immensely subtilizes the narrative of feeling, rebates none of the
secrecy of 'courtly love'—and at the same time excels Boccaccio
by admitting light and air into the stuffiness of the Italian dialogue
and imagery. Above all, he triumphs by placing the emotions
of the lover in a perspective to infinity.

Boccaccio first saw Maria d'Aquino in the church of St.
Lorenzo in Naples, and described his impression of her in five
different romances, including the poem *Il Filostrato*. 'Never
was there under white veil in dark gown', says Troilo, 'a lady so
beautiful'—

[1] III 479–80
[2] *Il Filostrato* II 74; *Proverbs* ix. 17
[3] *Il Filostrato* IV 138: 'And as in the new season the bird from leaf to leaf takes
delight in his song; so did they, speaking of many things between themselves'
*Troilus and Criseyde* IV 1432–5
*Yfeere* together      *Clere* bright

*non fu giammai*
*Sotto candido velo in bruna vesta*
*Sì bella donna . . .*

Chaucer, in effect, combines suggestions from three different contexts of the Italian to produce a new line:

Nor under cloude blak so bright a sterre . . .[1]

This is more than a particular circumstance—the penitential dress of Maria or Criseyde's widow's habit: it is the poetry of the appearance of his lady to *every* lover. It is not Chaucer's lady, for he denies her existence. It is an extension in the mind of Chaucer from all he has read in himself and the universe, and in books. As for Troilus,

. . . whoso axed hym wherof hym smerte,
He seyde, his harm was al aboute his herte.[2]

We must attend to associations within the whole poem in order to appreciate this: that here is a poet writing with the utmost sympathy of a humanly faithful and a faithless heart, and writing with the sympathy of understanding, which is not necessarily the sympathy of approval. The moralist impatient with our story can learn from it, if he cannot learn otherwise, that religion is greater than morality. The heart of Criseyde has been laid bare in two quotations that I have given. She was, as we shall hear, *slydynge of corage*. And her eyes were unsurpassed. The famous line of the last book *that Paradis stood formed in hire eyen* should be read with a whole development of the image in mind, and is still a little shocking to an age which rarely thinks of heaven. It appears Dantesque; and is beautiful not because it identifies Criseyde and Beatrice, but because it allows them to be divided. That is why it is Chaucerian.

And before I am too late let me praise a most distinguished plagiarist. I may do so very briefly, for the idea of systematic literary 'borrowing' causes less horror, at least among poets, than it did fifty years ago; even if some of us, in reading a poem like *Troilus and Criseyde*, are inclined to search out too curiously those verses for which editors have discovered no source. There is no harm in this, so long as we do not overlook the remarkable

[1] *Il Filostrato* I 38 (quoted); I 19; and the 'star' in III 29, IV 143 or V 44
*Troilus and Criseyde* I 175
[2] V 1224-5

and re-creative achievement of good translation of poetry, or the difficulty of establishing the exact point at which translation turns 'original', or the fine medieval art of poetic theft. Thus a Dantesque simile becomes first Boccaccian, and then Chaucerian:

> *Quali i fioretti dal notturno gelo*
> *chinati e chiusi, poi che il sol gl' imbianca,*
> *si drizzan tutti aperti in loro stelo:*
>
> *tal mi fec' io, di mia virtute stanca.*

Inferno

> *Quali i fioretti dal notturno gelo*
> *Chinati e chiusi, poi che 'l sol gl'imbianca,*
> *Tutti s'apron diritti in loro stelo;*
> *Cotal si fe' di sua virtude stanca*
> *Troilo allora, e riguardando il cielo,*
> *Incominciò come persona franca:*
> *Lodato sia il tuo sommo valore,*
> *Venere bella, e del tuo figlio Amore.*

Il Filostrato

> But right as floures, thorugh the cold of nyght
> Iclosed, stoupen on hire stalke lowe,
> Redressen hem ayein the sonne bright,
> And spreden on hire kynde cours by rowe,
> Right so gan tho his eighen up to throwe
> This Troilus, and seyde, 'O Venus deere,
> Thi myght, thi grace, yheried be it here!'[1]

*Troilus and Criseyde*

But I have no wish to repeat what has already been written upon the goods Chaucer stole direct from Dante, or the stolen goods he received; and I must now bring this introduction to an end. My end is comedy, for comedy is the end when certain kinds of poetry come together. One of these is the verse of direct action or downright idiom, and the other is the verse which everyone would call lyrical. We have them in sudden

---

[1] *Inferno* II 127–30: 'As little flowers by the cold night bowed and closed, when the sun whitens them, rise all open on their stems: thus I did, in my weakness'
   *Il Filostrato* II 80: 'As little flowers by the cold night bowed and closed, when the sun whitens them, all open straight upon their stems, so did Troilo then from his weakness, and glancing heavenward began as one freed: "Praised be thy supreme power, fair Venus, and that of thy son Love." '
   *Troilus and Criseyde* II 967–73
   *Kynde* natural      *Yheried* praised

61

succession on the third of May, when the swallow tells her ancient story, and Pandarus tosses in bed with a green lovesickness:

In May, that moder is of monthes glade,
That fresshe floures, blew and white and rede,
Ben quike agayn, that wynter dede made,
And ful of bawme is fletyng every mede;
Whan Phebus doth his bryghte bemes sprede
Right in the white Bole, it so bitidde,
As I shal synge, on Mayes day the thrydde,

That Pandarus, for al his wise speche,
Felte ek his part of loves shotes keene,
That, koude he nevere so wel of lovyng preche,
It made his hewe a-day ful ofte greene.
So shop it that hym fil that day a teene
In love, for which in wo to bedde he wente,
And made, er it was day, ful many a wente.

The swalowe Proigne, with a sorowful lay,
Whan morwen com, gan make hire waymentynge
Whi she forshapen was; and ever lay
Pandare abedde, half in a slomberynge,
Til she so neigh hym made hire cheterynge
How Tereus gan forth hire suster take,
That with the noyse of hire he gan awake . . .[1]

We have them both at once in the superb *aubade* of Troilus, which is written in a tradition returning to the *alba* of the troubadour, and to Ovid:

'O cruel day, accusour of the joie
That nyght and love han stole and faste iwryen,
Acorsed be thi comyng into Troye,
For every bore hath oon of thi bryghte yën!
Envyous day, what list thee so to spien?
What hastow lost, why sekestow this place,
Ther God thi light so quenche, for his grace?

[1] II 50–70
*And ful of bawme* . . . every meadow floats in balm
*Right in the white Bole* an astronomical reference to the date, with a light allusion to the snow-white bull in Ovid's description of Jupiter visiting Europa
*Shop* befell     *Teene* sorrow     *Wente* turn     *Proigne* is the Progne who as Ovid tells was *forshapen* from human form to a bird.     *Tereus*, the husband, put her away and took the sister who became a nightingale.     I shall return to the story in a chapter on Good Women.     *Waymentynge* lament

62

'Allas! what have thise loveris thee agylt,
Dispitous day? Thyn be the peyne of helle!
For many a lovere hastow slayn, and wilt—
Thy pourynge in wol nowher lat hem dwelle.
What profrestow thi light here for to selle?
Go selle it hem that smale selys grave;
We wol thee nought, us nedeth no day have.'[1]

This is a lyric of the sullen speaking voice, as Troilus curses the
crack of dawn; but it is still a lyric. One of day's bright eyes,
he says, is at every chink. But that splendid apparition is not
all of Chaucer's imagination of his scene. Day, to the lover, is
an inquisitive, absent-minded, Argus-eyed commercial traveller
trading in light. And the lover is no longer wilting. On the
contrary, he is quite as alive as Shakespeare's Troilus when
Shakespeare has written him a speech about day rousing the
ribald crows, and about wings more momentary-swift than
thought. The difference between Chaucer and Shakespeare is
a difference in development of the spirit; but if we are thinking
simply of the vitality of these two episodes, the only difference
that matters is that one bed is in a theatre and the other is not.

Put this passage for an instant at the centre, between the
verse of action and the verse of lyricism in the poem, then beyond
lyricism we have the excellent 'high style' of the invocation to
Venus, and beneath action the robust rumgumption of Pandarus.
But even Pandarus grows lyrical in excitement:

Thenk ek, how elde wasteth every houre
In ech of yow a partie of beautee;
And therfore, er that age thee devoure,
Go love, for old, ther wol no wight of thee.
Lat this proverbe a lore unto yow be:
'Too late ywar, quod Beaute, whan it paste';
And elde daunteth daunger at the laste.[2]

---

[1] III 1450–63
Chaucer may have remembered the *invida* of *Amores* I xiii, which has been suggested
as his source; but I am not convinced that there is any *literal* indebtedness to Ovid
in the passage.
*Accusour* revealer      *Faste iwryen* closely hidden      *Bore* hole showing light
*Ther God thi light so quenche* where I pray God to extinguish you      *Agylt* offended
'I much doubt', observed Hazlitt of the *smale selys*, 'whether there was such a profession as that of seal-engraver in the Trojan war'. I much hope that at this point
the reader will not bother to inquire.
[2] II 393–9
*Ek* too      *Elde* old age      *Partie* portion      *Ywar* aware      *Daunteth*
*daunger* overcomes disdain

This continues a theme common to Ovid and Jean de Meun, in both of whom Chaucer must have seen it; and his stanza is finer than the set songs of *Troilus and Criseyde*, even the songs of Troilus. And what is more remarkable than a critical moment for Pandarus, or a moment of hesitation for Criseyde, is the development of *rhythm* in verse of such quality. We can find a passage in which the very pattern of the flow of sentence and line expresses, as if with an equal balance of delicacy and reservation, the exact degree of union between the lovers:

> But thilke litel that they spake or wroughte,
> His wise goost took ay of al swych heede,
> It semed hire he wiste what she thoughte
> Withouten word, so that it was no neede
> To bidde hym ought to doon, or ought for-beede;
> For which she thought that love, al come it late,
> Of alle joye hadde opned hire the yate.[1]

And in the fourth book we can watch the rhythmic period stretched further and further, towards the great lament of Troilus. We shall find that the comedy of *Troilus and Criseyde* is not the moment only, of Pandarus and the swallow, but the whole enfilade of comedy, which includes what Chaucer called his *litel tragedye*, and ends in a laugh from the hollowness of the eighth sphere.

But I am jumping too far, and before I say more about Troilus's last laugh in the poem, we must turn to the reader who would like guidance through the preceding five books. Those impatient of conducted tours may read or re-read *Troilus and Criseyde* without my assistance, and glance through the next fifty pages. I shall in any case do my best to avoid doubling the tracks of earlier agents. And anyone who needs (let us say) a prospectus of Courtly Love will not have to look very long outside these chapters.

Once we have acquired an annotated edition and mastered a few hundred lines, Chaucer's language seems exceptionally easy, and is exceptionally clear; but if a reader is to digest the poem, he must learn to add salt in the right proportions. Everybody can appreciate Chaucer's irony here and there, but one must form the habit of relating not only lines or episodes, but whole

[1] III 463-9
*Goost* spirit    *Yate* gate

volumes which would otherwise appear inconsistent. Because Chaucer preferred to deal with one thing at once, and the most distinguished poet of 1950 is inclined to deal with two, we should not conclude that the former was defective in intelligence. Chaucer was aware of the passionate oxymoron of the love-poet, which was at least as old as Ovid: he had heard of living deaths and delicious pains, and had himself spoken about them. Such a line as

O quike deth, O swete harm so queynte

is burlesqued by Pandarus as he bustles in to Criseyde:

I have a joly wo, a lusty sorwe

and imitated in one of Troilus's paroxysms in the fifth book:

O herte myn, Criseyde, O swete fo![1]

On the other hand, it is not likely that a modern poet who had set himself to translate metres of Boethius, would carefully explain the sentence in which the first gobbets of gold and jewels are called 'precious perils'.[2] It is as if Chaucer was conscious of paradox as either a rhetorical figure inviting ridicule, or as a last resort of language when rational discourse has failed. And this consciousness has to do with a difference between the poetry of Chaucer and the poetry of Shakespeare to which I shall return. Chaucer has his own way of examining the sides of a question: he will look at them one by one, so that he can think of them all together. It is not merely that, as I have said, Chaucer tells a story with different layers. He tells it, as we shall see, from different points of view.

---

[1] I 411; II 1099; V 228
*Queynte* strange and difficult      *Lusty* happy
[2] *Pretiosa pericula*: BOETHIUS, *Consolatio Philosophiæ* II m. v 30

# IV

*Buona è la signoria d' Amore, perocchè trae lo intendimento del suo fedele da tutte le vili cose . . . non buona è la signoria d' Amore, perocchè quanto lo suo fedele più fede gli porta, tanto più gravi e dolorosi punti gli conviene passare.*

The lordship of Love is good, since it draws the mind of his liege from all evil things . . . the lordship of Love is not good, since the more faith his liege bears to him, the more heavy and grievous straits must he pass.

DANTE: *Vita Nuova XIII*

*This is the monstruosity in love, lady: that the will is infinite, and the execution confined: that the desire is boundless, and the act a slave to limit.*

SHAKESPEARE: *Troilus and Cressida III ii*

# TWO BOOKS OF THE BOOK OF TROILUS

THE INTRODUCTORY VERSES TO THE FIVE PARTS OF *Troilus and Criseyde* are not very reliable autobiography; but they do sometimes suggest how we should read what they introduce. I do not recommend anyone who is beginning the poem for the first time to trouble about Tisiphone. He would be better employed in enjoying the tone of the third stanza, the careful deference to courtly love, and solemn mockery of the lover out of grace.

> For I that god of Loves servantz serve,
> Ne dar to Love, for myn unliklynesse,
> Preyen for speed, al sholde I therfore sterve,
> So fer am I from his help in derknesse;
> But natheles, if this may don gladnesse
> To any lovere, and his cause availle,
> Have he my thank, and myn be this travaille![1]

The line about serving the servants of the god of love, recalling the Papal title *servus servorum dei*, is of the religion of *amour courtois*. The poet prays for success as a 'servant', imitates the lover's short expectation of life, reflects his audience's smiles on to himself. And if this succeeds in cheering any lover, the preface ends, acknowledgements are due to Cupid. But Chaucer's attitude to courtly love is not what we call a superior attitude; it is really superior. There was another religion, and a greater. There was also a smaller desire.

When, in his next introduction, he appeals to the Muse of History and apologizes for writing not from his own heart but 'out of Latin', he can avoid letting us see how much of his tongue is in his cheek:

> . . . of no sentement I this endite,
> But out of Latyn in my tonge it write.[2]

[1] I 15–21
*Unliklynesse* inability to please in consequence     *Al sholde I therfore sterve* even though I should die
[2] II 13–4

Perhaps that is why Chaucer was so fond of variations upon this joke. Another reason, I think, is that it hit a particular tone he wanted above all. He wished to be able to write an experience and at the same time deny, plausibly, that he had experienced it. This is an ambition for a master: to get some of the poetry within, so to speak, the very act—and to keep the poet, at least by the skin of his teeth, outside. And when he politely requests Venus to infuse passion into his *naked herte*, his intention, whatever it is, is not to write the third book in his own person.

> Ye in my naked herte sentement
> Inhielde, and do me shewe of thy swetnesse.
> Caliope, thi vois be now present,
> For now is nede; sestow nought my destresse,
> How I mot telle anonright the gladnesse
> Of Troilus, to Venus heryinge?
> To which gladnesse, who nede hath, God hym brynge![1]

So Chaucer's later inquiry, why he has not sold his soul for a night with Criseyde, is no more than an unusually large bubble floating down from the goddess of love towards her apparently dutiful poet. He knows: in a way greater than what we call experience.

But before these joys, there are prayers for the just expression of lovers' pains. None, says Chaucer, may destroy the natural law. And so he refuses to falsify human impulse. When he writes

> For evere it was, and evere it shal byfalle,
> That Love is he that alle thing may bynde,[2]

the poet is associating, not confusing, human love and the divine *amor che move il sole e l'altre stelle*. They are both to be respected, but not respected equally; and the extent to which 'courtly love' really respected either, is to be shown in his poem. Europeans, if they remain European, either disguise what Criseyde calls *lust voluptuous*, or desire to proceed beyond it. And at the outset, Chaucer will interpret the cult of love with the utmost generosity, and will even allow it a liturgy of its own.

We hear of the treachery of Calchas, who finds by divination that his city is to be destroyed, and therefore decides to leave:

---

[1] III 43–9
Calliope, the muse of epic poetry, is mentioned in Dante's invocation at the beginning of the *Purgatorio*. *Venus heryinge* the praise of Venus
[2] I 236–7

So whan this Calkas knew by calkulynge,
And ek by answer of this Appollo,
That Grekes sholden swich a peple brynge,
Thorugh which that Troie moste ben fordo,
He caste anon out of the town to go . . .[1]

*Calkas knew by calkulynge*: so much for the great divine's astrology.
Criseyde is left in Troy, but granted the protection of Hector.
She is one of the medievalized congregation at the feast of Pallas,
and staged with such brilliant lighting that the reports of commentators are strangely variant. One recalls Petrarch's Laura
at a service in Avignon; another remembers the Wife of Bath
(the dominant will and tingling flesh) at the funeral of her fourth
husband. A Florentine church known to Dante has been
mentioned, with heaven knows what propriety. Chaucer is in
no hurry to judge.

Then, in the manner descending from Provence, love is trans-
mitted through the glance of the lady, so that her knight will
long for what is *withinne the subtile stremes of hir eyen*, and will say

'What that I mene, O swete herte deere?'
Quod Troilus, 'O goodly, fresshe free,
That with the stremes of youre eyen cleere
Ye wolde somtyme frendly on me see . . .'[2]

By these eyes Troilus is to be trapped.[3] At the moment, he
must avoid suspicion; so he pretends to go on mocking love's
servants. They live in uncertainty and suffer disdain, no faith
is so exacting as theirs—or, he hints, so unrewarding—

. . . 'Lord, so ye lyve al in lest,
Ye loveres! For the konnyngeste of yow,
That serveth most ententiflich and best,
Hym tit as often harm therof as prow.
Youre hire is quyt ayen, ye, God woot how!
Nought wel for wel, but scorn for good servyse.
In feith, youre ordre is ruled in good wise!

[1] I 71–5
*Calkulynge* calculation, presumably astrological. The pun is surely deliberate.
[2] I 305; III 127–30
*Free* gracious
[3] III 1355, 1730ff.

71

'In nouncerteyn ben alle youre observaunces,
But it a sely fewe pointes be;
Ne no thing asketh so gret attendaunces
As doth youre lay, and that knowe alle ye.
But that is nat the worste, as mote I the!
But, tolde I yow the worste point, I leve,
Al seyde I soth, ye wolden at me greve.'[1]

He sounds like a very green youth trying to imitate the seasoned military duke who laughs at lovers in the *Knight's Tale* and remembers his own distant folly: but that story, as Chaucer tells it, is less serious than our present business. In suffering the torments he has laughed at, Troilus finds himself parodying his own earlier flippancy. He is as just as his lady, who before she can desert him considers how often women are betrayed. We receive the double irony of the sad dwellers in glasshouses, who aim so beautifully true: Chaucer himself more than once has his own version of the proverb.

And this, which we now follow, is our hero's 'new life'. Let him begin it with an exquisite image:

Thus gan he make a mirour of his mynde
In which he saugh al holly hire figure . . .[2]

Troilo is *speglio mio*[3] to Criseida when they have just retired for the night;-but there is nothing like this in Boccaccio. Chaucer is nearer to a Provençal purity of diction, and using one of the great elements or *topoi* which we mistakenly call 'commonplace'. After a *pitous vois* for Troilus, he returns to his calm narrative manner.

In hym ne deyned spare blood roial
The fyr of love—the wherfro God me blesse—
Ne him forbar in no degree, for al
His vertu or his excellent prowesse;
But held hym as his thral lowe in destresse,
And brende hym so in soundry wise ay newe,
That sixty tyme a day he loste his hewe.

---

[1] I 330–43
*Lest* delight    *Ententiflich* attentively    *Hym tit as often* . . . receives as much
evil as good    *Youre hire is quyt ayen* . . . you have your reward, God knows.    There
follow ironical allusions to religious orders and observance. *Sely fewe pointes* few
slight points    *As mote I the* so may I thrive    *Leve* believe
[2] I 365–6
[3] *Il Filostrato* III 31: 'mirror mine'

72

So muche, day by day, his owene thought,
For lust to hire, gan quiken and encresse,
That every other charge he sette at nought;
Forthi ful ofte, his hote fir to cesse,
To seen hire goodly look he gan to presse;
For therby to ben esed wel he wende,
And ay the neer he was, the more he brende.

For ay the ner the fir, the hotter is—
This, trowe I, knoweth al this compaignye.
But were he fer or neer, I dar sey this:
By nyght or day, for wisdom or folye,
His herte, which that is his brestes eye,
Was ay on hire, that fairer was to sene
Than evere was Eleyne or Polixene.[1]

At a first reading it is as well to hurry on from this point to the arrival of Pandarus, that fourteenth-century Polonius who is yet more hearty, more expansive, more alert, and happiest when his niece Criseyde is laughing with him at himself. He makes up for his own failure in love by sweating to bring Troilus down to earth and persuading Criseyde to meet him there. 'I am near death', says the excellent young knight:

'How hastow thus unkyndely and longe
Hid this fro me, thow fool?' quod Pandarus.
'Paraunter thow myghte after swich oon longe,
That myn avyse anoon may helpen us.'
'This were a wonder thing,' quod Troilus.
'Thow koudest nevere in love thiselven wisse:
How devel maistow brynge me to blisse?'[2]

The modern reader can easily recognize this situation. But he is less accustomed to admiring real sagesse and at the same time smiling at its plausibility—

'Ye, Troilus, now herke,' quod Pandare;
'Though I be nyce, it happeth often so,
That oon that excesse doth ful yvele fare
By good counseil kan kepe his frend therfro.

---

[1] I 435–55
*Forbar* spared     *Brende* burned     *Charge* care     *Eleyne* Helen of Troy
*Polixene* Polyxena, daughter of Hecuba
[2] I 617–23
*Paraunter* perhaps     *Swich oon* such a one     *Wisse* guide

I have myself ek seyn a blynd man go
Ther as he fel that couthe loken wide;
A fool may ek a wis man ofte gide.

'A whetstone is no kervyng instrument,
But yet it maketh sharpe kervyng tolis.
And there thow woost that I have aught myswent,
Eschuw thow that, for swich thing to thee scole is;
Thus often wise men ben war by foolys.
If thow do so, thi wit is wel bewared;
By his contrarie is every thyng declared.

'For how myghte evere sweetnesse have ben knowe
To him that nevere tasted bitternesse?
Ne no man may ben inly glad, I trowe,
That nevere was in sorwe or som destresse.
Eke whit by blak, by shame ek worthinesse,
Ech set by other, more for other semeth—
As men may see; and so the wyse it demeth.'[1]

Pandarus has failed through excess, but the wise can learn from him. This is, absolutely, a justification of his existence, though not of his operation. He is behovely.

But proverbs are no use to Troilus, who is still determined to die. *What knowe I of the queen Nyobe?* And a hundred lines further on, Pandarus is still unaware that his niece is the lady in question.

'Look up, I seye, and telle me what she is
Anon, that I may gon about thy nede—
Knowe ich hire aught? For my love, telle me this;
Thanne wolde I hopen rather for to spede.'
Tho gan the veyne of Troilus to blede,
For he was hit, and wax al reed for shame.
'A ha!' quod Pandare, 'here bygynneth game.'

And with that word he gan hym for to shake,
And seyde, 'Theef, thow shalt hyre name telle.'
But tho gan sely Troilus for to quake
As though men sholde han led hym into helle,
And seyde, 'Allas! of al my wo the welle,
Thanne is my swete fo called Criseyde!'
And wel neigh with the word for feere he deyde.

[1] I 624–44
*Nyce* foolish    *Doth ful yvele fare* leads far astray

And whan that Pandare herde hire name nevene,
Lord, he was glad, and seyde 'Frend so deere,
Now fare aright, for Joves name in hevene,
Love hath byset thee wel; be of good cheere!
For of good name and wisdom and manere
She hath ynough, and ek of gentilesse.
If she be fayr, thow woost thyself, I gesse.'[1]

The *game* continues:

'Now beet thy brest, and sey to God of Love,
Thy grace, lord, for now I me repente
If I mysspak, for now myself I love.
Thus sey with al thyn herte in good entente.'
Quod Troilus, 'A, lord! I me consente,
And preye to thee my japes thow foryive,
And I shal nevere more whyle I live.'

'Thow seyst wel,' quod Pandare, 'and now I hope
That thou the goddes wrathe hast al apesed;
And sithen thow hast wepen many a drope,
And seyd swych thyng wherwith thy god is plesed,
Now wolde nevere God but thou were esed!
And thynk wel, she of whom rist al thy wo
Hereafter may thy comfort be also.'[2]

Everybody is disposed to celestial or natural love, Troilus is
told, and it does not yet suit Criseyde to be celestial. Then
Pandarus remembers that as a peroration this will not do: so he
adds, in the courtly manner, that the new convert will henceforth
be the best pillar of love's religion, and the most formidable
adversary of love's enemies. Troilus is more than satisfied—but
he must emphasize that his intentions are entirely honourable.
Pandarus laughs: 'And I'm to guarantee it?—Good heavens,
nobody thinks otherwise!'

Tho lough this Pandare, and anon answerde,
'And I thi borugh? Fy! no wight doth but so;
I roughte naught though that she stood and herde
How that thow seyst! But farewel, I wol go.

---

[1] I 862–82
*Sely* poor    *Nevene* mentioned    *Woost* know
[2] I 932–45
*Rist* arises

Adieu! be glad! God speede us bothe two!
Yif me this labour and this bisynesse,
And of my spede be thyn al that sweetnesse.'[1]

Our English European, refining Boccaccio's narrative, so handles
the dialogue between Pandare and Troilus that the spark of
irony at this point is no prepared cynicism. Chaucer's aim is
to make the poem, to make the characters, not to undo them.
Their life is outside his, and they stand or fall of themselves, not
according to his personal judgement. He sets them down, and
watches them with compassion, with amusement. The name
which his Parson would give to the central act of his poem is
*fornication*, but Chaucer does not apply it to Troilus because it
would undo Troilus before he is made. And he is not made
until his *lighte goost* has risen, and he himself

held al vanite
To respect of the pleyn felicite
That is in hevene above.[2]

Chaucer was concentrating upon poetry and a story, and his
deference to the 'philosophical Strode' is not complete levity.
His work had its own order: the order of poetic fiction, which
is recorded knowledge of experience. And he is quite clear about
the relation between that order and the supreme order he recognized in theology. If the Parson is still unconvinced, tell him
this: could Pandare now congratulate Troilus on a lucky escape,
the lunar shade would remember neither luck nor escape here
below. He called his lady 'wife', and meant it.

After a bad night, Pandarus is nevertheless frisky on walking
out to solicit his niece. 'Where is my lady?' he asks; and
Criseyde has to remind him that he is not with his mistress—

'Wher is my lady?' to hire folk quod he;
And they hym tolde; and he forth in gan pace,
And fond two othere ladys sete, and she,
Withinne a paved parlour; and they three
Herden a mayden reden hem the geste
Of the siege of Thebes, while hem leste . . .

---

[1] I 1037–43
*Roughte naught* should not care     *Spede* success
[2] V 1817–9

'Ye, nece, ye shal faren wel the bet,
If God wol, al this yeer,' quod Pandarus;
'But I am sory that I have yow let
To herken of youre book ye preysen thus.
For Goddes love, what seith it? telle it us!
Is it of love? O, som good ye me leere!'
'Uncle,' quod she, 'youre maistresse is nat here.'

With that they gonnen laughe; and tho she seyde,
'This romaunce is of Thebes that we rede—
And we han herd how that kyng Layus deyde
Thorugh Edippus his sone, and al that dede;
And here we stynten at thise lettres rede,
How the bisshop, as the book kan telle,
Amphiorax, fil thorugh the ground to helle.'

Quod Pandarus, 'Al this knowe I myselve,
And al th'assege of Thebes and the care;
For herof been ther maked bookes twelve.
But lat be this, and telle me how ye fare.
Do wey youre barbe, and shewe youre face bare;
Do wey youre book, rys up, and lat us daunce,
And lat us don to May som observaunce.'

'I? God forbede!' quod she, 'be ye mad?
Is that a widewes lif, so God yow save?
By God, ye maken me ryght soore adrad!
Ye ben so wylde, it semeth as ye rave.
It sate me wel bet ay in a cave
To bidde and rede on holy seyntes lyves;
Lat maydens gon to daunce, and yonge wyves.'

'As evere thrive I,' quod this Pandarus,
'Yet koude I telle a thyng to doon yow pleye . . .'[1]

And with this scene, mirroring the reading of Chaucer's own
poem as Chaucer might have read it to his courtly audience,
contrasting the siege of Thebes, and the siege of Troy, with
laughter in the parlour and thin deceptions of a widow of society,

---

[1] II 79ff.
*While hem leste* for as long as they wished     *Yow let to herken of* stopped you listening
to     *Som good ye me leere* tell me something good     *Here we stynten at thise*
*lettres rede*—Criseyde indicates in the 'rose and gold' of the manuscript the place where
they had left off reading. The story seems to have been the *Thebaid* of Statius.
*Amphiorax* (Amphiaraus) was one of the Seven against Thebes who took up the cause
of Polynices when Polynices was expelled by his brother.     *Barbe* a widow's
covering     *Sate me* would become me

the intrigue of Pandarus has begun. The reader may tire of his ingenuity; but there is very little that we can skip if we are to follow, through all the finesse of dialogue, Criseyde's change of heart. And until the conclusion of the poem there is nothing finer than the rendering of her gradually weakening resistance. After righteous rebukes of Pandarus, she resists for no stronger reasons than a concern for her name, a fear for her freedom, and doubts of the constancy of men. She is less afraid of Shame than of Wicked-Tongue, and behaves like a medieval Olivia whose piety is as uncertain as her age. If we read Book II with attention, it is hard to call her volatile; but with the best will in the world a rootless flower will fail, or (as Criseyde herself says) *rooteles moot grene soone deye*. *I mene wel* might be another epitaph, for good intentions pave her way out of the story. The quality of the characterization is that every judgement is kept in the balance until her end; and *that*, with the finest tact, is edged off the page. I can only express, in literary terms, the value of this balance by saying that any person incapable of enjoying it (and do not let him try too hard) is not yet qualified in humanity to read Dante. And for that reading Chaucer kindly prepares us at the end of his poem.

Even Mr. C. S. Lewis's suggestion that fear is her frailty[1] causes a twinge or two of doubt: when we remember Chaucer with his Ovid and his Jean de Meun, and suspect Criseyde of trembling at will. And if Chaucer did not identify her with any of the worthy ladies of the court, the ladies of the court could very easily identify themselves with her. Criseyde is not deceived, but persuaded to accept the luxury of deceiving herself. She senses what is coming:

'Lat be to me youre fremde manere speche,
And sey to me, youre nece, what yow liste.'
And with that word hire uncle anoon hire kiste,
And seyde, 'Gladly, leve nece dere!
Tak it for good that I shal sey yow here.'

With that she gan hire eighen down to caste,
And Pandarus to coghe gan a lite,
And seyde . . .[2]

[1] *The Allegory of Love* p. 189. In Jean de Meun I have in mind *Le Roman de la Rose* ed. LANGLOIS, 13795ff., which in turn recalls feminine wiles in Ovid's *Art of Love*.
[2] II 248–55
*Fremde* strange

But it is in this that Chaucer shows himself a master: just before she relents, he gives her, in the speech condemning Pandarus, lines which are the most powerful she utters.

> And she began to breste a-wepe anoon,
> And seyde, 'Allas, for wo! Why nere I deed?
> For of this world the feyth is al agoon.
> Allas! what sholden straunge to me doon,
> When he, that for my beste frend I wende,
> Ret me to love, and sholde it me defende?
>
> 'Allas! I wolde han trusted, douteles,
> That if that I, thorugh my disaventure,
> Hadde loved outher hym or Achilles,
> Ector, or any mannes creature,
> Ye nolde han had no mercy ne mesure
> On me, but alwey had me in repreve.
> This false world, allas! who may it leve?
>
> 'What? is this al the joye and al the feste?
> Is this youre reed? is this my blisful cas?
> Is this the verray mede of youre byheeste?
> Is al this paynted proces seyd, allas!
> Right for this fyn? O lady myn, Pallas!
> Thow in this dredful cas for me purveye,
> For so astonied am I that I deye.'[1]

And when Pandarus has ranted in reply, Criseyde's blaze of righteousness has evaporated, leaving (it seems) a witless terror. She calms and compromises:

[1] II 408–27
*Nere I* should not I be     *Straunge* strangers     *Ret* advises     *Outher* either
*Repreve* reproach     *Leve* believe (Criseyde would also have some difficulty in *abandoning* the world, but that is not what she means)     *Feste* fun     *Reed* advice
*Cas* chance
*Paynted proces* 'dishonest procedure, colored so as to appear what it is not'—so F. N. Robinson. A little later on, I shall have something to say about William Empson's interpretation of this phrase. Meanwhile the reader may accept, partially accept, or reject the following extracts from Mr. Empson's *Seven Types of Ambiguity* (London: 2nd ed., 1947) pp. 62–3: 'Pandarus's great harangue is seen . . . as a brightly coloured procession . . . moving on, leading her on, to dusty death and the everlasting bonfire; and behind this simple frame-work . . . *proces* hints at a parallel with legal proceedings, ending where none of the parties wanted, when at last the lawyers, like Pandarus, stop talking and demand to be paid . . .'     *Fyn* end
*Pallas* the virgin goddess whose image is mentioned as an object of Trojan veneration in the first book     *Purveye* provide

Criseyde, which that wel neigh starf for feere—
So as she was the ferfulleste wight
That myghte be—and herde ek with hire ere
And saugh the sorwful ernest of the knyght,
And in his preyer ek saugh noon unryght,
And for the harm that myghte ek fallen moore,
She gan to rewe, and dredde hire wonder soore,

And thoughte thus: 'Unhappes fallen thikke
Alday for love, and in swych manere cas
As men ben cruel in hemself and wikke;
And if this man slee here hymself, allas!
In my presence, it wol be no solas.
What men wolde of hit deme I kan nat seye:
It nedeth me ful sleighly for to pleye.'

And with a sorowful sik she sayde thrie,
'A! Lord! what me is tid a sory chaunce!
For myn estat lith now in jupartie,
And ek myn emes lif is in balaunce;
But natheles, with Goddes governaunce,
I shal so doon, myn honour shal I kepe,
And ek his lif'; and stynte for to wepe.[1]

This transition is a Shakespearian leap executed in Chaucerian
stanzas. After the moment of consciousness, the moment of

Is al this paynted proces seyd, allas!
Right for this fyn?

Criseyde falls to

And if this man slee here hymself, allas!
In my presence, it wol be no solas.

And after the moment of intensity Chaucer has withdrawn with
a smile; *of no sentement I this endite* is written at the beginning of
the second book. *Laissez couler les grands mots*, wrote Taine of
our heroine: *vous serez édifiés tout à l'heure*,[2] We cannot say at
what precise hour Criseyde falls; she is sliding every minute.
This, in the end, Chaucer admits, with a supremely civilized
gesture, a beautiful balance of remoteness and regret—

[1] II 449–69
*Starf* died    *Emes* uncle's
[2] *Histoire de la littérature anglaise* (Paris, 1863), I iii, which contains the first substantial appreciation of *Troilus and Criseyde* from France

She sobre was, ek symple, and wys withal,
The best ynorisshed ek that mighte be,
And goodly of hire spech in general,
Charitable, estatlich, lusty, and fre;
Ne nevere mo ne lakked hire pite;
Tendre-herted, slydinge of corage;
But trewely, I kan nat telle hire age.[1]

I have referred several times to Shakespeare in the last few
pages, and it is high time that I explained myself. Chaucer is
not Shakespearian. And yet I do not know that one can find in
English, outside Shakespeare, a greater form of *inconsistent
probability* of characterization than Chaucer grasped: a fuller
understanding, I mean, of the saying in Johnson's *Rasselas*, that
inconsistencies cannot both be right, but imputed to man they
may both be true (add, only, that Chaucer is inclined to impute
them to woman). As we do not know all that we should like
to know about Chaucer's foreign travel, it is easy to guess: that
to send a major poet upon the King's service to the Italy of the
Visconti and Sir John Hawkwood—those astounding examples of
improbable inconsistency in real Renaissance life—must have
*some* effect beneath the lucent clarity of his verse. Of this verse
I have to confess that I cannot entirely accept the extremely
interesting analysis by Mr. Empson.[2] He has quoted admirably:

But now help God to quenchen al this sorwe!
So hope I that he shal, for he best may.
For I have seyn, of a ful misty morwe
Folowen ful ofte a myrie someris day;
And after wynter foloweth grene May.
Men seen alday, and reden ek in stories,
That after sharpe shoures ben victories.[3]

And the stanza, for me, is improved when I am shown a turn of
meaning upon the word *shoures*, so that the final image of conquest

---

[1] V 820–6
*Ynorisshed* bred          *Estatlich* with a dignity befitting her rank
*Lusty and fre* pleasant and gracious
One critic supposes *slydinge of corage* to mean 'with a heart quick to move in sympathy'.
It does not. *Mais sis corages li chanjot* wrote Benoît de Sainte-Maure, in the line which
Chaucer presumably had in mind (*Le Roman de Troie* 5286): the heart of Criseyde
was inconstant. *Slydinge* is Chaucer's translation of the Latin *lubrica* of Boethius.
Shakespeare would say *slippery*.
[2] WILLIAM EMPSON, *Seven Types of Ambiguity* pp. 58–67
[3] III 1058–64
*Seyn* seen          *Alday* constantly

after a storm of arrows is neatly attached to the sequence of changeable weather. But I am not convinced that a meaning of which his audience was less than half-conscious was for Chaucer a meaning at all. Part of the experience of enjoying Shakespeare's mature poetry is the appreciation of images further and further at the back of the mind, of secondary association in the context; and it is true that we might expect a few hints of the sort from a poet who was a very great experimenter and innovator in verse in his own language. At the climax of the dialogue that we have been following, between Pandarus and Criseyde, we might think we see not only the boldness of transition I mentioned, which can be said to anticipate Shakespeare, but also a poetry that dramatizes in Shakespeare's manner the state of mind of the character. And if such a poetry is present, Chaucer was not then setting down a question which is clearer than it would be in prose; he was using a phrase that is Shakespearian. Yet the meaning of the phrase *paynted proces* in Chaucer is not to be found by adding together all the definitions under an appropriate date in the Oxford Dictionary, and every reader must judge for himself, from the many occasions when Chaucer uses the word *proces*, how near Criseyde is to saying: 'Good heavens, is *that* what all your plausible rigmarole was leading up to?' (And this is a sentence which could have different shades of tone according to the occasion.) After Mr. Empson's attempt to demonstrate, in all his examples, a diction of multiple meanings, I remain with Chaucer's precise language and conversational ease. A suggestion of Chaucer's complexity, if it can be suggested at all in brief, is the *aubade* of Troilus which we have already praised. I remain also with a conviction that Chaucer is better qualified to criticize Shakespearian verse than any other English author; and the critic who has come nearest to writing what Chaucer, above all, was in a position to think, is Dr. Johnson. To guess what Chaucer might *say* would make an imaginary conversation. One thing that is possible is a quotation from *Troilus and Cressida*— 'I am too courtly, and thou art too cunning'. We can hear him speak highly of that bold and bitter satire of Shakespeare's, for the reason that it observes contradictions not only in Love but also in War. He would no doubt commiserate with a poet living at a time when pox had become so very prevalent. And he could sincerely call the Shakespeare of *Troilus and Cressida* what Chaucer himself had been called: noble *philosophical* poet.

To which Shakespeare replies: there is enough in Pandare for three characters of my own.

But the poets are not talking to each other. One is gaining in dramatic intensity while the other loses; and Chaucer gains the lucid intervals that Shakespeare will sometimes forgo. An act of imagination of the order of *Hamlet* risks a disturbance of balance of mind that may be fatal to a weak character. And so Chaucer, without hazard or Tragedy, gains less only than Shakespeare; and they divide English literature between them.

Criseyde, during this digression, has offered to please Troilus as long as her 'honour' is kept safe, and her uncle has reassured her: should he assent and abet to her dishonour, *the shame were to me*, he says, *as well as thee* . . . She asks, in the course of conversation, whether 'he' can speak well of love: Pandare smiles 'a little'. And when Pandare again speaks out, her rebuke this time is arch—

As helpe me God, ye shenden every deel![1]

'You're spoiling everything!'—It is more exciting to join the *olde daunce* blindfold, so that if she falls she can pretend, at least to herself, that she was not to blame. But women, reflects the sliding heart, are often betrayed: by a love which was nothing in the beginning, and is nothing in the end. *That erst was nothing, into nought it torneth*—*ex nihilo nihil fit*—the proverb has a meaning unknown to Criseyde, which she is to give to it. Meanwhile, her monologue continues to another wise saw. 'Nothing venture, nothing gain': Pandarus would be told off for that.

There follows, after the style of the romances, the garden scene, and Antigone sings of the joys of love as in a song from the *Paradis d'Amour* of Guillaume de Machaut. Criseyde is impressed, in a way that half-recalls her imagined love-potion.

> But every word which that she of hire herde,
> She gan to prenten in hire herte faste,
> And ay gan love hire lasse for to agaste
> Than it dide erst, and synken in hire herte,
> That she wex somwhat able to converte.[2]

That is, she was capable of changing her mind. The same

[1] II 590
[2] II 899–903
*Prenten* imprint

night, as she dreams of the Eagle, the royal lover, her heart is changed in her—

> A nyghtyngale, upon a cedir grene,
> Under the chambre wal ther as she ley,
> Ful loude song ayein the moone shene,
> Peraunter, in his briddes wise, a lay
> Of love, that made hire herte fressh and gay;
> That herkned she so longe in good entente,
> Til at the laste the dede sleep hire hente.
>
> And as she slep, anonright tho hire mette
> How that an egle, fethered whit as bon,
> Under hire brest his longe clawes sette,
> And out hire herte he rente, and that anon,
> And dide his herte into hire brest to gon,
> Of which she nought agroos, ne nothyng smerte;
> And forth he fleigh, with herte left for herte.[1]

So distant literary memories melt and coalesce, in the mind of the artist, to a new form—a Provençal nightingale, a hint from Troilo's dream of the Boar, perhaps suggestions from the later cantos of the *Purgatorio*: and not literary memories only. The third line alone, which exists in variously differing versions elsewhere,[2] shows Chaucer's constant habit of refashioning. And underneath the literary associations is the irony of their present application, the delicate irony which the *Owl and the Nightingale* had before made so illuminatingly indelicate: when the bird of love, charged with singing at the latrine, is uncomfortably aware that her opponent has scored a point. The Owl is in a stronger position when he is attacked for the filthy but natural habits of his brood. He is able to reply that he simply follows the sanitary arrangement of human beings, for babies (in this respect) are no better than owlets.

Pandare soon gives Troilus methodical instruction in the composition of a love-letter:

> Biblotte it with thi teris ek a lite[3]

—and, in high spirits, goes with the tear-stained note to Criseyde:

---

[1] II 918–31
*Peraunter* perhaps     *Hente* seized     *Hire mette* she dreamed     *Nought agroos* felt no terror
[2] *Knight's Tale* 1509, *Squire's Tale* 53, prologue to the *Legend of Good Women* A (G) 49
[3] II 1027, which has been compared with Ovid, *Heroides* III 3

This Pandare took the lettre, and that bytyme
A-morwe, and to his neces paleis sterte,
And faste he swor that it was passed prime,
And gan to jape, and seyde, 'Ywys, myn herte
So fressh it is, although it sore smerte,
I may naught slepe nevere a Mayes morwe;
I have a joly wo, a lusty sorwe.'

Criseyde, whan that she hire uncle herde,
With dredful herte, and desirous to here
The cause of his comynge, thus answerde:
'Now, by youre fey, myn uncle,' quod she, 'dere,
What manere wyndes gydeth yow now here?
Tel us youre joly wo and youre penaunce.
How ferforth be ye put in loves daunce?'

'By God,' quod he, 'I hoppe alwey byhynde!'
And she to laughe, it thoughte hire herte brest.[1]

When she has secretly read the letter, Criseyde frolics with him.

   . . . Pandarus, that in a study stood,
Er he was war, she took hym by the hood,
And seyde, 'Ye were caught er that ye wiste!'[2]

'Caught you!' The widow is forgotten.

   Pandarus, having instructed Troilus to pass by, now draws Criseyde to the window; and this episode, which I shall not follow further, is entertaining prologue to the higher comedy that Chaucer added, the intrigue at the house of Deiphobus. Helen, Hector, and other influential persons, are to gather together to comfort Criseyde and take up her cause against a certain Poliphete who, they are told, is threatening the security of Criseyde's position in Troy. Troilus is to be of the company and to retire early on a plea of sickness, which he can easily make plausible (*for I am sik*, he says, *in ernest*). Pandare, according to his own Polonian pun, is to drive the *deer* in the required direction. But the comedy rises as the company grows. It was at the suggestion

[1] II 1093–108
*Passed prime* after nine o'clock    *Ywys* certainly        *To laughe* laughs out so
loud        *It thoughte* it seemed        *Brest* would burst
[2] II 1180–2

of Deiphobus that Helen was invited, and now more than one intrigue is on foot: *God and Pandare wist al what this mente.*[1] Chaucer does not ponderously connect all this with the doom of Troy, though the association can hardly escape us, as we watch social comedy in the midst of a siege. The situation is given towards the beginning of the second book, when Criseyde and her friends listened to the story of another doomed city. This was also, beautifully, a medieval audience enjoying the art of literature in wartime, if not England preparing to meet invasion;[2] and a less civilized comedian would turn it to fiddling while Rome burns. Reading while Troy simmers has finer possibilities, when it is Chaucer amusing London. The collapse which is to come at the end of his poem is the fall of something larger than a city; and there will be time afterwards to expose the weakness of the foundations. At the moment there is much to be laughed at, much to enjoy. There are even one or two things to admire.

While everyone else is suggesting remedies for Troilus's 'sickness', Criseyde sits silent, thinking she is the one who could best cure him:

> Compleyned ek Eleyne of his siknesse
> So feythfully, that pite was to here,
> And every wight gan waxen for accesse
> A leche anon, and seyde, 'In this manere
> Men curen folk; this charme I wol yow leere.'
> But ther sat oon, al list hire nought to teche,
> That thoughte, 'best koud I yet ben his leche.'[3]

All but Troilus have heard Criseyde's case; so he must hear it, from the lady herself. Pandare leaps in to tell the patient that he is bringing a winding-sheet[4] and returns to inform Helen and Deiphobus that Troilus will listen to as much from Criseyde as he can stand, so long as there is not a crush. Now only a little shuffling is needed. Pandarus is speaking:

[1] II 1561
Mr. Charles Muscatine, writing in *Modern Language Notes* June 1948 on the whole scene, detects reminiscence of the scriptural story of Amnon's feigned illness, by means of which Tamar is raped at the suggestion of the 'very subtil man' Jonadeb.
[2] The poem seems to have been completed in 1385–6.
[3] II 1576–82
*Leere* teach       *Gan waxen for accesse* . . . turned leech for a touch of fever
[4] Pandare's joke, which I have slightly modernized, was *God have thi soule, ibrought have I thi beere* (II 1638); this I understand as a pun on the word for 'bier' and 'pillow-case'.

'I sey for me, best is, as I kan knowe,
That no wight in ne wente but ye tweye,
But it were I—for I kan in a throwe
Reherce hire cas unlik that she kan seye;
And after this she may hym ones preye
To ben good lord, in short, and take hire leve.
This may nought muchel of his ese hym reve.

'And ek, for she is straunge, he wol forbere
His ese, which that hym thar nought for yow;
Ek oother thing, that toucheth nought to here,
He wol yow telle—I woot it wel right now—
That secret is, and for the townes prow.'
And they, that nothyng knewe of his entente,
Withouten more, to Troilus in they wente.[1]

Troilus sends off Deiphobus and Helen to read a letter from
Hector which he happens to have by his bedside; and they *gonne
on it to reden and to poure* for a full hour, in a green arbour.   So the
intrigues are mortised.   Now let them 'read', says the narrator:

Now lat hem rede, and torne we anon
To Pandarus, that gan ful faste prye
That al was wel, and out he gan to gon
Into the grete chaumbre, and that in hye,
And seyde, 'God save al this compaynye!
Come nece myn; my lady queen Eleyne
Abideth yow, and ek my lordes tweyne.

'Rys, take with yow youre nece Antigone,
Or whom yow list; or no fors; hardyly
The lesse prees, the bet; com forth with me,
And loke that ye thonken humblely
Hem alle thre, and whan ye may goodly
Youre tyme see, taketh of hem youre leeve,
Lest we too longe his restes hym byreeve.'[2]

How neatly he verses Pandare's rush of talk, to make it more
specious!   Pandarus is a gas-bag, but almost as various as
Falstaff.   He has swift earth humour, and can be as learned as a

---

[1] II 1653–66
*In a throwe* in a short time          *Hym thar nought* he need not          *Prow* profit
[2] II 1709–22
*Prye* spy          *In hye* in haste          *No fors* never mind          *Hardyly* certainly
                                        *Prees* of a crowd

clerk. What is more, he is granted a free gift of the finest uncomprehended phrase in Chaucer:

'Nece, I conjure and heighly yow defende,
On his half which that soule us alle sende,
*And in the vertu of corones tweyne,*
Slee naught this man, that hath for yow this peyne . . .'[1]

Whatever that may mean, it is outrageous; and our author knew that the outrageous, also, can be poetical. The great ironist delighted to make it so. In the end Pandare dries up; he is futile, poor man. The last speech of his which has some sap in it, is his pungent Villonesque comment on Troilus waiting in vain for Criseyde:

'From haselwode, there joly Robyn pleyde,
Shal come al that that thow abidest heere;
Ye, fare wel al the snow of ferne yere!'[2]

*Di Mongibello,* says Pandaro, *aspetta il vento questo tapinello.* We have Pandarus.

---

[1] II 1733–6
*Half* behalf          *Sende* sent
The *corones tweyne* have been taken as nuptial crowns, the heavenly crowns of rose and lily bestowed in the *Second Nun's Tale,* crowns of chastity like the *corona dell' onestà mea* which Criseida in *Il Filostrato* II 134 proposes to keep, and crowns of Pity and Bounty. Other interpretations are possible.
[2] V 1174–6
Troilus has just said 'I bet you that she comes tonight'. Pandarus (under his breath): 'Tell the Marines and jolly sailor-boys what you're waiting for. It's goodbye to the snows of yesteryear . . .'
   That, I am afraid, is the modern equivalent. The Italian is *Il Filostrato* VII 10: 'The fellow expects a wind from Mongibello'.

# V

*Dico che quando ella apparia da parte alcuna,*
*per la speranza dell' ammirabile salute nullo*
*nemico mi rimanea, anzi mi giungea una fiamma*
*di caritade, la quale mi facea perdonare a*
*chiunque m' avesse offeso: e chi allora m'*
*avesse addiminandato di cosa alcuna,*
*la mia risponsione sarebbe state solamente,*
Amore, *con viso vestito d' umiltà.*

I say that when she appeared, from any direction, by the hope
of her wonderful salutation no enemy was left to me, but rather
a flame of charity possessed me which made me pardon whom-
soever had offended me: and to him who had then asked me of
any matter, my answer would have been simply, *Love*, with a
countenance clothed in humility.

DANTE: *Vita Nuova XI*

*Quand l'haleine douce vente*
*Qui vient du très doux pays*
*Où cil est qui m'atalente,*
*Volontiers y tourne mon vis;*
*Dieu! m'est vis que je le sente*
*Par dessous mon mantel gris.*

GUIOT DE DIJON, early XIIIth century

. . . *that bodily light which I spoke of seasons this world's life for her*
*blind lovers [caecis amatoribus] with an enticing and dangerous sweetness*
. . . *But thou pluckest me out, Lord, thou pluckest me out.*

ST. AUGUSTINE: *Confessions X xxxiv*

# THE BOOK OF TROILUS ENDS

THE PRAISE OF THE GODDESS AT THE BEGINNING OF BOOK III
is the most impressive *prohemium* in *Troilus and Criseyde*
Venus is addressed as the light of the third sphere of the.
heavens; she is the beloved of the sun, the daughter of Jove, the
delight of love. And through this commodious word of ours,
she is assimilated to that which moves and unites the universe,
and honoured by a phrase St. Bernard used of the Virgin.

O blisful light, of which the bemes clere
Adorneth al the thridde heven faire!
O sonnes lief, O joves doughter deere,
Plesaunce of love, O goodly debonaire,
In gentil hertes ay redy to repaire!
O veray cause of heele and of gladnesse,
Iheryed be thy myght and thy goodnesse!

In hevene and helle, in erthe and salte see
Is felt thy myght, if that I wel descerne;
As man, brid, best, fissh, herbe, and grene tree
Thee fele in tymes with vapour eterne.
God loveth, and to love wol nought werne;
And in this world no lyves creature
Withouten love is worth, or may endure . . .

Ye folk a lawe han set in universe,
And this knowe I by hem that lovers be,
That whoso stryveth with yow hath the werse:
Now, lady bright, for thy benignitee,
At reverence of hem that serven thee,
Whos clerc I am, so techeth me devyse
Som joye of that is felt in thy servyse.

Ye in my naked herte sentement
Inhielde, and do me shewe of thy swetenesse.
Caliope, thy vois be now present,

For now is nede; sestow nought my destresse,
How I mot telle anonright the gladnesse
Of Troilus, to Venus heryinge?
To which gladnesse, who nede hath, God hym brynge![1]

I do not think it unfortunate if a line or two of this brings to mind what is probably the finest poem of W. B. Yeats: *Sailing to Byzantium*. For memory is at once astonished by the difference in *scale* of *Troilus and Criseyde*. Chaucer has time to reach his own Byzantium, and can afford to mount a splendid prologue to the passing gladness of his hero. This is part of the poet's *destresse*: Troilus will not last long, so let him have his day, with the fullest poetic honours. Let us approve the association of divine and earthly love with a whole heart: and pray they may cease to be separate. There is no need to tell the audience what is absurd: praise Venus with allusions to St. Thomas Aquinas and to Dante, request her aid in composition, attend to the story—and wait for the moment when laughter explodes in the soul.

Fil Pandarus on knees, and up his eyen
To heven threw, and held his hondes highe,
'Immortal god', quod he, 'that mayst nought deyen,
*Cupid I mene*, of this mayst glorifie . . .'[2]

Or let Troilus respond to Criseyde in a manner of Dante before the Arch-Traitor:

*Io non morii, e non rimasi vivo*
Inferno

This Troilus, that herde his lady preye
Of lordshipe hym, wax neither quyk ne ded . . .[3]
*Troilus and Criseyde*

---

[1] III 1ff.
In the first two and a half stanzas here quoted, Chaucer was working over the invocation *O luce eterna* . . . of *Il Filostrato* III 74ff. But *love* . . . *In gentil hertes ay redy to repaire* is like the beginning of a canzone of Guinicelli: *Al cor gentil ripara sempre Amore*. *Thi benignitee* . . . recalls *la tua benignità* . . . of *Paradiso* XXXIII 16, and also the Prioress's address to the Virgin at the beginning of her Canterbury tale.
*Heele* health        *Tymes* seasons        *Vapour eterne* the divine effluence, the *dolce vapore* of Dante's paraphrase of the Lord's Prayer        *Werne* deny
[2] III 183–6
[3] *Inferno* XXXIV 25: 'I did not die, and did not remain alive'
*Troilus and Criseyde* III 78–9
*Of lordshipe hym* his patronage
The great line of Dante refers not to a physical state but to a metaphysical condition that is hardly imaginable. Chaucer is describing what we call 'loss of consciousness'. And when Gower in *Confessio Amantis* VIII 2451 writes *ne fully quik ne fully ded*, he could as well characterize most people in their ordinary waking lives. 'Consciousness', like 'health', is relative.

But such a collocation, for all I know, would have shocked even Chaucer (though he used his *Inferno* elsewhere, and to underline Criseyde for emphasis). The surprise of coincidence or innuendo —whichever you take it to be—is certainly, on another plane, comic; and the lady silently forgives her tongue-tied lover for not being too forward. *For she was wis, and loved hym neverethelasse.*

The rest of the narrative I shall not repeat at length. Troilus and Criseyde come together in intercourse, vow constancy, are divided. Calchas arranges the exchange through which Criseyde joins her father in the Grecian camp; but this circumstance may not be the whole cause of separation, may be only the occasion for Criseyde's infidelity. Her knight, loyal both to his lord and to his lady, will not weaken the cause of Troy by making her another Helen. Yet he accepts the services of Pandarus. He declares him no bawd; and gives the reason, with unconscious irony, that everyone knows a distinction between like things and the identical.[1] His love is illicit and therefore limited, but is not so easily judged. To the mind of Chaucer it has a double figure, which we can see as he reads of the copulation of Troilo and Criseida. As they enjoy *d'amor . . . l'ultimo valore*, Troilus and Criseyde, we are told, *felten in love the grete worthynesse.* The slight withdrawal, in that Chaucerian phrase, is not prudery but wisdom. In this poem we are aware of a convention of romance and also of what is being composed underneath it, so that even in the book of Venus the well-willy planet, the poet can stand aside and smile at the delights which in the end will seem empty to the spirit:

> Nil I naught swere, although he lay ful softe,
> That in his thought he nas somwhat disesed,
> Ne that he torned on his pilwes ofte,
> And wold of that hym missed han ben sesed.
> But in swich cas man is nought alwey plesed,
> For aught I woot, namoore than was he;
> That kan I deme of possibilitee . . .[2]

Now begins the longest passage in the poem that Chaucer

---

[1] III 403–6: with reference to the scholastic division between likeness and identity of substance.

[2] III 442–48

Troilus lay all the long night (III 399–441) and thought how he might serve his lady best.

sustained with no more than incidental reference to Boccaccio; and it contains, in the description of the night at the house of Pandarus, the best of Chaucerian humour. I quote without comment:

Now is ther litel more for to doone,
But Pandare up, and shortly for to seyn,
Right sone upon the chaungynge of the moone,
Whan lightles is the world a nyght or tweyne,
And that the wolken shop hym for to reyne,
He streght o morwe unto his nece wente;
Ye han wel herd the fyn of his entente.

Whan he was com, he gan anon to pleye
As he was wont, and of hymself to jape;
And finaly he swor and gan hire seye,
By this and that, she sholde hym nought escape,
Ne lenger doon hym after hire to gape;
But certeynly she moste, by hire leve,
Come soupen in his hous with hym at eve.

At which she lough, and gan hire faste excuse,
And seyde, 'It reyneth; lo, how sholde I gon?'
'Lat be,' quod he, 'ne stant nought thus to muse.
This moot be don! Ye shal be ther anon.'
So at the laste herof they fille at on,
Or elles softe he swor hire in hire ere
He nolde nevere comen ther she were.

Soone after this, she gan to hym to rowne,
And axed hym if Troilus were there.
He swor hire nay, for he was out of towne,
And seyde, 'Nece, I pose that he were,
Yow thurste nevere han the more fere;
For rather than men myghte hym ther aspye,
Me were levere a thousand fold to dye.'

Nought list myn auctour fully to declare
What that she thoughte whan he seyde so,
That Troilus was out of towne yfare,
As if he seyde therof sooth or no;
But that, withowten await, with hym to go
She graunted hym, sith he hire that bisoughte,
And, as his nece, obeyed as hire oughte.[1]

[1] III 547–81
*Shop hym* prepared                    *Rowne* whisper                    *Thurste* need
          *Me were levere* I would rather          *Nought list* it does not please

After supper and entertainment Criseyde is about to leave, but—

> The bente moone with hire hornes pale,
> Saturne, and Jove, in Cancro joyned were,
> That swych a reyn from heven gan avale,
> That every maner womman that was there
> Hadde of that smoky reyn a verray feere;
> At which Pandare tho lough, and seyde thenne,
> 'Now were it tyme a lady to gon henne!
>
> 'But goode nece, if I myghte evere plese
> Yow any thyng, than prey ich yow,' quod he,
> 'To doon myn herte as now so gret an ese
> As for to dwelle here al this nyght with me,
> For-whi this is youre owen hous, parde.
> For, by my trouthe, I sey it nought a-game,
> To wende as now, it were to me a shame.'
>
> Criseyde, which that koude as muche good
> As half a world, took hede of his preiere;
> And syn it ron, and al was on a flod,
> She thoughte, as good chep may I dwellen here,
> And graunte it gladly with a frendes chere,
> And have a thonk, as grucche and thanne abide—
> For hom to gon, it may nought wel bitide.[1]

This is the Comedy of Rain, of which Pandarus observes

> And if ye liggen wel to-nyght, com ofte,
> And careth nought what weder is alofte.[2]

When in his next move her uncle invents a story about Troilus's jealousy of 'Horaste', he produces from Criseyde a Boethian outburst which, if only she could mean it, anticipates Chaucer's epilogue. The situation in which Criseyde speaks to Troilus of his supposed distrust is another occasion for irony; and the lines are lit by one of the finest visual images of the whole poem.

> Quod Pandarus, 'Now wol ye wel bigynne:
> Now doth hym sitte, goode nece deere,
> Upon youre beddes syde al ther withinne,
> That ech of yow the bet may other heere.'

[1] III 624-44
*Avale* fall     I take the phrase about knowing *as muche good as half a world* to be somewhere between having one's head screwed on the right way, and being as cute as a cartload of monkeys.     *As good chep may I* I may as well     *Grucche* grumble
[2] III 669-70
*Liggen* lie

And with that word he drow hym to the feere,
And took a light, and fond his contenaunce
As for to looke upon an old romaunce.

Criseyde, that was Troilus lady right,
And cleer stood on a ground of sikernesse,
Al thoughte she hire servant and hire knyght
Ne sholde of right non untrouthe in hire gesse,
Yet natheles, considered his distresse,
And that love is in cause of swich folie,
Thus to hym spak she of his jalousie:

.        .        .        .

'And I, emforth my connyng and my might,
Have and ay shal, how sore that me smerte,
Ben to yow trewe and hool with al myn herte;

'And dredeles, that shal be founde at preve . . .'[1]

*And cleer stood on a ground of sikernesse*: that is the bright image of Criseyde confident that she is true, and we are to remember it when her sureness is broken.

. . . lasse thyng than othes may suffise
In many a cas; for every wyght, I gesse,
That loveth wel, meneth but gentilesse.[2]

To Troilus, meanwhile, *swetnesse* after *bitternesse* is a grace surpassing his deserts:

Criseyde, al quyt from every drede and tene,
As she that juste cause hadde hym to triste,
Made hym swich feste, it joye was to seene,
Whan she his trouthe and clene entente wiste;
And as aboute a tree, with many a twiste,
Bytrent and writh the swote wodebynde,
Gan ech of hem in armes other wynde.

And as the newe abaysed nyghtyngale,
That stynteth first whan she bygynneth to synge,
Whan that she hereth any herde tale,
Or in the hegges any wyght stirynge,
And after siker doth hire vois outrynge,
Right so Criseyde, whan hire drede stente,
Opned hire herte, and tolde hym hire entente.

---

[1] III 974ff.
*Feere* fire            *Fond his contenaunce* assumed the posture            *Sikernesse* security
*In cause of* to blame for            *Emforth* to the extent of            *At preve* by experience
[2] III 1146–8

And right as he that seth his deth yshapen,
And dyen mot, in ought that he may gesse,
And sodeynly rescous doth hym escapen,
And from his deth is brought in sykernesse,
For al this world, in swych present gladnesse
Was Troilus, and hath his lady swete.
With worse hap God lat us nevere mete!

Hire armes smale, hire streghte bak and softe,
Hire sydes longe, flesshly, smothe, and white
He gan to stroke, and good thrift bad ful ofte
Hire snowisshe throte, hire brestes rounde and lite:
Thus in this hevene he gan hym to delite,
And therwithal a thousand tyme hire kiste,
That what to don, for joie unnethe he wiste.

Than seyde he thus, 'O Love, O Charite!
Thi moder ek, Citherea the swete,
After thiself next heried be she,
Venus mene I, the wel-willy planete!
And next that, Imeneus, I thee greete;
For nevere man was to yow goddes holde
As I, which ye han brought fro cares colde.

'Benigne Love, thow holy bond of thynges,
Whoso wol grace, and list thee nought honouren,
Lo, his desir wol flee withouten wynges.
For noldestow of bounte hem socouren
That serven best and most alwey labouren,
Yet were al lost, that dar I wel seyn certes,
But if thy grace passed oure desertes . . .'

And therwithal Criseyde anon he kiste,
Of which, certein, she felte no disese,
And thus seyde he, 'Now wolde God I wiste,
Myn herte swete, how I yow myght plese!
What man,' quod he, 'was evere thus at ese
As I, on which the faireste and the beste
That evere I say, deyneth hire herte reste?

'Here may men seen that mercy passeth right;
Th'experience of that is felt in me,
That am unworthy to so swete a wight.

But herte myn, of youre benignite,
So thynketh, though that I unworthi be,
Yet mot I nede amenden in som wyse,
Right thorugh the vertu of youre heigh servyse . . .'[1]

*And lat hem in this hevene blisse dwelle* writes Chaucer, in the courtly manner. It is a grace of sense, he will grant. To set it off he will even show, with Boccaccio, the delight of the miser. 'Is that right?' he seems to say to the lovers; 'have I done you justice? Have I said too much, or too little?' *Amour courtois* is on trial, and must be given a fair hearing.

O blisful nyght, of hem so longe isought,
How blithe unto hem bothe two thow were!
Why nad I swich oon with my soule ybought,
Ye, or the leeste joie that was there?
Awey, thow foule daunger and thow feere,
And lat hem in this hevene blisse dwelle,
That is so heigh that al ne kan I telle!

But soth is, though I kan nat tellen al,
As kan myn auctour, of his excellence,
Yet have I seyd, and God toforn, and shal
In everythyng, al holly his sentence;
And if that ich, at Loves reverence,
Have any word in eched for the beste,
Doth therwithal right as youreselven leste.

For myne wordes, heere and every part,
I speke hem alle under correccioun
Of yow that felyng han in loves art,
And putte it al in youre discrecioun
To encrese or maken diminucioun
Of my langage, and that I yow biseche . . .[2]

---

[1] III 1226ff.
*Bytrent* twines        *Any herde tale* any shepherd talk        *Smale* slender
*Good thrift bad* blessed        *Unnethe* scarcely        *Wel-willy* beneficent
*Imeneus* Hymen the goddess of marriage    *Noldestow* wouldst thou not    *But if* unless
Again Chaucer recalls St. Bernard's prayer:

> . . . *qual vuol grazia ed a te non ricorre,*
> *sua disianza vuol volar senz'ali.*

> *La tua benignità non pur soccorre*
> *a chi domanda . . .*

'. . . who would have grace and comes not to thee, his desire wills to fly without wings. Your benignity not only succours whoso requests . . .'
[2] III 1317–36
*God toforn* before God
According to R. K. Root the reading *no man kan it telle* for *al ne kan I telle* in line 1323 is a revision, and also the later placing, after line 1414, of the remaining verses.
*In eched* added

Our poet has a genius for comparative valuation. He rarely says 'this is bad, this is evil', but often 'this is good, that is not so good, and this other is better'. His attitude accords with the Thomist principle that evil is deprivation of good: and there are degrees of deprivation. The impression which Chaucer conveys is that there will be time for the judgement: meanwhile there is no harm in amusing ourselves with an intermediate and generous prize-giving. The winners will find their own level, whether we are niggardly or not.

So Troilus wonderfully improves under the liberal education of love, and the praise of his largesse resounds *unto the yate of hevene*. But my last quotation from Book III occurs before this: it is Pandare's greeting to Criseyde the morning after the blissful night.

> Pandare, o-morwe which that comen was
> Unto his nece, and gan hire faire grete,
> Seyde, 'Al this nyght so reyned it, allas,
> That al my drede is that ye, nece swete,
> Han litel laiser had to slepe and mete.
> Al nyght,' quod he, 'hath reyn so do me wake,
> That som of us, I trowe, hire hedes ake.'
>
> And ner he com, and seyde, 'How stant it now
> This mery morwe? Nece, how kan ye fare?'
> Criseyde answerde, 'Nevere the bet for yow,
> Fox that ye ben! God yeve youre herte care!
> God help me so, ye caused al this fare,
> Trowe I,' quod she, 'for al youre wordes white.
> O, whoso seeth yow knoweth yow ful lite!'
>
> With that she gan hire face for to wrye
> With the shete, and wax for shame al red;
> And Pandarus gan under for to prie,
> And seyde, 'Nece, if that I shal be ded,
> Have here a swerd and smyteth of myn hed!'
> With that his arm al sodeynly he thriste
> Under hire nekke, and at the laste hire kyste.[1]

It is Chaucer's own.

\* \* \*

[1] III 1555-75
*Mete* dream    *Wordes white* deception    *Wrye* hide

A large part of Book IV was written in a dry month. Now we can generally say of the 'passage work' of the *Troilus* that it is at least well played, as in the third book, where even Criseyde's discourse on jealousy is in no great danger of losing an audience:

This Troilus, whan he hire wordes herde,
Have ye no care, hym liste nought to slepe . . .[1]

But the beginning of the fourth is out of practice. The complaint of Troilus, after the exchange of Criseyde and Antenor is ratified by the Trojan parliament, rises to eloquence in two stanzas; one of which has an interesting improvement of Boccaccio—

*O anima tapina ed ismarrita,*
*Che non ti fuggi dal più sventuroso*
*Corpo che viva? O anima invilita,*
*Esci del corpe e Criseida segui . . .*

Il Filostrato

'O wery goost, that errest to and fro,
Why nyltow fleen out of the wofulleste
Body that evere myghte on grounde go?
O soule, lurkynge in this wo, unneste,
Flee forth out of myn herte, and lat it breste,
And folowe alwey Criseyde, thy lady dere.
Thi righte place is now no lenger here . . .

'O ye loveris, that heigh upon the wheel
Ben set of Fortune, in good aventure,
God leve that ye fynde ay love of steel,
And longe mote youre lif in joye endure!
But whan ye comen by my sepulture,
Remembreth that youre felawe resteth there;
For I loved ek, though ich unworthy were.'[2]

Troilus

—for in this a dead Italian metaphor revives in a manner that is almost baroque, as if Chaucer, with his sorry lover, were anticipating the extremities of diction in Crashaw. Otherwise, the episode is disappointing. Troilus's pure sorrow is to come when there is occasion for it. Here his eyes are *woful*, his soul is

---

[1] III 1065–6
[2] *Il Filostrato* IV 34: 'O soul unhappy and dismayed, why do you not fly from the wretchedest body alive? O dejected soul, go forth from the body and follow Criseida'. *Troilus* IV 302ff.
*Leve* grant   An early hand found it necessary to explain, in MS Harley 2280 in the British Museum, that *unneste* meant *go out of thi nest.*

*woful*, his tears are *woful*; each of three successive stanzas repeat that he is *woful*. And the repetition is not rhetoric but merely accident, as if new disaster has bleared the poet's eye.

Pandarus—who meant well, we are told, although he was talking nonsense—suggests, without confidence, that Troilus should look for another lady; the town is full of them. He has the reply he deserves. Then he is obliged to stand by, half-pathetic, half-comic, listening to variations upon the lover's original moan. Chaucer adapts a figure from Reason's discourse on the folly of love.

> *Je vei maintes feiz que tu pleures*
> *Come alambic seur alutel*
>
> Romance of the Rose

> This Troylus in teris gan distille,
> As licour out of a lambic ful faste;
> And Pandarus gan holde his tunge stille,
> And to the ground his eyen doun he caste.
> But natheles, thus thought he at the laste:
> 'What, parde, rather than my felawe deye,
> Yet shal I somewhat more unto hym seye . . .'[1]
>
> *Troilus*

In medieval convention it is not necessarily unmanly to shed tears; the idea that immoderate grief is more contemptible than immoderate laughter is not much older than a century. But Troilus's inert despair is certainly dramatized against Pandare's downright proposals for action. Hold on to Criseyde and hang the consequences!—The reply is, such action would be impolitic and uncourtly. According to the Christian ethic Troilus might have done better from the start. According to his lights he does the Right Thing. He preserves the 'name' of Criseyde. This is the course of a literary lover who has a life of his own yet must love out of a book, in secrecy. He is constant. He would be a husband if he could. And he will have his reward.

As for the 'name' of Criseyde—

> Hire name, allas! is punysshed so wide,
> That for hire gilt it oughte ynough suffise.[2]

---

[1] *Le Roman de la Rose* ed. LANGLOIS, 6382–3: 'I often see you weep like an alembic on a furnace'
*Troilus* IV 519–25
[2] V 1095–6
For *punysshed* three MSS read *publisshed*

But we need not rush so far for a contrast. Pandarus says that
if Criseyde wants to leave, then she is false. And his conclusion
does follow, though not from his premise.

> Pandare answerde, 'Frend, thow maist, for me,
> Don as thee list; but hadde ich it so hote,
> And thyn estat, she sholde go with me,
> Though al this town criede on this thyng by note.
> I nolde sette at all that noys a grote!
> For whan men han wel cryed, than wol they rowne;
> Ek wonder last but nyne nyght nevere in towne.

> 'Devyne not in resoun ay so depe
> Ne corteisly, but help thiself anon.
> Bet is that othere than thiselven wepe,
> And namely, syn ye two ben al on.
> Ris up, for by myn hed, she shal not goon!
> And rather be in blame a lite ifounde
> Than sterve here as a gnat, withouten wounde.

> . . . .

> 'Thenk ek how Paris hath, that is thy brother,
> A love; and why shaltow nat have another?

> 'And Troilus, o thyng I dar thee swere,
> That if Criseyde, which that is thy lief,
> Now loveth thee as wel as thow dost here,
> God help me so, she nyl nat take a-grief,
> Though thow do boote anon in this meschief.
> And if she wilneth fro thee for to passe,
> Thanne is she fals; so love hire wel the lasse.

> 'Forthi tak herte, and thynk right as a knyght,
> Thorugh love is broken al day every lawe.
> Kith now somwhat thi corage and thi myght;
> Have mercy on thiself, for any awe.
> Lat nat this wrecched wo thyn herte gnawe,
> But manly sette the world on six and sevene;
> And if thow deye a martyr, go to hevene!'[1]

[1] IV 582ff.

*By note* in song     *I nolde sette* ... I shouldn't care     *Rowne* whisper
*Namely* especially     *Lief* love     *Do boote* find a remedy     *Kith* show
*Sette the world on six and sevene* risk all on the cast of a dice; or (in the modern sense of
'sixes and sevens') put everything to confusion

And when Troilus, after all, nerves himself to suggest to his lady that they should *stele away* together, her reply is one of the most transparent self-exposures that Chaucer's Criseyde is allowed:

'. . . thynketh on myn honeste,
That floureth yet, how foule I sholde it shende,
And with what filthe it spotted sholde be,
If in this forme I sholde with yow wende.
Ne though I lyved unto the werldes ende,
My name sholde I nevere ayeynward wynne.
Thus were I lost, and that were routhe and synne . . .'[1]

After the scene of the Trojan ladies taking their leave—that excellent Boccaccian and Chaucerian comedy of the social condolences—Criseyde is alone in her room, wringing her elegant hands (only Chaucer, it seems, saw her *fyngeres longe and smale*). Her tears fall delicately, like a shower in April. Her complaint is more poetical than Troilus's; it is in high style.

How myghte it evere yred ben or ysonge,
The pleynte that she made in hire destresse?
I not . . .[2]

To point out that such things are ironical is untrue if we apply a narrow sense, and truism if we regard Chaucer as a great ironist. For we have already been persuaded, in our preliminary conversation, to admit very much more differentiation of *degrees* of irony than the general usage implies. I prefer to say, particularly of the beautiful lines about Criseyde which follow, that Chaucer is capable of giving his full attention to one thing at once, but in reading him we are never made so passionately excited about one thing that everything else is driven out of the mind.

She was right swich to seen in hire visage
As is that wight that men on beere bynde;
Hire face, lik of Paradys the ymage,
Was al ychaunged in another kynde.
The pleye, the laughter men was wont to fynde

---

[1] IV 1576–82
Criseyde, in her world of 'romance', ignores an interesting tension of meaning in the word *honeste*. In the *Physician's Tale* 77 it is used in opposition to the *olde daunce* of love: in the *Compleynt to Pity* 40 it occurs along with Beauty, Delight and Pleasure as a desirable quality of the beloved. The net sense, to Criseyde, is 'reputation'.
*Shende* defile      *Ayeynward* back again
[2] IV 799–801
*Not* do not know

In hire, and ek hire joies everichone,
Ben fled; and thus lyth now Criseyde allone.[1]

And this is another distinction between the genius of Shakespeare and the genius of Chaucer; that Shakespeare could compress the whole of an experience into a single line or a single speech, where Chaucer kept in reserve, at a given point of his story, the completeness of the narrative and of possible attitudes towards it.

The soliloquy of Troilus on predestination, which is based on passages of the *Consolation of Philosophy*, was added, probably in a revision of the text, as an extension of Troilus's own disputes with Pandarus; and since it represents a single character struggling towards a philosophical conclusion, Philosophy's answer in defence of human freewill does not appear. Chaucer himself was certainly fascinated and puzzled by the logical problem as it was discussed by professional thinkers in his day, but I see no reason to suppose that in the order of faith he was determinist. What concerns us is the speech of Troilus; and I doubt whether any excuse for it will be convincing to a modern reader. Nothing, I hope, can induce him to read very much of verse like this—

> For if ther sitte a man yond on a see,
> Than by necessite bihoveth it
> That, certes, thyn opynyoun sooth be,
> That wenest or conjectest that he sit.
> And further over now ayeynward yit,
> Lo, right so is it of the part contrarie,
> As thus (nowe herkne, for I wol nat tarie):
>
> I sey, that if the opynyoun of thee
> Be soth, for that he sitte, than sey I this,
> That he mot siten by necessitee;
> And thus necessite in eyther is.
> For in hym nede of sittynge is, ywys,
> And in thee nede of sooth; and thus, forsothe,
> There mot necessite ben in yow bothe.[2]

[1] IV 862–8
*Beere* bier     Chaucer translates Boccaccio's *tututta si vedea trasfigurata* (*Il Filostrato* IV. 100) in a line which has also a fine version in the *Second Nun's Tale* 251–2:
> The sweete smel that in myn herte I fynde
> Hath chaunged me al in another kynde.

[2] IV 1023–36
*See* seat     The translation of Boethius in the Loeb Classical Library reads as follows: 'For if any man sitteth, the opinion which thinketh so must needs be true; and again on the other side, if the opinion that one sitteth be true, he must needs sit. Wherefore, there is necessity in both, in the one of sitting and in the other of truth.' I do not know whether the pun in *sooth . . . forsothe* was meant, or whether Chaucer was half asleep.

Even Professor Root has expressed the opinion that *And further over now ayeynward yit* is 'probably the least poetical line Chaucer ever wrote': for myself, I cannot recall a line of Chaucer's with less *sense*. The most charitable conclusion I can reach about the whole passage is that Chaucer was half sorry for, half amused by his philosophical lover, and deliberately bungled the versification of Boethius to show that Troilus, at least, was not sitting, but was standing (poor man!) on his head. Certainly, if we compare this paraphrase with the prose translation in *Boece*, the verse is Troilus *disputyng with hymself* rather than Boethius disputing with Philosophy.

There is time enough for a man to stretch out his neck when it is to come off, says Pandarus, and then he can deplore the necessity of execution. That is his answer. Chaucer, having read both philosophy and poetry, sees further than either Troilus or Pandare. And anyone who is bewildered and bored by Trojan philosophizing can have no doubt of what is meant by Troilus's play upon philosophical terms during his last night with Criseyde.

> '. . . lat us stele awey bitwixe us tweye;
> And thynk that folie is, whan man may chese
> For accident his substaunce ay to lese.

> 'I mene thus: that syn we mowe er day
> Wel stele awey, and ben togidere so,
> What wit were it to putten in assay,
> In case ye sholden to youre fader go,
> If that ye myghten come ayeyn or no?
> Thus mene I, that it were a gret folie
> To putte that sikernesse in jupertie.

> And vulgarly to speken of substaunce
> Of tresour, may we bothe with us lede
> Inough to lyve in honour and plesaunce,
> Til into tyme that we shal ben dede . . .'[1]

This highly cultivated speech is not 'out of character', for Troilus is a courtly lover, not Courtly Love. We hear his voice. Chaucer began not with an emotion or a moral, but with three persons and a story.

---

[1] IV 1503-16
*Chese, lese* choose, lose      *Accident* and *substaunce* are appearance and reality; but *accident*, opposed to *sikernesse*, also means 'uncertainty'.      *Mowe* may.

The first conversation between Diomede and Criseyde appears hasty, but Diomede is an efficient (if uncourtly) lover, and the hastiness is all Criseyde's:

> But natheles she thonked Diomede
> Of al his travaile and his goode cheere,
> And that hym list his frendship hire to bede;
> And she accepteth it in good manere,
> And wol do fayn that is hym lief and dere,
> And trusten hym she wolde, and wel she myghte,
> As seyde she, and from hire hors sh'alighte.[1]

His 'affair' is begun during her journey from Troy to the Grecian camp.

In this fifth book there is a gracious remoteness and reserve, so that as he speaks, Diomede's voice seems to be clear across a distance, the distance from Greek to Trojan and further—

> 'For though ye Troians with us Grekes wrothe
> Han many a day ben, alwey yet, parde,
> O god of love in soth we serven bothe . . .'[2]

Criseyde is on the horizon—

> I fynde ek in the stories elleswhere,
> Whan thorugh the body hurt was Diomede
> Of Troilus, tho wepte she many a teere,
> Whan that she saugh his wyde wowndes blede;
> And that she took to kepen hym good hede,
> And for to helen hym of his sorwes smerte.
> Men seyn—I not—that she yaf hym hire herte.[3]

'It is said—but I do not know—that she gave him her heart': she is almost out of sight. She does not return. Troilus waits.

> And whoso axed hym wherof hym smerte,
> He seyde, his harm was al aboute his herte.[4]

And before this extension of distance, Pandarus makes earthy eructations like an ancient troll at our feet.

This is the *completeness*. Troilus and Troy town *shall knotteles thorughout hire herte slide*—but first Chaucer will make a portrait

[1] V 183–9
*Bede* offer
[2] V 141–3
[3] V 1044–50
[4] V 1224–5

of Criseyde that is as balanced, as cool, as any in the *Prologue* to the *Canterbury Tales*. For Chaucer's Italian contemporary Petrarch, writes Mr. J. H. Whitfield, 'it is not only true to say that there are as many opinions as men; but also that each individual varies within himself from moment to moment.'[1] But Petrarch's is the rediscovery of an idea as old as Heraclitus; the character of Criseyde is a new demonstration in art. And after our doubts about verse of the fourth book, we find (and not only in prominent passages) that Chaucer reaches the ease and propriety that is the triumph of his latest stanzas. The reader must give himself to Chaucer to appreciate how exactly the length and shape of his verse has come to fit what he has to say, as it fits the small descriptions of three winters past, or of sunrise, which he adapts from Boccaccio's *Teseide*.[2] But the poetry of the fifth book is not here, or in the lines of Troilus as he waits for the change of the moon

> 'I saugh thyn hornes olde ek by the morwe,
> Whan hennes rood my righte lady dere . . .'[3]

It is the whole movement *sostenuto* of the lover's lament. Troilus, as Duke Theseus said of another, can go away and *pipe in an ivy leef*. At the same time nothing could be more sympathetic than this:

> Fro thennesforth he rideth up and down,
> And every thyng com hym to remembraunce
> As he rood forby places of the town
> In which he whilom hadde al his pleasaunce.
> 'Lo, yonder saugh ich last my lady daunce;
> And in that temple, with hire eyen cleere,
> Me kaughte first my righte lady dere.

> 'And yonder have I herd ful lustyly
> My dere herte laugh; and yonder pleye
> Saugh ich hire ones ek ful blisfully.
> And yonder ones to me gan she seye,
> 'Now goode swete, love me wel, I preye.'
> And yond so goodly gan she me biholde,
> That to the deth myn herte is to hire holde.

---

[1] J. H. WHITFIELD, *Petrarch and the Renascence* (Oxford: Blackwell, 1943) p. 79, referring to *Contra Medicum* IV 1232
[2] *Troilus* V 8–14, 274–9
[3] V 652–3

'And at that corner, in the yonder hous,
Herde I myn alderlevest lady deere
So wommanly, with vois melodious,
Syngen so wel, so goodly, and so clere,
That in my soule yet me thynketh ich here
The blisful sown; and in that yonder place
My lady first me took unto hire grace.'[1]

To propose a translation of such poetry into English is sheer
impertinence: though to attempt it may be innocent tribute.
And it is curious that this should be said of the poet who, in a
footnote of his Preface to the *Lyrical Ballads*, wrote that 'the
affecting parts of Chaucer are almost always expressed in language
pure and universally intelligible even to this day'.  We should
expect Wordsworth to admire the lament of Troilus; and the
impression which his reading of Chaucer made upon him, because
indirect and partial and difficult to estimate, is not sufficiently
admitted.  This is his version of the last stanza that I quoted:

And at the corner of that self-same house
Heard I my most beloved Lady dear,
So womanly, with voice melodious
Singing so well, so goodly, and so clear,
That in my soul methinks I yet do hear
The blissful sound; and in that very place
My Lady first me took unto her grace.[2]

Wordsworth has illustrated his own comment: there is no more
to explain than the word *alderlevest*.  And this verse, the best of
his three, is like the touched-up photograph of a detail from the
National Gallery.  Chaucer was extending a passage of *Il
Filostrato* reflecting Boccaccio's own experience, and added the
remembered song of Criseyde.  But it is the *movement* of the verse
that is so much his own.  We can find a hint of it as far back as
the black knight's memory of his lady's *carole*.  It is the rhythm
of the swan-song, the music of loss, in which Chaucer so delicately
excels: a theme that produced poetry in the artifice of *Anelida and
Arcite*, and will be beautiful again, at moments, in the new form
of the *Legend of Good Women*.  It will never be as in the fifth book
of *Troilus and Criseyde*.  This leaves his French contemporaries

[1] V 561–81
*Kaughte* perceived
[2] From the modernization of *Troilus and Criseyde* V 519–686 printed under the title
'Troilus and Cresida'.

far behind, and achieves, within its complicated art, the lyrical assurance of Guiot de Dijon.

I return, as I promised, to the hollowness of the eighth sphere. Slain by Achilles, Troilus himself has the last laugh:

> And whan that he was slayn in this manere,
> His lighte goost ful blisfully is went
> Up to the holughnesse of the eighthe spere,
> In convers letyng every element;
> And ther he saugh, with ful avysement,
> The erratik sterres, herkenyng armonye
> With sownes ful of hevenyssh melodie.
>
> And down from thennes faste he gan avyse
> This litel spot of erthe, that with the se
> Embraced is, and fully gan despise
> This wrecched world, and held al vanite
> To respect of the pleyn felicite
> That is in hevene above; and at the laste,
> Ther he was slayn, his lokyng down he caste;
>
> And in hymself he lough right at the wo
> Of hem that wepten for his deth so faste;
> And dampned al oure werk that foloweth so
> The blynde lust, the which that may nat last,
> And sholden al oure herte on heven caste.
> And forth he wente, shortly for to telle,
> Ther as Mercurye sorted hym to dwelle.[1]

These verses reach back through the *Teseide* of Boccaccio to Lucan and the *Dream of Scipio*, so that they are still within the illusion of antiquity: an illusion which Chaucer has preserved in terms that would impress themselves upon his own time. *Blinde lust* is a phrase which he will use of the rape of Lucretia, and which may be found in the Latin of St. Augustine's *Confessions*. It is not the same as 'blind lust'. We must beware of reading Chaucerian English with the excess of modern emotional emphasis. There is no need, now, for Troilus to be excited about *this litel spot of erthe*, or even *this wrecched world*. He is calmly looking and laughing, not cursing or moralizing. *Dampned* means, quite simply, 'condemned'. He is given, at last, cool

[1] V 1807–27
*Holughnesse* concavity     *In convers letyng* leaving on the other side

judgement. And this is the reward of Troilus, the great warrior and constant pagan: he rises, possibly to the sphere of the inconstant moon, at least to a classical heaven. He himself rejects those who, in the words of Scipio, 'have given themselves up to sensual pleasures', the 'lecherous folk' of Chaucer's version in the *Parliament of Birds*. This is the Chaucerian balance. It is *great comedy*. It can survive the promise of Nature's priest at the end of the *Romance of the Rose*—the Higher Garden from which faithful and fruitful multipliers of humanity may mock courtly lovers at the fountain of Narcissus. And Chaucer was a master in this: whether consciously or not, he allowed for the judgement that his age was not an age of Tragedy, of the Tragedy which is more than painful and pathetic wretchedness. Many comedians form outrageous characters, then trip them up; and the primitive comic act is 'all fall down' in the nursery rhyme, or the first laughter of Eve. But Chaucer does not trip his people. He often supports them (he props the Monk), and if they collapse, they fall naturally, and sometimes gracefully. The great landslide at the end of *Troilus and Criseyde* is much too comic, in the sense in which I am using the term, to be funny. It is an act of God which does not easily fit the classical divisions. Although Chaucer calls his poem in the medieval way a tragedy, there is a hint of divine comedy about the end of it, and that is to use the term 'comedy' in another sense. Here, in the last stanza, our poet reaches for the *Paradiso*, for he remembers that in these regions a greater has been before him.

> Swich fyn hath, lo, this Troilus for love,
> Swich fyn hath al his grete worthynesse;
> Swich fyn hath his estat real above,
> Swich fyn his lust, swich fyn hath his noblesse;
> Swich fyn hath false worldes brotelnesse.
> And thus bigan his lovyng of Criseyde,
> As I have told, and in this wise he deyde.

> O yonge, fresshe folkes, he or she,
> In which that love up groweth with youre age,
> Repeyreth hom fro worldly vanyte,
> And of youre herte up casteth the visage
> To thilke God that after his ymage
> Yow made, and thynketh al nys but a faire
> This world, that passeth soone as floures faire.

And loveth hym, the which that right for love
Upon a cros, oure soules for to beye,
First starf, and roos, and sit in hevene above;
For he nyl falsen no wight, dar I seye,
That wol his herte al holly on hym leye.
And syn he best to love is, and most meke,
What nedeth feynede loves for to seke?

Lo here, of payens corsed olde rites,
Lo here, what alle hire goddes may availle;
Lo here, these wrecched worldes appetites;
Lo here, the fyn and guerdoun for travaille
Of Jove, Appollo, of Mars, of swich rascaille!
Lo here the forme of olde clerkis speche
In poetrie, if ye hire bokes seche.

O moral Gower, this book I directe
To thee, and to thee philosophical Strode,
To vouchen sauf, ther nede is, to correcte,
Of youre benignites and zeles goode.
And to that sothefast Crist, that starf on rode,
With al myn herte of mercy evere I preye;
And to the Lord right thus I speke and seye:

Thow oon, and two, and three, eterne on lyve,
That regnest ay in three and two and oon,
Uncircumscript, and al maist circumscrive,
Us from visible and invisible foon
Defende; and to thy mercy, everichon,
So make us, Jesus, for thy mercy digne,
For love of mayde and moder thyn benigne.

Amen.[1]

*Repeyreth hom fro worldly vanite* advises Chaucer: recalling, as
elsewhere, strangers and pilgrims on the earth. And I observe
that the final completeness occurs in the silence, after three verses
sung by the prudent of paradise to the Trinity:

> *Quell' uno e due e tre che sempre vive,*
> *e regna sempre in tre e due e uno,*
> *non circonscritto, e tutto circonscrive . . .*[2]

[1] V 1828–69
*Estat real* royal rank    *Brotelnesse* fickleness    *Beye* buy    *Forme* 'forma' or
essential principle    *Strode* the fourteenth century Thomist philosopher and
opponent of Wiclif
[2] *Paradiso* XIV 28–30

For the end of *Troilus and Criseyde* is the more remarkable if Chaucer was unaware that these lines precede the *voce modesta* of Solomon expounding the fullness of human nature in the Resurrection of the Body.

This interpretation of the epilogue is an alternative to two views, neither of which convinces me: one, that it is a kind of moral appendix which would be better removed; the other, that it is a 'retraction' implying repentance of the supposed folly of writing the work.   I cannot believe that in his last page Chaucer has merely conformed to convention, though there is certainly a convention behind it.   On the other hand I cannot deny that Venus in Thomas Usk, and lovers in Lydgate and after, may take advantage of what is called the 'ambiguity' of the poem. A landslide does not crack nature's moulds.   Chaucer addresses *yonge fresshe folkes* in the hope that they will all understand what is the highest, and that those who are capable of following it will do so.   The rest could do worse than celebrate, in his manner, the fulfilment of desire.   They will be warned.   The poet can do only one thing more for them: he can write about marriage. But first he must arrange a procession of Good Women.

# VI

*A favourite flower of mine [the daisy]. It was a favourite with Chaucer, but he did not understand its moral mystery as I do.*

Preface to *Peter Bell*, a parody of Wordsworth's
poem published anonymously 1819

# PRELUDE TO A GLORIOUS LEGEND

IN THE PROLOGUE TO THE *LEGEND OF GOOD WOMEN* CHAUCER twice said goodbye to the courtly love vision—more emphatically, perhaps, the second time. The occasion for the whole poem, according to Lydgate, was a request of the Queen; the poet having expressed his willingness, after writing of Criseyde, to please the ladies of the court with *Penelopeës trouthe and good Alceste*. He has said very little about Penelope. The prologue is a sophisticated court-poem, a literary *tour de force*, and more; as we have discovered in our own day, the use in English poetry of the poetry of another language can go further than translation or pastiche, and the employment of a fresh verse-form further than prosodic novelty. And one legend (which we may be inclined to call *the* legend) is fine enough to justify a new judgement, and a new chapter, on what remains of Cupid's saints.

Chaucer's opening has been interpreted as expression of faith in authority by one, of scepticism by another, of agnosticism by a third expositor. 'Scepticism' is itself a term of more than one meaning, and therefore has its propriety. To me the passage is a prescription, by a comedian of high refinement, of the scepticism that is essential to a philosopher whatever he believes or does not believe, the scepticism without which thought on first principles is impossible; the scepticism of an advanced culture.[1] It is neither pyrrhonism, nor simple-minded credulity concerning *olde bokes*; and it takes into account the folly of the peasant who refused to accept a sermon on hell because he had not been there first to see it for himself.[2]

---

[1] Compare F. H. BRADLEY, *Appearance and Reality* (Oxford, 9th impression, 1930), p. x; T. S. ELIOT, *Notes Towards the Definition of Culture* (London: Faber, 1948), p. 29.
[2] G. R. OWST, *Literature and Pulpit in Medieval England* (Cambridge, 1933), p. 166. And compare JACOB BURCKHARDT, *The Civilization of the Renaissance*, tr. S. G. C. Middlemore, p. 512.

115

A thousand tymes have I herd men telle
That ther ys joy in hevene and peyne in helle,
And I acorde wel that it ys so;
But, natheles, yet wot I wel also
That ther nis noon dwellyng in this contree,
That eyther hath in hevene or helle ybe,
Ne may of hit noon other weyes witen,
But as he hath herd seyd, or founde it writen;
For by assay ther may no man it preve.
But God forbede but men shulde leve
Wel more thing then men han seen with yë!
Men shal not wenen every thing a lye
But yf himself yt seeth, or elles dooth;
For, God wot, thing is never the lasse sooth
Thogh every wight ne may it nat ysee.
Bernard the monk ne saugh nat all, pardee!
    Than mote we to bokes that we fynde,
Thurgh whiche that olde thinges ben in mynde,
And to the doctrine of these olde wyse,
Yeve credence, in every skylful wise,
That tellen of these olde appreved stories
Of holynesse, of regnes, of victories,
Of love, of hate, of other sondry thynges,
Of whiche I may not maken rehersynges.
And yf that olde bokes were aweye,
Yloren were of remembraunce the keye.
Wel ought us thanne honouren and beleve
These bokes, there we han noon other preve.[1]

By the next ten lines anyone reading the prologue from a modern edition will have been drawn to compare the two texts that are printed side by side. And since the doctors disagree about them, everybody will turn leech but the one person who knows the answer. I confess I am of the company.

And as for me, though that I konne but lyte,
On bokes for to rede I me delyte,
And to hem yive I feyth and ful credence,

---

[1] B(F) 1–28
*Leve* believe      *Bernard the monk ne saugh nat all,* a proverb common in various medieval Latin forms, and traditionally supposed to refer to St. Bernard of Clairvaux. F. N. Robinson quotes the variant *Multa sunt quae bonus Bernardus nec vidit, nec audivit* ('there are many things which the good Bernard has neither seen nor heard'). *In every skylful wise* in every way that is reasonable      *Regnes* kingdoms      *Yloren* lost
*Preve* proof, experience

And in myn herte have hem in reverence
So hertely, that ther is game noon
That fro my bokes maketh me to goon,
But yt be seldom on the holiday,
Save, certeynly, whan that the month of May
Is comen, and that I here the foules synge,
And that the floures gynnen for to sprynge—
Farewel my bok, and my devocioun!

> And as for me, though that my wit be lite,
> On bokes for to rede I me delyte,
> And in myn herte have hem in reverence,
> And to hem yeve swich lust and swich credence
> That there is wel unethe game non
> That fro my bokes make me to gon,
> But it be other upon the halyday,
> Or ellis in the joly tyme of May,
> Whan that I here the smale foules synge,
> And that the floures gynne for to sprynge—
> Farwel my studie, as lastynge that sesoun![1]

But I shall not be talkative.

*Swich lust and swich credence* . . . might be what Coleridge called a 'willing suspension of disbelief', and the phrase a revision; on the other hand *ful credence* and *reverence* need not be taken as literal statement. So let us read on. Finesse is more perceptible at the return to the theme, after the poet has revered a French daisy, a *marguerite*, a fashionable literary image for a worshipful lady, and has drawn on half a dozen French poems for the purpose. There are many things, Chaucer tells us, that we have to take on trust from books: here is one of them, and not the most trustworthy.

But wherfore that I spak, to yive credence
To olde stories and doon hem reverence,
And that men mosten more thyng beleve
Than men may seen at eye, or elles preve?
That shal I seyn, whanne that I see my tyme;
I may not al at-ones speke in ryme.

---

[1] B(F); A(G) 29–39
*Konne but lyte* know but little       *To hem yeve swich lust* . . . take such pleasure in
them and give them such credence . . .

But wherfore that I spak, to yeve credence
To bokes olde and don hem reverence,
Is for men shulde autoritees beleve,
There as there lyth non other assay by preve.
For myn entent is, or I fro yow fare,
The naked text in English to declare
Of many a story, or elles of many a geste,
As autours seyn; leveth hem if yow leste![1]

At this point a willing suspension of disbelief in Good Women is possibly in question, and such a delicate suspicion of a hint is of the very essence of the best in the poem.

As I have implied, it is not certain in what order the two versions of the prologue were composed;[2] but if we accept the conclusions of Professor Lowes, we can imagine Chaucer going over the piece after the lapse of a decade. There is an apparent technical revision, which includes improvement of line, alteration of repeated words, tightening of the whole construction.[3] But the poet has done more than look to the working of his poem. I am inclined to think, if Professor Lowes' dating is correct, that Chaucer re-wrote the prologue from memory, and that the result is good criticism rather than finished re-creation; but it is difficult to convince even oneself about the merits of a text based on a single, not very reliable manuscript. This Cambridge text gives a poem with more movement, though much of it moves in dream. The *ballade* becomes a dance-song in which the whole assembly takes part; and then, the Court of Love seated with due ceremonial in order of precedence, the movement is suddenly still. One is held by a slightly uncomfortable illusion of reality in the dialogue. The dreamer is polite, helpless, less than life-size under the eye of the blind god:

---

[1] B(F) 97–102; A(G) 81–8
*Or I fro yow fare* before I leave you          *Geste* exploit or tale of exploits
          *If yow leste* if you care to do so
[2] These were described as A and B when it was supposed that A was the earlier; but since Bernhard ten Brink, J. L. Lowes and some other scholars have held the opposite view, A has been printed as 'G' (after the single MS Gg. 4.27 in the Cambridge University Library) and B as 'F' (after MS Fairfax 16 in the Bodleian).
[3] There is also the deletion of lines reminiscent of *Troilus* and *Il Filostrato* (B.F 68–71; 84–8) and of lines which might have been later adapted for the opening of the Canterbury *Prologue* (B.F 171–4). These four verses are in turn a development of the *Book of the Duchess* 402–4. The association of Zephyrus with Flora occurs in the *Romance of the Rose* but his *sweete breeth* does not.

The god of love on me his eye caste
And seyde 'Who restith there?' and I answerde
Unto his axynge, whan that I hym herde
And seyde, 'Sire, it am I', and cam hym neer,
And saluede hym. Quod he, 'What dost thow heer
In my presence, and that so boldely?
For it were better worthi, trewely,
A worm to comen in my syght than thow.'
'And why, sire,' quod I, 'and it lyke yow?'
'For thow,' quod he, 'art therto nothyng able.
My servaunts ben alle wyse and honourable.
Thow art my mortal fo and me werreyest,
And of myne olde servauntes thow mysseyest,
And hynderest hem with thy translacyoun,
And lettest folk to han devocyoun
To serven me, and holdest it folye
To truste on me. Thow mayst it nat denye.
For in pleyn text—it nedeth nat to glose—
Thow hast translated the Romauns of the Rose,
That is an heresye ageyns my lawe,
And makest wise folk fro me withdrawe;
And thynkest in thy wit, that is ful cool,
That he nys but a verray propre fool
That loveth paramours, too harde and hote.
Wel wot I therby thow begynnyst dote
As olde foles, whan her spiryt fayleth;
Thanne blame they folk, and wite nat what hem ayleth.[1]

In these last lines Cupid might be addressing a diminished Duke
Theseus; and when Alceste rebukes him, there is both a fear of
the irrational situation of the dream, and the amusement of the
waking mind. Yet even the dreamer, forgiven, gains enough
courage to be sharply silenced:

I ros, and doun I sette me on my knee,
And seyde thus, 'Madame, the God above
Foryelde yow, that ye the god of love
Han maked me his wrathe to foryive,
And yeve me grace so longe for to live,
That I may knowe soothly what ye be,
That han me holpen and put in swich degre.
But trewely I wende, as in this cas,

---

[1] A(G) 237–63: compare *Knight's Tale* A 1799, 1812: *Who may been a fool, but if he love?* says Theseus. Yet *a man moot ben a fool, or yong or oold* . . .
*Therto nothyng able* not qualified to do so      *Werreyest* make war
*Lettest . . . to han* prevent . . . having      *Paramours* with passionate devotion

Naught have agilt, ne don to love trespas.
For-why a trewe man, withoute drede,
Hath nat to parte with a theves dede;
Ne a trewe lovere oghte me nat to blame,
Thogh that I speke a fals lovere som shame.
They oughte rathere with me for to holde,
For that I of Criseyde wrot or tolde,
Or of the Rose; what so myn auctour mente,
Algate, God woot, yt was myn entente
To forthere trouthe in love and yt cheryce,
And to ben war fro falsnesse and fro vice
By swich ensaumple; this was my menynge.'
And she answerde, 'Lat be thyn arguynge . . .
Thow hast thy grace, and hold thee ryght therto.
Now wol I seyn what penaunce thow shalt do
For thy trespas, and understond it here:
Thow shalt, whil that thow livest, yer by yere,
The moste partye of thy tyme spende
In makynge of a gloryous legende
Of goode women, maydenes and wyves,
That were trewe in lovynge al her lyves . . .'[1]

The poet, as we shall see, is not entirely suppressed.

But I believe that what would have embarrassed Chaucer most of all, if he reconsidered his prologue in the 1390's, was the 'religion of love' that it contained, the too delicate imitation of real religion. He no longer wished to commix the natural world (that *men han seen with eye*) and the supernatural world (*hevene or helle*) with the imaginary world of allegiance to Cupid, in which *ne shal no trewe lover come in helle*. In the *Canterbury Tales* he had come to distinguish the various levels of experience more and more *dramatically*; and narrative in his own name was now inconvenient, unless he could dramatize himself also. This indeed he had begun to do, within the dream convention, as long ago as the *Book of the Duchess*; and one way of dealing with the prologue to the *Legend of Good Women* was to erect a bed much earlier in the poem, put some of the embarrassing stuff, the beautiful nonsense, in a dream, and make it still more beautiful. If that is what he did, the imaginary, the 'ideal' May day, which one can enjoy without bothering about an unreliable English spring, became a 'real' *someres day* on which

---

[1] A(G) 445ff; parallel to B(F) 455ff.
*Foryelde* reward     *I wende . . . naught have agilt* I did not think I had done wrong
                      *Hath nat to parte with* has no part in

the poet could describe with verisimilitude his preparations for reclining out of doors.—The line

> And this was now the firste morwe of May

became

> Whan passed was almost the month of May . . .[1]

In *Troilus and Criseyde* Chaucer had already tested a particular case of courtly love: now he tries the conventional literary mode, and it is found wanting. What was wanted the poet himself shows in the superb *ballade* 'To Rosemounde', which is usually dated between, or after, the two versions of our prologue.

> Madame, ye ben of al beauté shryne
> As fer as cercled is the mapemounde,
> For as the cristal glorious ye shyne,
> And lyke ruby ben your chekes rounde.
> Therwith ye ben so mery and so jocounde
> That at a revel whan that I see you daunce,
> It is an oynement unto my wounde,
> Thogh ye to me ne do no daliaunce.
>
> For thogh I wepe of teres ful a tyne,
> Yet may that wo myn herte nat confounde;
> Your seemly voys that ye so smal out-twyne
> Maketh my thoght in joye and blis habounde.
> So curtaysly I go, with love bounde,
> That to myself I sey, in my penaunce,
> 'Suffyseth me to love you, Rosemounde,
> Thogh ye to me ne do no daliaunce.'
>
> Nas never pyk walwed in galauntyne
> As I in love am walwed and ywounde,
> For which ful ofte I of myself devyne
> That I am trewe Tristam the secounde.
> My love may not refreyde nor affounde;
> I brenne ay in an amorous plesaunce.
> Do what you lyst, I wyl your thral be founde,
> Thogh ye to me ne do no daliaunce.[2]

---

[1] B(F) 108; A(G) 89

[2] *Mapemounde* map of the world      *So smal out-twyne* so delicately unthread    *Pyk . . . in galauntyne* pike soused    *Refreyde* (Kökeritz's reading) cool      *Affounde* founder    J. M. Manly suggested that 'To Rosemounde' was written for Princess Isabel of France when she married Richard II, in 1396, at the age of seven. Whether he guessed right or not, that is precisely the sort of occasion which might have produced from Chaucer great comic poetry.

Mr. C. S. Lewis formerly wondered whether we should smile at this,[1] but I cannot quite seriously see Chaucer producing, even in imagination, a barrelful of tears, no matter how 'conventional' his phrase may be. As for comparing a man in love and a fish in sauce, one could as easily translate thus a comparison in Jack Donne or the *Love Song of J. Alfred Prufrock* to make them appear contributions to an anthology of comic verse; whereas the original poetry in each of these different pieces gave something like an electric shock. In the case of Chaucer we have a court poet of unsurpassed accomplishment giving authoritative expression to the *vitality* of a feeling which, according to vogue, ought at this stage to be languishing; and doing so with frisky joy. And whatever the courtly Duc de Berry made of fat in 1389, *Merciles Beaute*, probably by Chaucer, is an amusing trifle obviously flouting convention—

> Sin I fro Love escaped am so fat,
> I never thenk to ben in his prison lene;
> Sin I am free, I counte him not a bene.

> He may answere, and seye this and that;
> I do no fors, I speke right as I mene.
> Sin I fro Love escaped am so fat,
> I never thenk to ben in his prison lene.

> Love hath my name ystrike out of his sclat,
> And he is strike out of my bokes clene
> For evermo; ther is non other mene.
> Sin I fro Love escaped am so fat,
> I never thenk to ben in his prison lene;
> Sin I am free, I counte him not a bene.[2]

And when in the witty 'envoy' to Scogan the poet comically feigns horror at a friend's apostasy against cupid, it is not difficult to perceive the tone of his repetition of the name:

> Allas! Scogan . . .

> Hastow not seyd, in blaspheme of the goddes,
> Thrugh pride, or thrugh thy grete rekelnesse,

---

[1] *The Allegory of Love* p. 171. 'As serious poetry it is bathos: as jest it is flat. What effect Chaucer intended is just one of those things which, as I conceive, we shall never know . . .'
This seems to be a latter-day XIXth-century view of wit in verse, and a view which perhaps Mr. Lewis himself would not now defend with great enthusiasm.

[2] The poem is the triple roundel with the opening line *Your yen two wol slee me sodeynly*. I quote only the last part.
*I do no fors* I do not care    *Sclat* slate    *Mene* course, 'thing to do'

Swich thing as in the lawe of love forbode is,
That, for thy lady saw nat thy distresse,
Therfore thow yave hir up at Michelmesse?
Allas! Scogan, of olde folk ne yonge
Was never erst Scogan blamed for his tonge!

And, Scogan . . .

Nay, Scogan . . .

Scogan, that knelest at the stremes hed
Of grace . . .[1]

In the beautiful image of the envoy the 'stream' is, I think, both the Thames and the time of love—*in th'ende of which strem*, says Chaucer, *I am dull as ded*.[2]

To Bukton Chaucer addressed a complementary envoy about marriage; and by the time this was written the *Canterbury Tales* were well under way. When he returned to our present prologue, it was not, I think, to pretend to spend the rest of his life on the hagiography of courtly love, but rather to dissociate himself from the cult. The act of revision might be seen as parallel to the ending of *Troilus and Criseyde*; Chaucer has allowed the courtly mode a generous probation, and has found it, as I said, wanting. If he had come to think it worthless, the poem would have been suppressed. There is something in it still: and our magistral poet, even if Good Women are too much for him, excels in the defence of difficult cases.

> . . . at the laste a larke song above:
> 'I see', quod she, 'the myghty god of love!
> Lo, yond he cometh! I see his wynges sprede!'
> Tho gan I loke endelong the mede,
> And saw hym come, and in his hond a quene
> Clothed in ryal habyt al of grene.
> A fret of gold she hadde next hyre her
> And upon that a whit corone she ber
> With many floures, and I shal nat lye;
> For al the world, ryght as the dayesye
> Ycorouned is with white leves lite,
> Swiche were the floures of hire coroune white.
> For of o perle fyn and oryental

---

[1] 13ff.
*Rekelnesse* rashness        *Erst* before
[2] Against this line in the MSS is written *Grenewich*, at one time Chaucer's residence; and against the *stremes hed* is written *Windesore*. These may be later additions.

Hyre white coroun was ymaked al;
For which the white coroun above the grene
Made hire lyk a dayesye for to sene,
Considered eek the fret of gold above.
Yclothed was this myghty god of love
Of silk, ybrouded ful of grene greves;
A garlond on his hed of rose-leves,
Stiked al with lylye floures newe.
But of his face I can not seyn the hewe;
For sikerly his face shon so bryghte
That with the gleem astoned was the syghte . . .[1]

In what I am at present assuming to be the revised text, he achieves at moments a beautiful balance between *To Rosemounde* and the *ballade* to Alceste, a balance that we can see as we watch him trying to look repentant before the god of love, and apparently thinking of a lively speech of Theseus in a tale perhaps just completed for the Knight. All I suggest is that this is one way of reading the prologue to the *Legend of Good Women*. Chaucer's language is clear; but there is a double image behind it, an elusive dramatic irony that you can interpret or not, as you wish.

The *ballade* danced and sung *in carole-wyse* is Chaucer's Ballade of Great Names, of famed ladies, of Good Women whose stories he is to tell; and all their beauties, and Absalom's, and Jonathan's, must now give place to the admirable Alceste. This has every air of a piece of fashionable French artifice, yet it can stand up to a great poem which Villon wrote in France a century later.

Hyd, Absalon, thy gilte tresses clere;
Ester, ley thow thy meknesse al adoun;
Hyd, Jonathas, al thyn frendly manere;
Penelope and Marcia Catoun,
Mak of youre wyfhod no comparisoun;
Hyde ye youre beautes, Ysoude and Eleyne:
Alceste is here, that al that may desteyne.

Thy fayre body, lat it nat apeere,
Laveyne; and thow, Lucresse of Rome toun,
And Polixene, that boughte love so dere,
Ek Cleopatre, with al thy passioun,

<hr>

[1] A(G) 141–64
*Ryal* royal        *Greves* boughs
I am inclined to prefer the line *For of o perle fyn, oriental* in the other version, though not the whole passage.

Hide ye youre trouth in love and youre renoun;
And thow, Tysbe, that hast for love swich peyne:
Alceste is here, that al that may desteyne.

Herro, Dido, Laodomya, alle in-fere,
Ek Phillis, hangynge for thy Demophoun,
And Canace, espied by thy chere,
Ysiphile, betrayed with Jasoun,
Mak of youre trouthe in love no bost ne soun;
Nor Ypermystre or Adriane, ne playne:
Alceste is here, that al that may disteyne.[1]

Here is the highest point reached in Chaucer's early pure lyrical strain: the *cantabile* line. Villon did not forget that he was employing a musical form, but Villon has that unexpected twist of the lip and of the heart which is outside the circle of the *carole* of the court of love:

*Ou est la tres sage Helloïs,*
*Pour qui fut chastré et puis moyne*
*Pierre Esbaillart a Saint Denis?*
*Pour son amour ot ceste essoyne.*
*Semblablement, ou est la royne*
*Qui commanda que Buridan*
*Fust geté en ung sac en Saine?*
*Mais ou sont les neiges d'antan? . . .*

Where's Heloise, the learned nun,
    For whose sake Abeillard, I ween,
Lost manhood and put priesthood on?
    (From Love he won such dule and teen!)
    And where, I pray you, is the Queen
Who willed that Buridan should steer
    Sewed in a sack's mouth down the Seine? . . .
But where are the snows of yester-year?

Dante Gabriel Rossetti has been admired, but Villon is untranslatable. I have quoted only one verse, and his withering directness has escaped. Indeed, he has about as much chance in English as Chaucer in Czech. And whatever we may make of Absalom's golden hair, Chaucer's *ballade* remains within the prelude to a 'glorious legend'.

[1] A(G) 203–23
If, as F. N. Robinson suggests, Chaucer remembered the line about golden-haired Absalom in *Le Roman de la Rose* (ed. LANGLOIS, 13870), he has taken a pinch from a passage about Venus and free love, out of the *heresye* of Jean de Meun, to aid the rites of the god.
The return of *Marcia* to Cato was treated as allegory by Dante in the *Convivio*.
*Desteyne* distain, bedim          *In-fere* together          *With Jasoun* by Jason

Chaucers *bookes shall this yeere proove more witty then ever they were: for there shall so many suddayne, or rather sodden wittes steppe abroad, that a Flea shall not friske foorth unless they comment on her.*

SIMON SMEL-KNAVE (STUDIENT IN GOOD-FELOWSHIP): *Feareful and Lamentable Effects of Two Dangerous Comets, which shall Appear in the Yeere of our Lord* 1591, *the* 25 *of March*

# OF WOMEN THAT WERE CALLED GOOD

IT IS CUSTOMARY, IN COMMENTING ON OUR 'GLORIOUS LEGEND', to remark on the sameness of female virtue and pass on;[1] whereas one reason why Chaucer persevered to a tenth heroine was that he had some interest in the *difference*. If he set out to press his women into one set mould of goodness he soon began to fail: they are all 'Cupid's saints' but at the same time various approximations to real sanctity, and many of them not even approximations. I do not think it is often observed[2] that Chaucer had an *arrière-pensée* all through the work, otherwise he could not have shown even the degree of interest which I shall try to indicate. Four of the nine stories he completed occur in the *Rose*,[3] for the translation of which he has been soundly

---

[1] What is now the critical commonplace of Chaucer's growing boredom with the series may be traced to T. R. LOUNSBURY: *Studies in Chaucer* (New York, 1892) III pp. 335ff. But Lounsbury had read them. And, aside from this particular poem, he seems to have been the first modern critic to emphasize Chaucer's *urbanity*.

[2] When this chapter was drafted I knew of the papers by H. C. Goddard, *Journal of English and Germanic Philology*, VII iv 87ff. (1908), VIII 47ff. (1909), and R. M. Garrett, XXII 64ff. (1923), but was not then able to consult them. And the short essay in Mr. Nevill Coghill's *The Poet Chaucer* (Oxford, 1949) appeared later. J. L. Lowes, in the journal mentioned (VIII 513ff.), criticized with some justice but no mercy H. C. Goddard's over-emphasis, his comparison of the two prologues, and his neglect of the 'stock *exempla* of fidelity in love'; and was well advised to disown, in the end, the view 'that Chaucer saw no irony in any of the situations he portrayed'. R. M. Garrett called the legends 'a masterly set of humorous sketches'; but with Mr. Garrett's reading of Ariadne's proposal as 'farce' I agree, and he has observed Chaucer's ironical bluster against his own sex. F. N. Robinson warns us (apparently with reference to the articles by H. C. Goddard and R. M. Garrett) that 'in the mind of Chaucer and his contemporaries the heroines he celebrates were good in the only sense that counted for the purpose in hand—they were faithful followers of the god of Love' (*Complete Works of Geoffrey Chaucer* p. 567). I grant that Chaucer was not 'perpetrating a huge joke upon critics and patrons'; and it is clear that the word *good*, of the title of the poem, is used in a special convention. It is equally clear that Chaucer did not accept Cupid as an absolute of goodness.
When Mr. Coghill speaks of 'the exquisite performance of a solemn *badinerie*' and of 'a ballet written and danced in a spirit of graceful comedy', with 'moments of serious tenderness and other moments of burlesque' (*op. cit.* p. 88), he seems to me to answer a modern inquirer very well on the subject of the prologue.

[3] *Le Roman de la Rose*, ed. LANGLOIS (Paris, 1914–23), 8608ff. (Lucretia), 13173ff. (Dido), 13211ff. (Phyllis), 13229ff. (Medea). That is, of course, in the part by Jeun de Meun which the god of love, if he had read it, could call *an heresye ageyns my lawe*. He appears to be unaware of his servant Guillaume de Lorris, who began the poem. It is an amusing detail of balance of comedy that more than one of the books mentioned could be used in a sense opposed to that which is assumed.

rated by the god of love; and in the *Book of the Duchess* the dreamer, as if acting the part of Reason personified in the *Romance*, condemned suicidal madness in Medea, Phyllis and Dido as a warning to the distraught lover.

> 'A, goode sir! . . .
> Remembre yow of Socrates,
> For he ne counted nat three strees
> Of aught that Fortune koude doo . . .
> Thogh ye had lost the ferses twelve,
> And ye for sorwe mordred yourselve,
> Ye sholde be dampned in this cas
> By as good ryght as Medea was,
> That slough hir children for Jasoun;
> And Phyllis also for Demophoun
> Heng hirself, so weylaway!
> For he had broke his terme-day
> To come to hir. Another rage
> Had Dydo, the quene eke of Cartage,
> That slough hirself, for Eneas
> Was fals; which a fool she was! . . .'[1]

No one will take this quite literally as Chaucer's attitude to human love, though it is nearer to the classical Latin view of love as a *rage* than to the view that Chaucer is set to defend in the *Legend of Good Women*. In the Man of Law's notice of what he calls the *Seintes Legende of Cupide*, the most virtuous ladies are apostrophized *with the beste*—the 'best' including suicides and murderesses:

> Whoso that wole his large volume seke,
> Cleped the Seintes Legende of Cupide,
> Ther may he seen the large woundes wyde
> Of Lucresse, and of Babilan Tisbee;
> The swerd of Dido for the false Enee;
> The tree of Phillis for hire Demophon;
> The pleinte of Dianire and of Hermyon,
> Of Adriane, and of Isiphilee;
> The bareyn yle stondynge in the see;
> The dreynte Leandre for his Erro;

---

[1] 714ff. Compare *Le Roman de la Rose* 5847–56; and, on the other hand, Chaucer's own legends of Dido, Medea and Phyllis.
*Ferses twelve* all the pieces of chess except the king (referring to the terms of the knight's complaint against Fortune).

The teeris of Eleyne, and eek the wo
Of Brixseyde, and of thee, Ladomya;
The crueltee of thee, queene Medea,
Thy litel children hangynge by the hals,
For thy Jason, that was of love so fals!
O Ypermystra, Penelopee, Alceste,
Youre wifhod he comendeth with the beste![1]

This is rather too inaccurate, even for a 'blurb'; it is also too well written. (*The bareyn yle stondynge in the see* might have gone somewhere in the finer passages of the *Knight's Tale*, not far from *the smylere with the knyf under the cloke*.) But these lines, together with those to which I referred in the *Romance of the Rose* and the *Book of the Duchess*, suggest a flexibility of mind which it is unreasonable to suppose was entirely ossified during the composition of the *Legend of Good Women*. Chaucer thought of the ethic of the Church beside the ethic of chivalric love as one might think of two tunes, frequently dissonant, sometimes in concord, but occasionally, and perhaps by accident, in unison.

If we look through the legends with an eye to what is admirable by the poet's highest standards, we can make, at once, three observations. The first is that he skips over Cleopatra with a momentary interest in an actual sea-fight; second, he finds one or two shivering lines for Piramus and Thisbe; and, third, he is at his best in a passage of the story of Dido. This last is of very much greater interest than his impression of the *Æneid* in the *House of Fame*. It is true that part of the beginning of the legend is another insipid verse abstract; but when he has paid his homage to Virgil, he treats Dido afresh, in a way which is Chaucer and English poetry. In order to enjoy it we have to be aware that this is no competition, but deliberately confined to proportions delicate, sensitive, amusing beside the vast intention of the Latin. The first descriptions of Dido can hardly be referred to Virgil; they are 'conventionally' medieval in diction, and in rhythm Chaucerian. She is seen as a *fresshe lady* capable of love, and not in relation to the politic of Rome or to myth. In the alteration the stature of Virgil's queen is inevitably reduced —but her raging, murderous fury in the *Æneid* is of course outside

---

[1] *Canterbury Tales* B 61–76
*The swerd* . . . the sword with which Dido killed herself   *The tree*, on which Phyllis hanged herself, or into which she was transformed   *The pleinte* . . . the epistles of Deianira, Hermione, Ariadne, and Hypsipyle, from Ovid.   *The bareyn yle* apparently Naxos, on which Ariadne was abandoned

Chaucer's commission.  He has the poetic problem of directing our sympathy towards Dido and against Æneas, and at the same time he has the ironist's consciousness of what he is doing.  He assumed that his readers would know, perhaps their Virgil, certainly their *Romance of the Rose*, in which the story is told by La Vieille to show that in the opinion of the decrepit quean One Lover is Not Enough.  He keeps at a distance from the deities who produce epic crises—

> I can nat seyn if that hit be possible,
> But Venus hadde him maked invisible—
> Thus seith the book . . .[1]

—and makes no miraculous apparition of Æneas in celestial splendour; only the bare statement,

> Unto the quene appered Eneas,
> And openly biknew that it was he.[2]

Where Virgil's hero appears radiant from the circling cloud, Chaucer makes a note of the facial muscles and skull formation, as dispassionately as if he were observing the Miller—

> . . . he was lyk a knyght,
> And suffisaunt of persone and of myght,
> And lyk to been a verray gentil man;
> And wel his wordes he besette can,
> And hadde a noble visage for the nones,
> And formed wel of braunes and of bones.[3]

—and then adds, without great conviction,

> For after Venus hadde he swich fayrnesse
> That no man myghte be half so fayr, I gesse.

Thus he plays his game of carrying out instructions of the court of love.

The two outstanding passages of poetry show the action of Eros: first in the munificence of Dido, which Chaucer, passing over the golden splendour of the feast, develops in his own way:

[1] 1020–2
[2] 1057–8
*Biknew* confessed
[3] 1066–71
*Besette* employ
  Compare the Canterbury *Prologue* A 545–6, quoted below, p. 174, together with a parallel couplet from the popular romance *Ipomydon*.  I do not think we need assume that Chaucer misunderstood *Os humerosque deo similis* (*Æneid* I 589).

To daunsynge chaumberes ful of paramentes,
Of riche beddes, and of ornementes,
This Eneas is led, after the mete.
And with the quene whan that he hadde sete,
And spices parted, and the wyn agon,
Unto his chambres was he led anon . . .
There nas courser wel ybrydeled non,
Ne stede, for the justing wel to gon,
Ne large palfrey, esy for the nones,
Ne jewel, fretted ful of ryche stones,
Ne sakkes ful of gold, of large wyghte,
Ne ruby non, that shynede by nyghte,
Ne gentil hautein faucoun heroner,
Ne hound, for hert or wilde bor or der,
Ne coupe of gold, with floreyns newe ybete,
That in the land of Libie may be gete,
That Dido ne hath it Eneas ysent;
And al is payed, what that he hath spent.[1]

So Dido is expressed through her gifts, with a vitality that reaches
a point of aristocratic excellence in the line *Ne gentil hautein
faucoun heroner.*   This quality is still clearer in the finest passage
of the legends, Chaucer's handling of *Oceanum interea surgens
Aurora reliquit* . . .

The dawenyng up-rist out of the see:
This amorous queen chargeth hire meynee
The nettes dresse, and speres brode and kene;
An huntyng wol this lusty freshe queene,
So priketh hire this newe joly wo.
To hors is al hir lusty folk ygo;
Into the court the houndes been ybrought;
And upon coursers, swift as any thought,
Hire yonge knyghtes hoven al aboute,
And of hire women ek an huge route.
Upon a thikke palfrey, paper-whit,
With sadel red, enbrouded with delyt,
Of gold the barres up-enbossed hye,
Sit Dido, al in gold and perre wrye;
And she as fair as is the bryghte morwe,
That heleth syke folk of nyghtes sorwe.[2]

[1] 1106–25
*Paramentes* rich hangings       *Sete* sat          *Wyghte* weight
*Hautein* proud          *Heroner* for herons
[2] 1188–203
*Meynee* retinue          *Hoven* hover          *Thikke* stout          *Perre* precious
stones          *Wrye* covered

In Virgil it is the queen, not the princes of Carthage, who linger; and her *sonipes* here becomes *a thikke palfrey, paper-whit*.   Chaucer's last couplet, with its beautiful double rhyme, and its imagery in the troubadour tradition, is his own—and so, in effect, is the whole passage.

What is positive in this comes of a natural impulse renewing life, creative as in the Spring movement of the Canterbury *Prologue*.   The sensitive physical excitement of the scene is in the mettle of Æneas's horse, set off by the virility of *these yonge folk*.

> Upon a courser stertlynge as the fyr—
> Men myghte turne hym with a litel wyr—
> Sit Eneas, lik Phebus to devyse,
> So was he fressh arayed in his wyse.
> The fomy brydel with the bit of gold
> Governeth he, ryght as hymself hath wold.
> And forth this noble queen thus lat I ride
> On huntynge, with this Troyan by hyre side.
>    The herde of hertes founden is anon,
> With 'hey! go bet! pryke thow! lat gon, lat gon!
> Why nyl the leoun comen, or the bere,
> That I myghte ones mete hym with this spere?'
> Thus seye these yonge folk, and up they kylle
> These bestes wilde, and han hem at here wille.[1]

When they are surprised by the thunderstorm,

> She fledde hireself into a litel cave,
> And with hire wente this Eneas also.
> I not, with hem if there wente any mo;
> The autour maketh of it no mencioun.[2]

Chaucer can smile without suspicion of archness: he has done his job admirably.

The tragic conflict in Virgil's Dido, between the new desire and the old duty, must not of course be attempted; and certain passages remain to be smoothed over.

> . . . *neque enim specie famave movetur*
> *Nec iam furtivum Dido meditatur amorem;*
> *Coniugium vocat; hoc prætexit nomine culpam.*
>
> Æneid

[1] 1204–17
*Stertlynge as the fyr* leaping like flame          *Wyr* bit          *Wold* wished
[2] 1225–8
*Not* do not know

For there hath Eneas ykneled so,
And told hire al his herte and al his wo,
And swore so depe to hire to be trewe,
For wel or wo, and chaunge hire for no newe,
And as a fals lovere so wel can pleyne,
That sely Dido rewede on his peyne,
And tok hym for husbonde, and becom his wyf
For evermo, whil that hem laste lyf.[1]

*Legenda Didonis Martiris*

It is as if Chaucer translated Virgil's *enim*, and then saw that the rest simply would not do. And so, soon after this, he may plead for Good Women:

O sely wemen, ful of innocence,
Ful of pite, of trouthe, and conscience,
What maketh yow to men to truste so?
Have ye swych routhe upon hyre feyned wo,
And han swich olde ensaumples yow beforn?
Se ye nat alle how they ben foresworn?
Where sen ye oon, that he ne hath laft his leef,
Or ben unkynde, or don hire som myscheef,
Or piled hire, or bosted of his dede?
Ye may as wel it sen, as ye may rede.
Tak hede now of this grete gentil-man,
This Troyan, that so wel hire plesen can,
That feyneth hym so trewe and obeysynge,
So gentil, and so privy of his doinge,
And can so wel don alle his obeysaunces
And wayten hire at festes and at daunces
And whan she goth to temple and hom ageyn
And fasten til he hath his lady seyn
And beren in his devyses, for hire sake,
Not I not what; and songes wolde he make,
Justen, and don of armes many thynges,
Sende hire lettres, tokens, broches, rynges—
Now herkneth how he shal his lady serve! . . .[2]

---

[1] *Æneid* IV 170–3: thus translated by Dryden:
The queen, whom sense of honour could not move,
No longer made a secret of her love,
But called it marriage; by that specious name
To veil the crime and sanctify the shame.
*Legend of Good Women* 1232–9
*Sely* innocent
[2] 1254–76
*Leef* beloved     *Piled* despoiled     *And beren in his devyses* . . . carry I do not know what tokens in his heraldic decoration.

This is entirely medieval; and the ironical reserve is Chaucer's. For the moment he is like an actor trying very hard to be out of breath, and succeeding.

At the end of the poem, the furious majesty of Virgil's queen is changed to Chaucerian pathos and grace:

> She axeth hym anon what hym myslyketh—
> 'My dere herte, which that I love most?'
> 'Certes', quod he, 'this nyght my faderes gost
> Hath in my slep so sore me tormented,
> And ek Mercurie his message hath presented,
> That nedes to the conquest of Ytayle
> My destine is sone for to sayle;
> For which, me thynketh, brosten is myn herte!'
> Therwith his false teres out they sterte;
> And taketh hire withinne his armes two.
>    'Is this in ernest?' quod she, 'wole ye so?
> Have ye nat sworn to wyve me to take?
> Allas! what woman wole ye of me make?
> I am a gentile woman and a queen.
> Ye wole nat from youre wif thus foule fleen?
> That I was born, allas! What shal I do?'
>    To telle in short, this noble quen Dydo,
> She seketh halwes and doth sacryfise;
> She kneleth, cryeth, that routhe is to devyse;
> Conjureth hym, and profereth hym to be
> His thral, his servant in the leste degre;
> She falleth hym to fote and swouneth ther,
> Dischevele, with hire bryghte gilte her . . .[1]

Perhaps there is something here, even if it is only a line, which is not entirely obliterated by the nightmare and the horror in the *Æneid*.

This music is successful with a 'dying fall': let him steal Ovid's *albus olor* for the purpose—

> 'Ryght so', quod she, 'as that the white swan
> Ayens his deth begynnyth for to synge,
> Right so to yow make I my compleynynge.
> Not that I trowe to geten yow ageyn,
> For wel I wot that it is al in veyn,
> Syn that the goddes been contraire to me.

[1] 1293–315
*Halwes* shrines

136

But syn my name is lost through yow,' quod she,
'I may wel lese a word on yow, or letter,
Al be it that I shal ben nevere the better;
For thilke wynd that blew youre ship awey,
The same wynd hath blowe awey youre fey.'[1]

The white swan had already sung in Anelida's *compleynt*, but in these closing couplets she has a new voice.

The second part of the next legend is also told by La Vieille in Jean de Meun, with the 'moral' that women should take warning from the folly of Medea, and not rely on a mere Jason: Medea's mistake was in having only one string to her bow. Hypsipyle and Medea, in Chaucer, are simply tender chickens for the wicked fox, and the story comes to a deliberate and abrupt end before Medea's terrible vengeance.[2]   Chaucer's own introduction is the liveliest passage:

Thow rote of false lovers, Duc Jasoun!
Thow sly devourere and confusioun
Of gentil wemen, tendre creatures,
Thow madest thy recleymyng and thy lures
To ladyes, of thy statly aparaunce
And of thy wordes, farced with plesaunce,
And of thy feyned trouthe and thy manere,
With thyn obeysaunce and humble cheere,
And with thy contrefeted peyne and wo.
There othere falsen oon, thow falsest two!
O, often swore thow that thow woldest dye
For love, whan thow ne feltest maladye
Save foul delyt, which that thow callest Love!
Yif that I live, thy name shal be shove
In English, that thy sekte shal be knowe!
Have at thee, Jason! now thyn horn is blowe!
But certes, it is bothe routhe and wo
That love with false loveres werketh so;
For they shal have wel betere love and chere
Than he that hath abought his love ful dere,
Or hadde in armes many a blody box.
For evere as tendre a capoun et the fox,
Thow he be fals and hath the foul betrayed,

---

[1] 1355–65: Chaucer is paraphrasing Ovid: *Heroides* VII 1–8
*Fey* faith
[2] This was described in Chaucer's day by John Gower in the *Confessio Amantis*, which has the tale of Jason and Medea in Book V.

As shal the good-man that therfore hath payed;
Al have he to the capoun skille and ryght,
The false fox wol have his part at nyght.
On Jason this ensaumple is wel ysene
By Isiphile and Medea the queene.[1]

In the attacks on Jason, in the imprecations elsewhere against Wicked Men, Chaucer is fulfilling his contract as Cupid's own *jongleur*, and dramatizing his own antics: without, of course, suggesting that the hero's unfaithfulness is to be condoned. It is the serio-comic attitude of his address to the audience:

. . . Jason is as coy as is a mayde;
He loketh pitously, but nought he sayde,
But frely yaf he to hire conseyleres
Yiftes grete, and to hire officeres.
As wolde God I leyser hadde and tyme
By proces al his wowyng for to ryme!
But in this hous if any fals lovere be,
Ryght as hymself now doth, ryght so dide he,
With feynynge, and with every subtil dede.[2]

The poet is not digging his neighbour in the ribs; he is implying that no more exposure of Jason is needed, for Jason's ways are only too well known in others. And male triflers in the audience had already received a home thrust, when Alceste said that *in youre world* the score of seduction is considered *game*.[3] Jason is another who knew all the *olde daunce:* a wicked uncle to the Wife of Bath.

Chaucer is a little more concerned about Lucretia than about his last two heroines, but there is nothing of poetic interest in her legend except, here and there, an internal rhyme. The story was told in the *Romance of the Rose* by the jealous husband of Friend's imagination, with an envoy, which I imagine Chaucer had in mind when he completed the *Clerk's Tale*, to the effect that there are no women of her virtue left. Chaucer takes pleasure in making out a *prima facie* case on the other side: 'I tell the tale', he says,

---

[1] 1368–95
*Of thy statly aparaunce* recalls Dante's line on Jason in the *Inferno* (XVIII 85): *quanto aspetto reale ancor ritiene!* ('what a regal aspect he yet retains!') Chaucer is constrained to pass over the Lemnian women's murder of their men, to which Dante refers.
*Recleymyng* enticement    *Manere* courtesy    *Shove* pushed forward, advertised
*Rote* root    *Thyn horn* the hunting call    *Therfore hath payed* has paid for it
[2] 1548–56
[3] A(G) 476–9

. . . for she was of love so trewe,
Ne in hir wille she chaunged for no newe;
And for the stable herte, sadde and kynde,
That in these wymmen men may alday fynde.
Ther as they kaste hir herte, there it dwelleth.
For wel I wot that Crist himselve telleth
That in Israel, as wyd as is the lond,
That so gret feyth in al that he ne fond
As in a woman; and this is no lye.
As of men, loke ye which tirannye
They doon alday; assay hem whoso lyste
The trewest ys ful brotel for to triste.[1]

'As for men', the centurion was not the only male commended
by Christ for faith. And Christ also praised the faith of a
Woman who was not Good; 'this is no lie' either. But if Chaucer
did not really regard Lucretia as representative of womanhood,
he showed proper deference to St. Augustine's commentary on
her story[2] and thought the legend an impressive *exemplum*. The
manner of her death recalls the Parson's sermon, and a tale the
Monk kept in his cell:

But pryvely she kaughte forth a knyf,
And therwithal she rafte hirself hir lyf;
And as she fel adoun, she kaste hir lok,
And of hir clothes yet she hede tok.
For in hir fallynge yet she had a care,
Lest that hir feet or suche thyng lay bare;
So wel she loved clennesse and eke trouthe.[3]

This is certainly not flippant or irreverent; nor is it entirely
earnest. St. Augustine had no illusions about the suicide of the
noble Roman matron, whom he contrasts with Christian women
who suffered as she did and yet 'declined to avenge upon themselves the guilt of others'. 'If you extenuate the homicide',
said Augustine, 'you confirm the adultery; if you acquit her of

---

[1] 1874–85
This recalls the Syro-phœnician woman (*Matthew* xv. 21–9); the centurion (*Matthew*
viii. 5–13, *Luke* vii. 1–10) and blind Bartimæus (*Mark* x. 46–52, *Luke* xviii. 35–43); and
the woman 'which was a sinner' (*Luke* vii. 36–50).
*Sadde* steady        *In al that*, i.e., *in al the lond* (the reading of some manuscripts)
*Brotel* frail
[2] *De Civitate Dei* I 19
[3] 1854–60   Compare *Parson's Tale* I 422–9 (a vigorous treatment, for which Dr.
Owst finds a parallel in a sermon on the Magdelene by Master Rypon); *Monk's Tale*
B 3902–5.
*Clennesse* purity

adultery, you make the charge of homicide heavier'. Chaucer is aware of this larger problem of casuistry, and therefore looks for something small to admire. The whole of his legend, with its melodramatic villain, would no doubt go down better, as a preacher's anecdote, than Gower's more independent version.[1] Gower, on the other hand, does express a certain feline progression and suspense in assault, but attempts more than Chaucer without bringing it off. We are drawn by the suspicion that, with this subject, no Englishman has been very happy, because no Englishman happens to have been very serious. The author of *Othello* and *Macbeth*, like Chaucer, could have grasped its difficulties, and unlike Chaucer could have demolished them; but at the time in question, after the early brilliance of *Venus and Adonis*, Shakespeare was pursuing words and ideas and temptations of a teeming theatrical brain, leaving narrative poetry far behind him. In our own day, much as I enjoy the best of Mr. Benjamin Britten, in *Lucretia* I do not find his echoes of Puccini sufficiently conscious. And if it is not absurd to compare a tale and an opera, this failure of Mr. Britten's seems, in contrast to Chaucer's, a failure of detachment.

The next legend has three verses to praise. A line about Androgeus may be an accidental success:

. . . he was slayn, lerning philosophye

but I suspect that felicities in poetry are sometimes even less deliberate than we suppose. Gower on the same character conveys a rather different impression.

. . . and so befell that he
Unto Athenes forto lere
Was send, and so he bar him there,
For that he was of hih lignage,
Such pride he tok in his corage,
That he foryeten hath the Scoles
And in riote among the foles
He ded manye thinges wronge
And useth thilke life so longe
Til ate laste of that he wroghte
He fond the meschief which he soghte,
Whereof it fell that he was slain.[2]

[1] *Confessio Amantis* Book VII, the Rape of Lucrece
[2] *Confessio Amantis* V 5234–45: *Legend of Good Women* 1898

There are hints of life in the treatment of the two ladies, and Ariadne, unexpectedly forward, appears to take Theseus by surprise:

> 'Yit were it betere that I were youre wyf,
> Syn that ye ben as gentil born as I . . .'
> 'Ye, lady myn', quod he, 'or ellis torn
> Mote I be with the Mynotaur to-morwe! . . .
> Upon my trouthe, I swere and yow assure
> This sevene yer I have youre servaunt be.
> Now have I yow, and also have ye me,
> My dere herte, of Athenes duchesse!'
> This lady smyleth at his stedefastnesse,
> And at his hertely wordes, and his chere,
> And to hyre sister seyde in this manere,
> Al softely: 'Now, syster myn', quod she,
> 'Now be we duchesses, bothe I and ye . . .'[1]

This, Mr. Garrett has pointed out, is sheer farce; but there is little more of the sort. At the crisis, in two good lines of adaptation of Ovid, Chaucer was clearly struck by *reddebant nomen concava saxa tuum*:

> Ryght in the dawenyng awaketh she,
> And gropeth in the bed, and fond ryght nought.
> . . . to the stronde barefot faste she wente,
> And cryed, 'Theseus! myn herte swete!
> Where be ye, that I may nat with yow mete,
> And myghte thus with bestes ben yslayn?'
> *The holwe rokkes answerde hire agayn.*
> No man she saw, and yit shyned the mone
> And hye upon a rokke she wente sone,
> And saw his barge saylynge in the se . . .
> And in the signe of Taurus men may see
> *The stones of hire corone shyne clere.*[2]

So *le grant translateur* thought, after the bed and the bare feet, of Tennyson to come.

The legend of Philomela begins with dignity:

---

[1] 2089ff.
*Hertely wordes* heartfelt words (I have omitted a number of them).
[2] 2185ff. Compare Ovid: *Heroides* X
The last line alludes to the story that Bacchus placed the crown of Ariadne in the heavens. She is ever a 'duchess'.

Thow yevere of the formes, that hast wrought
This fayre world, and bar it in thy thought
Eternaly . . .[1]

In the rest, Chaucer can scarcely hide his yawns:

. . . I am wery of hym for to telle . . .

O sely Philomene, wo is thyn herte!
God wreke thee, and sende thee thy bone!
Now is it tyme I make an ende sone.[2]

For once a contemporary has beaten him on his own ground, and must be given credit for it. Chaucer is bored by an outlandish story and a character who, he says, ought never to have been born; Gower, in his unprepossessing style, goes behind the events to a strange and real world of folklore, playing an antique flute that sounds both remote and close. Even the metamorphoses, which are surprising, are also in some way, in John Gower's telling of the tale, inevitable. Philomene is birdlike from the beginning.[3] She denounces Tereus:

‘. . .
And if I to the wodes wende,
Ther schal I tellen tale and ende,
And crie it to the briddes oute,
That thei schul hiere it al aboute.
For I so loude it schal reherce,
That my vois schal the hevene perce . . .’[4]

I doubt whether it is fair to quote this poet, unless one quotes several pages. He needs time. On the other hand, he should not be read for too long at a stretch. But the extracts which follow may convey to those who are not able to see a text something of what Gower, at his best, can do.

Sche lay swounende unto the deth,
Ther was unethes any breth;

[1] 2228–30
Professor Karl Young has shown (*Speculum* January 1944) that this impressive address to the Platonic deity *deus dator formarum* is derived at first or second hand from a medieval comment upon the Latin text of the *Metamorphoses*.
[2] 2258, 2339–41
*Sende thee thy bone* answer your prayer
[3] *Confessio Amantis* V 5637–56
The quotations are taken from *The English Works of John Gower*, ed. G. C. MACAULAY (London: Kegan Paul, 1901), Volume II.
[4] V 5669–74

Bot yit whan he hire tunge refte,
A litel part therof belefte,
Bot sche with al no word mai soune,
Bot chitre and as a brid jargoune.[1]

At the climax: Tereus is about to slay the sisters

And in a twinclinge of an yhe
The goddes, that the meschief syhe,
Here formes changen alle thre . . .
The ferst unto a nyhtingale
Was schape, and that was Philomene,
Which in the winter is noght sene,
For thanne ben the leves falle
And naked ben the buisshes alle . . .[2]

In Spring, how beautifully is introduced the traditional paradox
of love, the bittersweetness, from somewhere the other side of
the *reversaris* of the troubadours:

To wode comth this Philomene
And makth hir ferste yeres flyght;
Where as sche singeth day and nyht,
And in hir song al openly
Sche makth hir pleignte and seith, 'O why,
O why ne were I yit a maide?'
For so these olde wise saide,
Which understoden what sche mente,
Hire notes ben of such entente.
And ek thei seide how in hir song
Sche makth gret joie and merthe among,
And seith, 'Ha, nou I am a brid,
Ha, nou mi face mai ben hid:
Thogh I have lost mi maidenhede,
Schal noman se my chekes rede.'
Thus medleth sche with joie wo
And with hir sorwe merthe also,
So that of loves maladie
Sche makth diverse melodie
And seith love is a wofull blisse,
A wisdom which can noman wisse,

[1] V 5695–700
[2] V 5935ff.

A lusti fievre, a wounde softe:
This note sche reherceth ofte
To hem which understonde hir tale.[1]

There is no Ovid in these lines, except by accident; we read with a shock of surprise, in an earlier passage, that Progne prays *unto Cupide and to Venus*.[2] Gower is employing the love convention in a fashion of his own, and with an effect which in my experience is only paralleled in certain Appalachian folksongs. And this, if it is not a private fancy, is a tribute to the real purity of feeling that can be reached by a courtly poet, good but not great, consciously refining his diction in the vulgar tongue.

I return to Chaucer, who has made up for his feeble conclusion to the last story by thus closing the legend of Phyllis:

Be war, ye women, of youre subtyl fo,
Syn yit this day men may ensaumple se;
And trusteth, as in love, no man but me.[3]

Beside the noble letter of Dido, Phyllis descends to a tedious caterwauling; and with an illusion of *perpetuum mobile* the *Legend* breaks off—at a paragon of female virtue.

Towards the beginning of my last chapter I spoke of the 'fresh verse-form' of the prologue to the *Legend of Good Women*, but without mentioning the probability, long ago argued by Professor Lowes, that Chaucer had previously conducted his experiments in many of the legends themselves. Their duller tracts are so often reminiscent of the wicked knight in *Anelida and Arcite* that until decisive evidence turns up no more need be said. The stories, whenever they were written, remain unequal; remove the dust, and a few passages look very well in daylight. They are certainly not *satire* against women, or even inverted satire. What they are, Lydgate knew:

This poete wrote at Request of the quene
A Legende of parfight hoolynesse
Off goode women to Fynden out nyntene
That did excelle in bounte and fayrnesse,
But for his labour and his besynesse
Was inportable his wittes to encoumbre
In al this world to Fynde so greet a noumbre . . .

[1] V 5974–97
[2] V 5819
[3] 2559–61

. . . Redith the legende of martyrs of Cupide
Which that Chauncer in Ordre as they stood,
Compyled of women that wer callyd good.[1]

This, in spite of Lydgate's reputation, is not humourless; and
poets, in their verse, may be critics of other poets in other ways.
They may also be critics of themselves. We have the first form
of criticism in the legends, and the second in their prologue.
This critical activity will not alone make a masterly poem,
though it is a condition of any fruitful experiment or poetic
advance. The greater progress here is underground, showing
itself, now and again, in new achievement of rhythm and imagery.
Chaucer can sing praises—

Glorye and honour, Virgil Mantuan,
Be to thy name!

—and arrange to look smaller than he really is behind a pre-
eminent classical master. On the other hand, the *Legend of
Good Women*, or a great deal of it, may be read as criticism of
Ovid, even if rather more than has so far been proved is closer
to a French or Italian version of the Latin. It would be difficult
to find in English a more exquisite homage to the *Heroides* than
Dido's letter, or the conclusion of the legend of Ariadne: and
at the same time no Englishman of Chaucer's sense would pass
a simile which distracts attention to faulty plumbing in a Roman
bathroom.[2] Professor Shannon tells us that Chaucer had chosen
the best of Ovid's stories by the time he abandoned the *Legend*,
and had learnt the art of brief narrative in the process. The
poet of Criseyde, bringing Ovid and classical story into English,
could have found nowhere else a complete analysis of female
emotion: refined and sophisticated, and fitting the ladies of the
court.[3] But—and this is the criticism—his poetry at the beginning of the legend of Philomela, upon Tereus and God the giver
of forms, is also a comment on Ovid's relish of horrors that still
have power to corrupt. There is no farcical engagement, here,
with the naughty male. Chaucer is propounding a serious
problem: the problem of evil. As for Good Women, Ovid
would have told him that they knew too little (poor dears) of
either the Art of Love or its Remedies.

[1] Prologue to Book I of the *Fall of Princes*
*For his labour* . . . he was driven near to distraction for his pains
[2] *Metamorphoses* IV 121–4: altered in *Legend of Good Women* 851–2.
[3] EDGAR FINLEY SHANNON, *Chaucer and the Roman Poets* (Harvard University Press,
1929: O.U.P.) pp. 168, 176, 300

# VIII

*It is those that cannot connect who hasten to cast the first stone.*

E. M. FORSTER: *Howards End XL*

*Children should not see a carpet on the loom till the pattern is made plain.*

RUDYARD KIPLING: *Kim VI*

*If you would not be deceived, and would love the brethren, bear in mind that every vocation in the Church has its hypocrites.*

ST. AUGUSTINE: *Enarrationes in Psalmos XCIX xiii*

# CANTERBURY PROLOGUE

WE SHOULD LIKE, NO DOUBT, TO CALL CHAUCER'S *CANTERBURY Tales* the crown of his achievement, the sustained example of the master's later manner, and what we have is a vast incomplete pattern enclosing some work of the early middle period. Those who look in it for perfect mature Chaucer are asking for something much smaller than Chaucer intended to give: that was a design in which the mature though imperfect Chaucer should have a place, in which the imperfect and not so mature Chaucer should have a place also. And it may be thought to fit the condition of society in late fourteenth-century England that the design was not finished, that a work which on one plane represents the variety of human functions in its time recalls also their failure to achieve the medieval idea of organic unity, the reflection of celestial order. But the fact remains that a large number of tales were written, and partially arranged in a way which does not always appear accidental.

So we should like, still more, to see the whole architecture; and the manuscripts give us a confusion of fragments. Walter Skeat, following Bradshaw and Furnivall, adopted an order geographically correct but without authority, and arranged his Oxford edition as best he could along the route to Canterbury according to indications of time or place left by the pilgrims. This is a conjecture, from circumstantial evidence, of the author's plan at we do not know what point in the course of composition. Professor Robinson, following the famous Ellesmere manuscript, retains the order of the best early copies. Now one result of this is that certain tales of similar kind—like those of the Man of Law and the Clerk, or the Prioress and the Second Nun— are not so widely dispersed; and another is that the Knight's group draws nearer the explosion of the Wife of Bath, and appears related to its consequences in a way we may call dramatic. But the recent researches of the late J. M. Manly and the late Edith Rickert support Tatlock's view that none of the extant

149

manuscripts has an authorized arrangement, and we can see on our own that the best of them leave the second half of the journey too heavily prosed. We are therefore left to ourselves, having pried into the editor's business just long enough to discover that he cannot help us, and that we ought to be heartily thankful to have anything to read at all.[1]

In this matter critics have been unusually docile. Only one, and one of the most learned, has made any bold proposal; and if we persist in regarding an unfinished book of variously shuffled chapters as a work of literature, it is to him we must go. I refer to Professor Kittredge, who earlier in the present century made a neat parcel of half a dozen tales begun by the Wife of Bath, and labelled it 'Marriage Group'. The sequel to his initiative has been disappointing. Let us see what we can do.

But first we must recognize that Chaucer's way of adapting his tales to particular pilgrims was both new and various. It was a new thing, in panchatantra and decameron, to move so far in the direction of drama, of storytellers becoming active through their stories, and through their stories acting upon one another, and exactly how much further Chaucer would have gone if he had completed his work is not for us to decide. We can probably come nearer to a definition of the point at which he left off.[2] Pilgrims and plots and speech are related in a variety of degrees, and even by no more than the doubtful certificate of a manuscript-heading. Yet so long as this is admitted, we may without too many assumptions distinguish four kinds of arrangement within *Canterbury Tales*. At the moment I shall do no more than sketch them in a few sentences: and these can be safely ignored by anyone who is anxious to get to Chaucer.

There is the conflict and collision between personalities coming forward with their attitudes to a particular theme: love and lust in the introductory group, marriage in Professor Kittredge's. There is one sequence with such a miscellany of form and style that tales seem to be contrasted in every way and tellers to reveal

---

[1] The editor's difficulties may be gathered from C. R. Kase's 'Observations on the Shifting Positions of Groups G and DE in the Manuscripts of the Canterbury Tales': *Three Chaucer Studies* (New York: O.U.P., 1932). Carleton Brown, in *Publications of the Modern Language Association* (New York), LVII 29ff. (1942), infers from manuscript variations the order of the series as it was developed and revised by the author.

[2] The latest discussion at the time of writing is J. R. HULBERT, 'The *Canterbury Tales* and their Narrators', *Studies in Philology*, XLV 565ff. (1948).

themselves, if at all, indirectly: so that the Shipman and the Poet and their company do so very much less or so very much more than express themselves, that they remain the least known of all. There is, third, the ironical contrast between tale and teller in Physician and Pardoner, and also perhaps in the Man of Law;[1] fourth, the contrast between the self-effacing manner of the Second Nun and the way the Yeoman gets the Canon off his chest—between quasi-anonymous restraint and a personal outburst. These last may not have been intended as self-sufficient parts of the whole, for like contrasts are to be found within the two larger groups. And this is as much as I wish to guess of the sort of pattern Chaucer was working towards: to say more would over-emphasize the unity of the tales we have. My prologue must not be longer than Chaucer's, and to the real *Prologue* I now turn.

> Whan that April with his shoures soote
> The droughte of March hath perced to the roote,
> And bathed every veyne in swich licour
> Of which vertu engendred is the flour;
> Whan Zephirus eek with his sweete breeth
> Inspired hath in every holt and heeth
> The tendre croppes, and the yonge sonne
> Hath in the Ram his half cours yronne,
> And smale foweles maken melodye,
> That slepen al the nyght with open eye
> (So priketh hem nature in hir corages);
> Thanne longen folk to goon on pilgrimages,
> And palmeres for to seken straunge strondes,
> To ferne halwes, kowthe in sondry londes;
> And specially from every shires ende
> Of Engelond, to Caunterbury they wende,
> The hooly blisful martir for to seke
> That hem hath holpen whan that they were seeke.[2]

The relation between this poetry of Spring and the pilgrimage that follows is in one way the relation between leaves on a Gothic capital and the whole fabric. I do not intend to compare *Canterbury Tales* to a cathedral; only to suggest that the opening

---

[1] F. N. Robinson, in *Complete Works of Geoffrey Chaucer* p. 1005, mentions articles supporting an arrangement which would underline this view of the *Man of Law's Tale*.

[2] A 1–18

| | | | |
|---|---|---|---|
| *Soote* sweet | *Vertu* power | *The Ram* Aries in the zodiac | |
| *Corages* hearts | *Strondes* strands, shores | | *Ferne halwes* distant shrines |
| | *Kowthe* known | *Seeke* sick | |

of the *Prologue*, like decoration in stone, is both 'natural' and 'conventional'. It is perfectly fresh, yet has been done as often as foliage has been carved, and is being done again, as Chaucer writes, in a tradition reaching back at least as far as the *Pervigilium Veneris*. In whatever sense you may insist upon the formality of such beginning, the sap is in it still, and nature urging creation to procreation, and even the young man that *slepte namoore than dooth a nyghtyngale*. The time of pagan rejoicing is also the time of pilgrimage; and there is an irony of circumstance which cannot have been imperceptible to a fourteenth-century reader, in the association of a recurring springtide, always the same, with an occasion that was of his own age and, for some in his age, an escape from religious observance. On a late medieval pilgrimage it was your affair how holy you made your holiday, and Chaucer's worldlings, unlike Boccaccio's, made it no holier than they could help. And every reader, like every traveller, will find what he seeks: no more and no less: and we may find more than I have said. Now this happens for the reader only when the writer can see what he writes as something outside himself, being written for more than one person and even *by* more than one person, and therefore admitting at least a double interpretation. Our poet has mastered his precedents to this end: to keep out Geoffrey Chaucer until he lets in the Spring and the Canterbury pilgrims.

A recent monument of American scholarship,[1] to which I shall refer again, allows us to assume that for reality and comprehensiveness no true literary antecedent has been found of the series of characters now to arrive. Chaucer in the first place *saw* persons, but what he heard and read about them was also experience that he could use. The Host, master of ceremonies, is called Harry Bailly; one Harry Bailly, Host of the Tabard, represented the borough of Southwark in the Parliament of Chaucer's own day; and according to the contemporary preacher John de Bromyard, innkeepers ran to meet pilgrims of the road, 'talking and gaming with them until the time comes for reckoning up the bill'.[2] Chaucer had met friars; in youth he is said to have beaten a friar in Fleet Street; he had heard the satirical attacks of the preachers and knew those of Jean de Meun; and

---

[1] *Sources and Analogues of Chaucer's Canterbury Tales* ed. w. f. BRYAN and GERMAINE DEMPSTER (Chicago, 1941).
[2] G. R. OWST, *Literature and Pulpit in Medieval England* (Cambridge, 1933) p. 25

it was probably at the time of writing when an Austin friar called Peter Pateshul left his order to preach against the vices of its members, some of whom objected from the body of the congregation, were attacked by the crowd, and chased back to their friary through the London streets. The mob threatened to burn it to the ground, but were dissuaded by two respected friars and a city sheriff. Chaucer was acquainted with some of those who supported Pateshul's case.[1] In different ways, directly or indirectly, the poet could play such facts as these against one another, in a social art, a civilized verse.

For the style of the *Prologue* has ease; even nonchalance, as when Chaucer throws out conventional compliments to see whether they stick. He apologizes with mock naïveté for arranging his people informally, in the wrong order; he is as witty in placing a word or a line as in placing a pilgrim and, later, a tale. Here, first, is his own voice:

> Bifel that in that seson on a day,
> In Southwerk at the Tabard as I lay
> Redy to wenden on my pilgrimage
> To Caunterbury with ful devout corage,
> At nyght was come into that hostelrye
> Wel nyne and twenty in a compaignye,
> Of sondry folk, by aventure yfalle
> In felaweshipe; and pilgrimes were they alle,
> That toward Caunterbury wolden ryde.
> The chambres and the stables weren wyde,
> And wel we weren esed atte beste.
> And shortly, whan the sonne was to reste,
> So hadde I spoken with hem everichon
> That I was of hir felawshipe anon,
> And made forward erly for to ryse,
> To take oure wey ther as I yow devyse.
>   But nathelees, whil I have tyme and space,
> Er that I ferther in this tale pace,
> Me thynketh it acordaunt to resoun
> To telle yow al the condicioun
> Of ech of hem, so as it semed me,
> And whiche they weren, and of what degree,
> And eek in what array that they were inne;
> And at a knyght than wol I first bigynne.[2]

[1] Chronicled in WALSINGHAM: *Historia Anglicana*
[2] A 19–42
*Everichon* every one          *Forward* agreement

Then we have the Knight, representing chivalry of the old school (now a little besmutted); the Squire, demonstrating how to win a lady; the Yeoman, suggesting the might of England on the soil of France. The ecclesiastical sequence is a *crescendo* with Friar as climax. Jean de Meun had employed drums and trumpets in vituperation of this character: Chaucer prefers a *piano subito* for harp and voice—

> And in his harpyng, whan that he hadde songe,
> His eyen twynkled in his heed aryght,
> As doon the sterres in the frosty nyght.[1]

The Oxford student of philosophy looks uncomfortable between an unscrupulous business man and a judge, accompanied by a representative of the smaller landed gentry who is a connoisseur of food and wine. A naval gentleman is so disreputable and at the same time so proficient that it is amusing merely to proceed, with some ceremony, to the qualifications of the doctor. The lady from Bath is as unambiguous as a pillar-box. There are the two good brothers, parson and ploughman; and the remainder, in various ways, live by their wits.

This is a glance only, and we can see that the arrangement so apologetically offered is not after all haphazard. The design is first a visual one, a pattern of colour on the road to Canterbury, and even, as the early illustrators observed, a pattern of good and bad horses. It is the manuscript artist who can often tell us more than anyone else about how the *Tales* used to be read.[2] Then, as there is an effective order of persons, in relation and contrast, so there is an effective order of detail in each character. And the observer is constantly varying his distance and angle of vision, so as to produce more than two dimensions. In a dozen lines on the Merchant, one is about boots, another about shady finances, and a third about the man's name, which we are to understand is either forgotten or withheld. This is not photography of fourteenth-century England, or fashionable portrait painting: but the freedom of the artist to invent composite figures, to range between the *hæcceitas* of the Friar and the Idea of a Christian Priest. And justifying this freedom begins with a simple exercise like describing a commercial racketeer, which is

[1] A 267–9
*Sterres* stars
[2] Mr. Earle Birney has been observant on this point in his article ' Is Chaucer's Irony a Modern Discovery?' *Journal of English and Germanic Philology*, July 1942.

an exercise in detachment. This, for the writer, is a logical beginning. The reader starts elsewhere.

It is surprising that no one, so far as I remember, has tried to persuade us that Chaucer was criticizing his *verray parfit gentil knyght*, and that we should refuse to take certain lines at their face value:

> And though that he were worthy, he was wys,
> And of his port as meeke as is a mayde.
> He nevere yet no vileynye ne sayde
> In al his lyf unto no maner wight.[1]

Is not the Merchant's *worthy knyght* also *wys*?[2] And the villain Jason, if not *meeke*, was *as coy as is a mayde*.[3] Furthermore, it is easy enough to *love*

> chivalrie,
> Trouthe and honour, fredom and curteisie.[4]

As for saying *no vileynye unto no maner wight*, that is a safely negative virtue. The Knight, it could be supposed, was no more 'perfect' than the *verray parfit praktisour*. *La cavalleria*, wrote Francesco Sacchetti at this time, *è morta*: knighthood is dead.[5] They were knights who slew the *hooly blisful martir* at Canterbury; and some of the latest, said a fourteenth-century preacher, seemed to belong to the order that crucified Christ.[6] But Chaucer begins with one who was not of this order; and I remark only the very different uses to which he put the same words. The Knight is five times called *worthy*—not, I believe, because we are to consider him the reverse, but because the worth of knights in his day could hardly be taken for granted. They were open to criticism by the virtue of their own code. There is no need to invoke absolute perfection; it is the perfection of a knight that is in question—the highest point that could be reached by the Knight in his time. We shall not deny that people like the Knight have been the backbone of the nation, and to the extent that he fights for the Cross rather than the Crown Chaucer's Knight is the backbone of a larger body than the nation. All

---

[1] A 68–71
*Worthy . . . wys* brave . . . prudent      *Vileynye* churlish speech
[2] E 1266
[3] *Legend of Good Women* 1548
[4] A 45–6
*Fredom* liberality
[5] *Novella* 153, quoted by Burckhardt
[6] G. R. OWST, *Literature and Pulpit in Medieval England* p. 336

this is admitted. But we are not to confuse the backbone with the whole anatomy.

The *Squier* is a character that both represents his contemporary kind and at the same time revives the person of Mirthe in the *Romaunt of the Rose*. The description is a luminous and illuminated portrait of a young man who might turn out to be the Merchant's Damian who seduced May or, on the other hand, the Franklin's Aurelius who refrained from seducing Dorigen. Chaucer's coeval, the monastic preacher Master Rypon of Durham, said that many knights spent more time upon the ornamentation of their clothing than upon 'the endurance of labours'; Bishop Thomas Brunton had condemned their adultery.[1] On the whole, a fourteenth-century moralist might feel doubtful about the Squire's chances of following his father. A homilist spoke against the extravagant pride of the knightly class, as a result of which *now a pore squyer wole ride with* 9 *or* 10 *yemen, alle of sute of as gret araie as sumtyme weren full worthi squyers.*[2] Chaucer's Knight brings one good servant. And the *Yemen* has the colour and definition of a manuscript miniature:

> . . . he was clad in cote and hood of grene;
> A sheef of pecok arwes bright and kene
> Under his belt he bar ful thriftily,
> (Wel koude he dresse his takel yemanly:
> His arwes drouped noght with fetheres lowe),
> And in his hand he baar a myghty bowe.
> A not heed hadde he, with a broun visage.
> Of wodecraft wel koude he al the usage.
> Upon his arm he baar a gay bracer,
> And by his syde a swerd and a bokeler,
> And on that oother syde a gay daggere
> Harneised wel and sharp as point of spere;
> A Cristopher on his brest of silver sheene.
> An horn he bar, the bawdryk was of grene;
> A forster was he, soothly, as I gesse.[3]

The *Prioresse* is one of the two most delicately balanced pieces of female characterization in Chaucer. There are therefore nearly as many views about it as there are critics and editors. The

[1] *Op. cit.*, p. 332 and note
[2] *Op. cit.*, p. 337
[3] A 103–17
*Not heed* close-cropped head     *Bracer* arm-guard     *Cristopher* talisman of
travellers, an image of the patron saint of foresters     *Sheene* bright
*Forster* forester and gamekeeper

most valuable comment I have seen was not written by a critic or an editor, but by a historian: and she is speaking about the critics.

One interprets it as a cutting attack on the worldliness of the Church; another thinks that Chaucer meant to draw a charming and sympathetic picture of womanly gentleness; one says that it is a caricature, another an ideal; and an American professor even finds in it a psychological study of thwarted maternal instinct, apparently because Madame Eglentyne was fond of little dogs and told a story about a schoolboy. The mere historian may be excused from following these vagaries . . .
Many truly spiritual men and women still took the vows, but with them came others who were little suited to monastic life, and who lowered its standard, because it was hard and uncongenial to them. Eglentyne became a nun because her father did not want the trouble and expense of finding her a husband, and because being a nun was about the only career for a well-born lady who did not marry.[1]

'How many readers of the *Prologue*', asks Dr. Power, 'know that the smale houndes, like the fair forehead and the brooch of gold full sheen, were strictly against the rules? . . . How many of the literary critics, who chuckle over her, know that she never ought to have got into the *Prologue* at all? The Church was quite clear in its mind that pilgrimages for nuns were to be discouraged.' But by now the critics have learnt Dr. Power's lesson, and readers of Chaucer may find it summarized by Professor Robinson. Here is her conclusion:

This then was Chaucer's prioress in real life . . . aristocratic, tender-hearted, worldly, taking pains to 'countrefete chere of court'; liking pretty clothes and little dogs; a lady of importance, attended by a nun and three priests; spoken to with respect by the none too mealy-mouthed host . . . Was she religious? Perhaps; but save for her singing the divine service and for her lovely address to the Virgin, at the beginning of her tale, Chaucer can find but little to say on the point . . .

That is very just; and to Dr. Power's strictures upon the unhistorical critics there is no reply—except to say that Dr. Power and Chaucer were not talking about the same thing. Dr. Power

[1] EILEEN POWER, *Medieval People* (London: Methuen, 2nd edition, 1925), pp. 60, 68

has tried to describe a type of fourteenth-century nun, and produced an abstraction. Chaucer was imagining a very particular lady (particular in more than one sense), who should be approached with circumspection and tact, and portrayed with reticence. Madame Eglentyne—unless in the anonymous *Tale of Beryn*—does not dance with the Friar, or gossip with the Wife of Bath.[1]

Yet she is strangely reminiscent of Ydelnesse in the garden of Guillaume de Lorris:

> . . . by mesure large were
> The openyng of hir yen clere;
> Hir nose of good proporcioun,
> Hir yen grey as a faucoun,
> With swete breth and wel savoured;
> Hir face whit and wel coloured,
> With litel mouth and round to see . . .
>
> *Romaunt of the Rose*

> Hir nose tretys, hir eyen greye as glas;
> Hir mouth ful smal, and therto softe and reed . . .[2]
>
> *Prologue*

It has often been unkindly observed that her table manners are taken from the mouth of the *vekke*, the prostitute *manquée* in the *Romance of the Rose*, who like the Wife of Bath *knew al the olde daunce*. There is also Fraunchise, whose nose was *tretys* and whose *herte wolde have full gret pitee*—not when she saw a mouse caught in a trap, but when

> a man were in distresse,
> And for her love in hevynesse . . .[3]

---

[1] 'Chaucer told us how the friar loved harping and how his eyes twinkled like stars in his head when he sang, but failed perhaps to observe that he had lured Madame Eglentyne into a dance.'

'It is really quite disturbing to think what additional details the Wife of Bath may have given the prioress about her five husbands.'

*Medieval People* pp. 81–3

[2] *Romaunt* 543–49

*Prologue* A 152–3

*Tretys* well-proportioned (the *traitis* of Guillaume de Lorris)

*Eyen greye* are *iex vairs* to the trouvère, *uelhs vairs* to the troubadour: all describe changing light in the eyes of the lovely lady. *Vair* is also dovegrey-and-white; *greye*, at least in old English *græge*, what we call sea-'blue'. And *glas*, as Muriel Kinney pointed out in *Romanic Review* X 322ff. (1919), may be the clear glass of Venice or the darker glass of England. Possibly—I do not know—Chaucer was aware of English glass as well as Venetian, of the soul of the Prioress behind the sparkle.

[3] *Romaunt of the Rose* 1223–4

Here Chaucer seems to be using what is called the 'modern' poetic device of allusion as a mode of sophisticated comedy, which is an interesting development of the approved medieval habit of systematic plagiarism. And it is amusing to watch a gentleman who could have no illusions about the height of fashion, observing what courtly elegance looked like when it had travelled to Stratford atte Bowe and back. It looked—and Professor Manly has reminded us, there is no suggestion of coquetry about *coy*— quite charming; one could not help taking a second glance.

> But sikerly she hadde a fair forheed;
> It was almost a spanne brood, I trowe;
> For, hardily, she was nat undergrowe.
> Ful fetys was hir cloke, as I was war.
> Of smal coral aboute hire arm she bar
> A peire of bedes, gauded al with grene,
> And theron heng a brooch of gold-ful sheene,
> On which ther was first writen a crowned A,
> And after *Amor vincit omnia.*[1]

Beneath, this is serious: for the particular difficulties of a court poet who is trying to preserve or to achieve integrity (I am thinking now of Chaucer's possible estimate of himself, not of our estimate of him) are the difficulties of the Prioress in reverse. It is here that the problem of the forgiveness of one's neighbour becomes acute. In order to be 'objective' one must possess a high degree of self-knowledge; as, in a station, it is difficult to be sure of the speed and direction of a train on the adjacent line without looking to see how fast, and which way, the bookstall appears to be moving. I do not mean that Chaucer is trying to interest us in his personal motion or emotion. It would have been easy (vulgarly easy) to get a louder laugh at the expense of Madame Eglentyne. But in order to understand the Prioress, Chaucer had first to know himself. And it is because he so neatly avoided both self-satisfaction and self-pity that we are left thinking how beautifully he has caught the object. *Voici donc la réflexion qui commence à poindre*, wrote Taine, *et aussi le grand art. Chaucer ne s'amuse plus, il étudie.* On the one hand there is

[1] A 154–62
*Sikerly* certainly romances) attractive large beads were green  *Hardily* surely *A peire of bedes, gauded al with grene* a rosary, of which the  *Fetys* (another word recalling the

the person who, as we say, has 'more than one side to his character'; on the other hand there is the deceiver. We can see the Knight in different aspects, which do not necessarily contradict one another. The Pardoner has a duplicity fully revealed in his tale, which is a superb sermon from a revolting man. And here Chaucer gives us both the private and the public view, both the *yvel entencioun* and the *noble ecclesiaste*.[1] We are not yet in the reduced world of the modern novel. Now the Prioress has her place between the Knight and the Pardoner, nearer to the Knight than to the Pardoner, in this larger vision of the *Canterbury Tales*. She can sing the divine office properly, whether you like her nasal intonation or not; and when she follows the Shipman Madame Eglentyne, exactly, excels herself.

I have spent some time over one portrait, and in the rest of this Canterbury Prologue I shall try to keep out historical information which can be got from the editors.[2] But some important facts about the very lively art of contemporary preaching, published some years ago by Dr. G. R. Owst, cannot. If we imagine the Church in control of broadcasting in an age without a printing press, we have some idea of the power of the medieval vernacular sermon. And as Dr. Owst has shown, the vices touched by Chaucer, including the ecclesiastical corruption, were vigorously satirized by the regular preachers. So Chaucer has no new targets to display; only a new sort of archery, which quietly transfixed the object without contorting it. Sometimes he hit the mark while looking in an *elvish* manner at the wrong thing; at, let us say, an Oxford man who slept by Aristotle and not with Alison. There will be time for a sermon (and he did not neglect to finish it); there is also a time for civilized amusement. And so we are given a *lord* of a *Monk*, a hunting up-to-date monk (*How shal the world be served?*), anxious to dissociate himself from certain views of St. Augustine; and not to be lightly baited, the Host discovers. The innuendo which follows the jingling bridle has been justly praised—

---

[1] I find this distinction made by Leigh Hunt (1846), but with a different emphasis: 'Humour deals in incongruities of character and circumstance . . . Such is the melting together . . . of the professional and the individual or the accidental and the permanent, in the Canterbury pilgrims'.

[2] A good deal of scattered material has been collected in Miss Muriel Bowden's *Commentary on the General Prologue to the Canterbury Tales* (New York: Macmillan, 1949), whose publication has enabled me to abbreviate some of the notes in this chapter. Much of her annotation is not fully given in editions before the date of her book, and she has taken into account the work of Dr. Owst.

And whan he rood, men myghte his brydel heere
Gynglen in a whistlynge wynd as cleere
And eek as loude as dooth the chapel belle.[1]

But what is particularly remarkable about this character, I
think, is the way the man's downright tone comes through to
our own time; and his interlocutor is there, playing with him,
letting him have his head, trying out the Socratic irony,

The reule of seint Maure or of seint Beneit,
By cause that it was old and somdel streit,
This ilke Monk leet olde thynges pace
And heeld after the newe world the space.
He yaf nat of that text a pulled hen,
That seith that hunters ben nat hooly men;
Ne that a monk, whan he is recchelees,
Is likned til a fissh that is waterlees—
This is to seyn, a monk out of his cloystre.
But thilke text heeld he nat worth an oystre;
And I seyde, his opinion was good.
What sholde he studie and make hymselven wood,
Upon a book in cloystre alwey to poure,
Or swynken with his handes, and laboure,
As Austyn bit?  How shal the world be served?
Lat Austyn have his swynk to hym reserved!
Therfore he was a prikasour aright;
Greyhoundes he hadde as swift as fowel in flight;
Of prikyng and of huntyng for the hare
Was al his lust, for no cost wolde he spare.[2]

There is in these lines a whole social mode, a way of approxi-
mating to charity in a casual encounter.  They imply the logical
position that without irony everyday intercourse may be reduced
either to silence or to egregious falsehood.  It is a position which
a great and simple soul like Tolstóy could not approve.  And
in an age when no plain speaking was to be heard and moral
standards were not familiar, Tolstóy would be right.  But a
strong piece of invective from John de Bromyard sets off Chaucer's
way of dealing with the greyhounds.  It is about hunting
parsons:

[1] A 169–71
[2] A 173–92

| | | |
|---|---|---|
| *Beneit* Benedict | *Streit* strict | *Pace* pass away |
| *Recchelees* negligent | *What* why | *Prikasour* riding huntsman |

They knew that those substitutes [whom they had placed in their parishes] were too slothful and insufficient to guard the souls [committed to their care] and to rescue the prey from the Devil's mouth. They knew, too, on the other hand, that the Devil carries off souls by earth and by air, by water and by fire. Therefore they have provided themselves with the swiftest hounds that run upon the earth, so that the Devil should not make away with the souls of parishioners by that route . . .[1]

When there is orthodox preaching of this kind, a distinguished poet with a genius for comedy does not need to devote his energies to the task of lashing evils; unless, like Langland, he feels called to do so. Why should Chaucer be 'moral' about the Monk? In due course he shall be moral indeed; for there is to be a good deal of apposite morality from the Monk himself, about the fall of pride and the refinements of vanity. And we are to have the Monk's outraged pride, hidden behind the dignity of a *grand seigneur*, in his reticence before the Host.

It is not easy, with the Reformation between us and Chaucer, to understand his assured serenity in face of the Monk and the Friar: one modern apology is to praise his 'satire', another to praise his 'tolerance', and both miss the mark. The Friar, for a reader today, is the more difficult case; here Chaucer was taking the original course of reviving a figure done to death, not only in pulpit prose,[2] but in verse as long ago as the *Romance of the Rose* even before its later instalment. Instead of flogging a dead horse, he was brilliantly reanimating it. One way of appreciating Chaucer's *Frere* more fully is to examine the cathedral building of fourteenth-century England, and consider whether it was produced by a people quaking at schism, heresy and corruption: another way is to read the lines to which Chaucer alludes in Jean de Meun, who uses his allegorical figure False-Seeming as the occasion for attack:

---

[1] G. R. OWST, *Literature and Pulpit in Medieval England* p. 264. The Monk's pleasures were also condemned by one of his own order, Robert Rypon of Durham (p. 270). Preachers commonly objected to hunters trampling down poor men's corn: Thomas Gascoigne and John of Mirfield pitied the animals (p. 329).

[2] For example, by the Dominican friar John de Bromyard: G. R. OWST, *Preaching in Medieval England* (Cambridge, 1926), pp. 90-1. Dr. Owst notes (*op. cit.*, p. 13) that a sermon of Archbishop Fitzralph of Armagh at St. Paul's Cross in 1356 was so violent that 'the battle over "ecclesiastical poverty" and the privileges of the friars was to rage more fiercely than ever in city pulpit and University schools for years to come'.

'Sir, I wole fillen, so mote I go,
My paunche of good mete and wyn,
As shulde a maister of dyvyn;
For how that I me pover feyne,
Yit alle pore folk I disdeyne.
I love bettir th'acquayntaunce,
Ten tymes, of the kyng of Fraunce
Than of a pore man of mylde mode,
Though that his soule be also gode.
For whanne I see beggers quakyng,
Naked on myxens al stynkyng,
For hungre crie, and eke for care,
I entremete not of her fare.
They ben so pore and ful of pyne,
They myght not oonys yeve me dyne,
For they have nothing but her lyf.
What shulde he yeve that likketh his knyf?
It is but foly to entremete,
To seke in houndes nest fat mete . . .
I wole no lyf but ese and pees,
And wynne gold to spende also.
For whanne the grete bagge is go,
It cometh right with my japes.
Make I not wel tumble myn apes?
To wynnen is alwey myn entente;
My purchase is bettir than my rente.
For thought I shulde beten be,
Overal I entremete me;
Withoute me may no wight dure . . .[1]

Chaucer's Pardoner has the same ancestor in the *Romance of the Rose*,[2] yet the verses I have just quoted come nearer to anticipating Langland. Here is Chaucer's first transformation of False-Seeming:

A Frere ther was, a wantowne and a merye,
A lymytour, a ful solempne man.
In alle the ordres foure is noon that kan
So muche of daliaunce and fair langage.

[1] *Romaunt of the Rose* 6486–504; 6832–41
*Dyvyn* divinity    *How that* although    *Pover* poor    *Entremete* meddle
*Fare* business    *Go . . . cometh right* empty . . . is replenished    *Apes* dupes
*Purchase* money 'picked up'    *Rente* regular income    *Dure* survive
[2] *Le Roman de la Rose* ed. LANGLOIS, 11065ff. . . . *en quelque leu que je viegne*: *Romaunt of the Rose* 6201ff.

He hadde maad ful many a mariage
Of yonge wommen at his owene cost.
Unto his ordre he was a noble post.
Ful wel biloved and famulier was he
With frankeleyns over al in his contree,
And with worthy wommen of the toun;
For he hadde power of confessioun,
As seyde hymself, moore than a curat,
For of his ordre he was licenciat.
Ful swetely herde he confessioun,
And plesaunt was his absolucioun:
He was an esy man to yeve penaunce,
Ther as he wiste to have a good pitaunce.
For unto a povre ordre for to yive
Is signe that a man is wel yshryve;
For if he yaf, he dorste make avaunt,
He wiste that a man was repentaunt;
For many a man so hard is of his herte,
He may nat wepe, althogh hym soore smerte.
Therfore, in stede of wepynge and preyeres,
Men moote yeve silver to the povre freres.
His typet was ay farsed ful of knyves
And pynnes, for to yeven faire wyves.
And certeinly he hadde a murye note:
Wel koude he synge and pleyen on a rote;
Of yeddynges he baar outrely the pris.
His nekke whit was as the flour-de-lys;
Therto he strong was as a champioun.
He knew the tavernes wel in every toun
And every hostiler and tappestere
Bet than a lazar or a beggestere;
For unto swich a worthy man as he
Acorded nat, as by his facultee,
To have with sike lazars aqueyntaunce.
It is nat honest, it may nat avaunce,
For to deelen with no swich poraille,
But al with riche and selleres of vitaille.
And overal, ther as profit sholde arise,
Curteis he was and lowely of servyse.
Ther was no man nowher so vertuous.
He was the beste beggere in his hous:
For thogh a wydwe hadde noght a sho,
So plesaunt was his *In principio*,
Yet wolde he have a ferthyng, er he wente.
His purchas was wel bettre than his rente.

And rage he koude, as it were right a whelp.
In love-dayes ther koude he muchel help,
For ther he was nat lyk a cloysterer
With a thedbare cope, as is a povre scoler,
But he was lyk a maister or a pope.
Of double worstede was his semycope,
That rounded as a belle out of the presse.
Somwhat he lipsed, for his wantownesse,
To make his Englissh sweete upon his tonge;
And in his harpyng, whan that he hadde songe,
His eyen twynkled in his heed aryght,
As doon the sterres in the frosty nyght.[1]

The irony has precisely the right degree of sharpness to clean the system and leave it sweet.

The medieval merchant was also a butt for satire, as we should guess from the *Romaunt of the Rose*[2] and the *Shipman's Tale*; but the *Marchant* on pilgrimage is a slight sketch that has been sufficiently admired. I have admired it a little myself, earlier in this chapter. I suspect that if the poet could now look over our text he would stop the rattle of the last line but one, as in revising the prologue to the *Legend of Good Women* he may have altered words accidentally repeated. The *Frere* is the last major portrait before Parson and Ploughman and their contraries, Pardoner and Summoner; the Merchant is one of several persons arranged briefly in a corridor of the *Prologue*, who later expand in the open air. Chaucer varied his whole series by issuing, unexpectedly, a description of a dangerous character like the Knight or the scholar of Oxford or the Parson, a character whose very existence was a threat to the peace of mind of the less virtuous. On the *Clerk of Oxenford* he permits himself a mild pun,

> But al be that he was a philosophre,
> Yet hadde he but litel gold in cofre . . .[3]

and for the rest verses facts which are sufficiently remarkable in themselves, sufficiently unlike the Miller's *hende Nicholas*. Arch-

---

[1] A 208–68
*Lymytour* friar licensed to beg within a definite limit    *Farsed* stuffed
*Rote* early form of lute       *Yeddynges* popular songs       *Tappestere* barmaid
*Honest* seemly       *Rage* wanton       *Love-dayes* days appointed for the settlement of disputes by arbitration, in which the clergy were not at this time supposed to take part except to help the poor       *Wantownesse* winning affectation
[2] 5697ff.
[3] A 297–8
Alluding to the 'philosophers' stone'

bishop Fitzralph of Armagh, who spoke out on the 'getting of benefices', suggests to us that such a one might be an innocent who would not long resist the ways of the world:

> For he hadde geten hym yet no benefice,
> Ne was so worldly for to have office.[1]

But the *Prologue* is not Chaucer's last word.

Contemporary readers would no doubt have found incidental amusement in the attempt to spot the original of the *Man of Lawe*:[2] and we can still watch a nice variation of emphasis upon the word *semed*—

> A Sergeant of the Lawe, war and wys,
> That often hadde been at the Parvys,
> Ther was also, ful riche of excellence.
> Discreet he was and of greet reverence—
> He semed swich, his wordes weren so wise . . .
> Nowher so bisy a man as he ther nas,
> And yet he semed bisier than he was.[3]

—or contrast the lines about Virginia in the *Physician's Tale*:

> No countrefeted termes hadde she
> To seme wys . . .[4]

Again we hear a counterpoint to Jean de Meun:

> Phisiciens and advocates
> Gon right by the same yates;
> They selle her science for wynnyng,
> And haunte her craft for gret getyng.[5]

The *Frankeleyn* is a simple study in crimson and white, Epicurism and rich cooking: to be considered in relation to what the Merchant has to say about January, and the Parson about *delit* and *delicat* meat.

---

[1] A 291–2
G. R. OWST, *Literature and Pulpit in Medieval England*, pp. 243ff.
[2] According to J. M. Manly, only Thomas Pynchbek, of the score of Sergeants, fits the description. Pynchbek was a *nouveau riche* who had offended Chaucer's friend Sir William Beauchamp; and if we accept this reference it is possible that there is a pun on his name in A 326 (*Ther koude no wight pynche at his writyng*).
[3] A 309ff.
*Parvys* probably at St. Paul's, where experienced Sergeants assisted at new investitures.
[4] C 51–2
[5] *Romaunt of the Rose* 5721–4
*Right* exactly

A Frankeleyn was in his compaignye.
Whit was his berd as is the dayesye;
Of his complexioun he was sangwyn.
Wel loved he by the morwe a sop in wyn;
To lyven in delit was evere his wone,
For he was Epicurus owene sone,
That heeld opinioun that pleyn delit
Was verray felicitee parfit . . .
It snewed in his hous of mete and drynke,
Of alle deyntees that men koude thynke . . .
An anlaas and a gipser al of silk
Heeng at his girdel, whit as morne milk . . .[1]

The Squire, the Friar and the Franklin all have something *whyt*
about them, a gay plausibility.[2] *Epicurus owene sone* would—
nearly does—father the Squire; and both remind Chaucer of
bright blossom. They wither, but have at least bloomed. A
European poet in the age of Petrarch could contemplate the
Franklin with neither stiffness nor excessive respect, and above
all without indifference. For Epicure was coming to life, yet
'austerity' meant more than a government order.

There follow two manifestations of medieval culture: the
*solempnitee* of the guild festival, and some examples of fourteenth-
century cuisine, with which art I understand Mr. Layton has
recently experimented.[3] Chaucer smiles upon the social ambitions of the wives of the *Haberdasshere, Carpenter, Webbe, Dyere,
Tapycer*; and finds that the *Cook* has produced a dry-scabbed
ulcer and a very good *fricassée* of chicken. None of this is in
itself of great importance; but these people have a right to use
the road to Canterbury, and the right to a place in the *Prologue*.
The place of the five guildsmen is to exhibit their own careful
bourgeois pride next to men of considerable substance; in a
social comedy which we can easily appreciate. On the other

---

[1] A 331ff.
*Frankeleyn* franklin, a wealthy landowner, of the gentry *Complexioun* . . .
*sangwyn* medieval shorthand for a category of 'free-handed, full-bodied, kind-hearted,
cheerful people' (J. L. Lowes)    *By the morwe* in the morning
*A sop in wyn* a rich wine sauce over the best white bread    *Anlaas* hunting dagger;
*gipser* purse; only the most wealthy and distinguished wore both.
    Petrarch, in Chaucer's time, stands at a turning-point in the reputation of *Epicurus*,
who was condemned by Dante, and rehabilitated in the XVth century.
[2] Compare *Troilus* III 901 and 1567. I do not of course mean that Chaucer
necessarily had this connotation in mind whenever in the *Prologue* he used the word
*whyt*: the first thing is the brilliance of *floures, flour-de-lys, dayesyes*, snow, and *morne
milk*.
[3] T. A. LAYTON, *Five to a Feast* (London: Duckworth, 1948)

hand it is difficult even for the expert to estimate the relative positions of the Man of Law and that *worthy vavasour* his companion, in the scale of social *worthinesse*. Chaucer plays that scale against another, profounder, order of values, just as he conjures with the ambiguity of the term *worthy*. And this is a comedy which is not possible without consciousness of definite class distinctions, of what is and of what ought to be typical of a particular group, trade, or profession. There was in the first place the three-fold division of society, into nobility, clergy and commons, each with peculiar virtues: bravery and fidelity proper to the first, industry and meekness to the third.[1] There were the many gradations within the three classes, and in what was expected of them. The whole was a part of the beautiful order of the medieval mind, and the defect of the whole a tendency to petrifaction. Set against this neat pattern the actual reputation of the species, not often favourable. It is said that an honest miller has a thumb of gold; the doctor in a misericord is an ape; specific vices are exposed in detail in the pulpit; and the preacher himself may be a fox. None of this need surprise. Because men are not perfect, social institution is imperative,

> Onde convenne legge per fren porre;
> convenne rege aver, che discernesse
> delle vera cittade almen la torre.[2]

But in fourteenth-century England the old order is shaken; Archbishop Sudbury is murdered by the mob; and Chaucer quietly re-affirms the proper virtues of knight, priest and peasant. The *Prologue* gives us a 'real' England, and rather more than we should get in a fourteenth-century group. We can also see, in a glimpse, an ideal England, not so that people could dream about it after dinner, but in order that they might desire it.

> And specially from every shires ende
> Of Engelond, to Caunterbury they wende . . .

The consciousness of nationality was new and exciting; and though it did not turn the head of 'Ser Geoffreddo', I cannot

---

[1] The proper virtue of a priest is specially illustrated in a moving little treatise of the Three Estates which Mr. A. I. Doyle has transcribed from the British Museum MS Harley 2339 and published in *Dominican Studies*, October 1950.
[2] *Purgatorio* XVI 94–6
'Therefore law was needed as a curb; a ruler was needed, who might discern at least the tower of the true city.'

read these two lines without a certain emphasis. They have their relation to the contemporary preaching about St. Thomas of Canterbury, St. Thomas of *yngelonde*.[1] And if we desire this Yngelonde, the Engelond that is always 'Now and in England', then the opening of Chaucer's *Prologue* contains even more than Englishmen going towards Augustine's Canterbury, and trying to find, in the art of *felaweshipe*, the good life: it contains also the waters of life quenching the drought, it contains death and resurrection, Lent and Easter, a new Spring that may come to all pilgrims.[2]

It may not impossibly come to Chaucer's *Shipman*, who is not troubled by patriotism either. His latest 'original', I believe, is Miss Galway's Basque mariner John Piers, who captured the *Magdeleyn* of Bristol and finished off her crew.[3]

By water he sente hem hoom to every lond.[4]

In the opinion of Professor Lowes, one line alone—*With many a tempest hadde his berd been shake*—puts Chaucer's figure in the company of the Ancient Mariner and the Flying Dutchman;[5] but the Ellesmere illustrator understood this line to mean that the weather had blown away most of the Shipman's whiskers. *And certeinly*, the poet remarks, *he was a good felawe*: that is, he was a shady customer. He was also an efficient seaman. And he seems to possess the first two of the qualities which according to his tale women naturally desire, and which the great sailor Jason commanded:

---

[1] '. . . Thus took holy Thomas of Cauntebury his dethe full mekely, for right of holy chirche and the welfare of yngelonde.'
                    MS Harley 2247 fol. 23v, quoted by G. R. Owst
[2] I am indebted in this sentence to a communication by Miss Margaret Galway to the *Times Literary Supplement* of 6 October 1950, which states, much more directly than on my own initiative I should have been inclined to do, feelings I believed implicit in Chaucer's lines, though sufficiently hidden to anyone not open to them. I have to add Miss Galway's intention, which was to propose that Chaucer's Human Comedy, like Dante's *Divine Comedy*, has an ideal date in the past: 1378, in the first year of the reign of Richard II. April 18, when the storytelling began, was in that year the date of Easter, as it was in 1367, when the new King was born. This, whether it is a good guess or not, is what would be called at a fourteenth-century banquet an apt *sotelte*.
[3] *Modern Language Review* XXXIV 497ff. (1939). Manly's man was Piers Resselden, who joined with the notorious pirate John Hawley of Dartmouth.
[4] A 400
He made them walk the plank (after the custom of the country).
[5] J. L. LOWES, *Geoffrey Chaucer* (Oxford, 1934) p. 162, referring to A 406. To pull or shake someone's beard was commonly regarded as an insult.

They wolde that hir housbondes sholde be
Hardy, and wise, and riche, and therto free . . .[1]

This is a character that Hollywood is still seeking, and to Chaucer
a simple enjoyment of the problem of appearance and reality.
There was a good deal of satire at the expense of the irreligion,
cupidity and incompetence of physicians of the time: John
Arderne, a fourteenth-century surgeon of integrity, was perhaps
a rare bird. Yet medicine in late fourteenth-century England
could rise to a local anæsthetic, and also to legal protection against
negligence.[2] We can see Chaucer's tactic more clearly if we
set it beside Jean de Meun's straightforward invective:

> Her wynnyng is of such sweetnesse
> That if a man falle in seknesse,
> They are full glad, for her encres;
> For by her wille, withoute lees,
> Everich man shulde be sek,
> And though they die, they sette not a lek.
> After, whanne they the gold have take,
> Full litel care for hem they make.
> They wolde that fourty were seke at onys,
> Ye, two hundred, in flesh and bonys,
> And yit two thousand, as I gesse,
> For to encrecen her richesse.[3]

The *Doctour* begins with a flourish of qualifications, which are in
due course just perceptibly stained by the customary vitriol.

> Ful redy hadde he his apothecaries
> To sende hym drogges and his letuaries,
> For ech of hem made oother for to wynne—
> Hir frendshipe nas nat newe to bigynne . . .
>    Of his diete mesurable was he,
> For it was of no superfluitee,
> But of greet norissyng and digestible.
> His studie was but litel on the Bible.

---

[1] B 1365–6: *Legend of Good Women* 1528
*Free* generous
  Probably the *Shipman's Tale* was originally intended for the Wife of Bath, but her
requirements (compare B 1365–7 and D 1258–9) were less exacting. Those of
Pertelote the hen, however, were similar (B 4104): she wanted a perfect Courtly
Lover.
  [2] *Chaucer's World* compiled by EDITH RICKERT, ed. CLAIR C. OLSON and MARTIN M.
CROW (New York: Columbia University Press, 1948: O.U.P.) pp. 178ff.
  [3] *Romaunt of the Rose* 5725–36
  *Withoute lees* truly    *Sette not a lek* don't care a rap

In sangwyn and in pers he clad was al,
Lyned with taffata and with sendal;
And yet he was but esy of dispence;
He kepte that he wan in pestilence.
For gold in phisik is a cordial,
Therfore he lovede gold in special.[1]

The *Wyf of Bathe* hints and glances at what is to be out-
rageously and coolly and copiously confessed by the woman
herself. *She koude muche of wandrynge by the weye*[2]—and to her a
pilgrimage was a Cook's Tour. She had her five husbands 'at
the altar', not to mention *autre compaignie*,

She was a worthy womman al hir lyve:
Housbondes at chirche dore she hadde fyve,
Withouten oother compaignye in youthe—
But therof nedeth nat to speke as nowthe.[3]

The Old Hag in the *Romance of the Rose* was a progenitor of hers,
and so was the woman of Samaria. But our first impression of
the Wife is of Pride—pride in her provincial weaving, conceit in
her imagined precedence, and vanity in her ostentatious dress.
Alice, like Falstaff, can be admired: and like Falstaff, has been
admired. I prefer Blake's statement that she is 'useful as a
scarecrow'. And the *Persoun* could hardly be placed to better
advantage:

A good Wif was ther of biside Bathe . . .

A good man was ther of religioun
And was a povre Persoun of a toun,
But riche he was of hooly thoght and werk.
He was also a lerned man, a clerk,
That Cristes gospel trewely wolde preche;
His parisshens devoutly wolde he teche.
Benygne he was, and wonder diligent,
And in adversitee ful pacient,
And swich he was ypreved ofte sithes.
Ful looth were hym to cursen for his tithes,
But rather wolde he yeven, out of doute,

[1] A 425ff.
*Letuaries* electuaries, remedies          *In sangwyn and in pers* in rich cloths of red and
persian blue          *Taffata . . . sendal* expensive silks
*Esy of dispence* moderate in expenditure
[2] A 467
I find it difficult to believe that this means *simply* that she had travelled abroad, as
Skeat suggests. Moral aberration is surely implied.
[3] A 459–62
*O other compaignye* cf. *Le Roman de la Rose* 12781: *La Vieille.*          *As nowthe* at present

Unto his povre parisshens aboute
Of his offryng, and eek of his substaunce.
He koude in litel thyng have suffisaunce.
Wyd was his parisshe, and houses fer asonder,
But he ne lefte nat, for reyn ne thonder,
In siknesse nor in meschief, to visite
The ferreste in his parisshe, muche and lite,
Upon his feet, and in his hand a staf.
   This noble ensample to his sheep he yaf,
That first he wroghte, and afterward he taughte.
Out of the gospel he tho wordes caughte;
And this figure he added eek therto,
That if gold ruste, what shal iren do?
For if a preest be foul, on whom we truste,
No wonder is a lewed man to ruste;
And shame it is, if a prest take keep,
A shiten shepherde and a clene sheep.
Wel oghte a preest ensample for to yive,
By his clennesse, how that his sheep sholde lyve.
   He sette nat his benefice to hyre
And leet his sheep encombred in the myre
And ran to Londoun unto Seinte Poules
To seken hym a chauntrye for soules,
Or with a bretherhed to been withholde;
But dwelte at hoom, and kepte wel his folde,
So that the wolf ne made it nat myscarie;
He was a shepherde and no mercenarie.
   And though he hooly were and vertuous,
He was to synful men nat despitous,
Ne of his speche daungerous ne digne,
But in his techyng discreet and benygne.
To drawen folk to hevene by fairnesse,
By good ensample, this was his bisynesse.
But it were any persone obstinat,
What so he were, of heigh or lowe estat,
Hym wolde he snybben sharply for the nonys.
   A bettre preest I trowe that nowher noon ys.
He waited after no pompe and reverence,
Ne maked him a spiced conscience,
But Cristes loore and his apostles twelve
He taughte, and first he folwed it hymselve.[1]

[1] A 445; 477–528
*Ofte sithes* many times     *Take keep* take heed
*A chauntrye* an endowment for a priest to sing Mass daily for the deceased
*With a bretherhed to been withholde* to be retained as a guild chaplain
*Despitous* scornful     *Daungerous* disdainful     *Digne* haughty

There follows Chaucer's model peasant:

> With hym ther was a Plowman, was his brother,
> That hadde ylad of dong ful many a fother;
> A trewe swynkere and a good was he,
> Lyvynge in pees and parfit charitee.
> God loved he best with al his hoole herte
> At alle tymes, thogh him gamed or smerte,
> And thanne his neighebor right as hymselve . . .[1]

The *Plowman* is unobtrusive, but elaboration was needless. No other English poet reveals so clearly as Chaucer the essence of his virtue. The question has been asked, and variously answered, whether Chaucer's idealized knight, priest and peasant are not in fact inverted satire. We are reminded that to praise a plough-man was unfashionable; and indeed Chaucer had no earthly reason to love him. He had only a commandment, and a con-science. But to search in such a case for the personal predilections of Geoffrey Chaucer is to ignore what was impersonal in the poet, what is impersonal in the poetry. With no suspicion of quibbling, Chaucer has set up a balance of conflicting attitudes, which is not the same as compromise, and which has courtly tact as a condition, not a cause. It may be figured as a projection, in art, of the habit of mind of a medieval subject in a high position of trust, even of a justice of the peace for Kent; and the reverse of the mental processes of Bernard Shaw. It is conceivably the reply of the human spirit at the centre of the aristocracy of London to the terror and instability of fourteenth-century politics. It is the poetry of the knowledge that human judge-ments of human character are not final; but that some interim reports are better than others. It is, finally, at the height of the comedy of the *Prologue*. Comedy both unites and classifies; and the comedy of Chaucer extends charity as far as it will go without contamination.

Chaucer introduced the *Millere*, I think, by remodelling two lines about a hero of the kind of bourgeois minstrelsy that he later burlesqued in *Sir Thopas*.

> He ys a myghty man for the nonys
> And wele ishape with grete bonys.
> > *Ipomydon*

---

[1] A 529–35
*Thogh him gamed or smerte* in pleasure or pain

The Millere was a stout carl for the nones;
Ful byg he was of brawn, and eek of bones.[1]
*Prologue*

Like Gamelyn in 'romance', and like Sir Thopas, the Miller
distinguished himself at the low sport of wrestling; his physique
has to be seen to be believed—

> . . . over al ther he cam,
> At wrastlynge he wolde have alwey the ram.
> He was short-sholdred, brood, a thikke knarre;
> Ther was no dore that he nolde heve of harre,
> Or breke it at a rennyng with his heed.
> His berd as any sowe or fox was reed,
> And therto brood, as though it were a spade.
> Upon the cop right of his nose he hade
> A werte, and theron stood a toft of herys,
> Reed as the bristles of a sowes erys;
> His nosethirles blake were and wyde.
> A swerd and a bokeler bar he by his syde.
> His mouth as greet was as a greet fourneys.
> He was a janglere and a goliardeys,
> And that was moost of synne and harlotries.
> Wel koude he stelen corn and tollen thries;
> And yet he hadde a thombe of gold, pardee . . .[2]

The mouth is manifestly caricatured; the features of the Summoner and the Pardoner are more repulsive, and more probable.
It is not only that Chaucer has brought off his jokes.   The humour
is in the right place.

The *Prologue* exposes all sides of Efficiency by admiring it both
without reserve, and with a variety of ironical emphasis.   There
is the dignity of the ploughman who is *a trewe swynkere and a good*,
there is the vocation of the priest, and the worth of the *parfit
knyght*.   And there are the special abilities of the wicked, including
the Wife of Bath's certificate in the domestic arts: but Chaucer

---

[1] MS Harley 2252, ed. KÖLBING (Breslau, 1889), 77–8; A 545–6   *For the nonys* (or
*nones*) is nothing more here than a minstrel's rhyme-tag.
[2] A 547–63
*Over al ther he cam* . . . he would beat all the wrestlers in the district, and win the prize.
*Knarre* tree-knot—hence thickset sturdy fellow (when the *k* is pronounced, as of course
it should be, definition is hardly needed).   *Of harre* off its hinges   *The cop right* the
very summit: our phrase 'was surmounted by . . .' embalms a similar metaphor.
*A janglere and a goliardeys* full of idle talk and coarse tales   *Tollen thries* take three
times his legal allowance of corn   *And yet he hadde a thombe of gold* he was honest,
as millers go (alluding to the proverb 'An honest miller hath a thumb of gold')

does not deal in black and white. The *Maunciple* and the *Reve* exemplify in their degree the kind of subordinate who by a combination of astuteness and deceit has found a shady corner for himself, like the Reeve's *with grene trees shadwed.*

> Ther nas baillif, ne hierde, nor oother hyne,
> That he ne knew his sleighte and his covyne;
> They were adrad of hym as of the deeth.
> His wonyng was ful faire upon an heeth;
> With grene trees shadwed was his place.
> He koude bettre than his lord purchace.
> Ful riche he was astored pryvely:
> His lord wel koude he plesen subtilly,
> To yeve and lene hym of his owene good,
> And have a thank, and yet a cote and hood.[1]

Such a person is still both subject and object to Chaucer. I mean that Chaucer is not merely aiming at a target; he is (never wholly, but in varying degrees) identifying a part of himself with the object. The advertised 'tolerance' of Chaucer has large, firm bounds. Before he was, they are.

Only so, it seems to me, can we account for the natural manner in which he writes about the unnatural beings that follow: even the surprising comparison, in the *Somonour*, between leprous flesh and the faces of cherubim becomes less surprising when we remember its origin. Thus, to a contemporary, the irony would be so unforced as to appear an accident of reporting:

> A Somonour was ther with us in that place,
> That hadde a fyr-reed cherubynnes face,
> For saucefleem he was, with eyen narwe.
> As hoot he was and lecherous as a sparwe;
> With scalled browes blake and piled berd;
> Of his visage children were aferd.
> Ther nas quyk-silver, lytarge, ne brymstoon,
> Boras, ceruce, ne oille of tartre noon;
> Ne oynement that wolde clense and byte,
> That hym myghte helpen of his whelkes white,
> Nor of the knobbes sittynge on his chekes.[2]

[1] A 603–12
*Hierde* herdsman          *Hyne* farm worker          *Covyne* deceitfulness
*Lene* lend          *Yet* besides
[2] A 623–33
The painted face of a cherub was commonly fire-red, and phrases like the French *il a une face de cherubin* and *rouge comme un cherubin* became current.
          *Saucefleem* pustular          *Piled* scanty          *Whelkes* pimples

175

In this character of a corrupt officer of the ecclesiastical court there are all the materials for a savage *grotesquerie* and a dramatization in the satirical manner of Ben Jonson. But the more we watch, the clearer it becomes that the object is in no theatrical colours, but a white Chaucerian light. We are kept just so far away as not to be distracted by the onion-laden breath:

> Wel loved he garleek, oynons, and eek lekes,
> And for to drynken strong wyn, reed as blood;
> Thanne wolde he speke and crie as he were wood.
> And whan that he wel dronken hadde the wyn,
> Thanne wolde he speke no word but Latyn.
> A fewe termes hadde he, two or thré,
> That he had lerned out of som decree—
> No wonder is, he herde it al the day;
> And eek ye knowen wel how that a jay
> Kan clepen 'Watte' as wel as kan the pope.
> But whoso koude in oother thyng hym grope,
> Thanne hadde he spent al his philosophie;
> Ay *Questio quid iuris* wolde he crie.
> He was a gentil harlot and a kynde;
> A bettre felawe sholde men noght fynde.
> He wolde suffre for a quart of wyn
> A good felawe to have his concubyn
> A twelf month, and excuse hym atte fulle;
> Ful prively a fynch eek koude he pulle.
> And if he foond owher a good felawe,
> He wolde techen him to have noon awe,
> In swich caas, of the ercedekenes curs,
> But if a mannes soule were in his purs;
> For in his purs he sholde ypunysshed be.[1]

There is no heat here; only light, revealing and exposing a medieval Sweeney Erect. The observer himself stays apart, and the only gesture is the Summoner's 'gesture of orang-outang': *ful prively a fynch eek koude he pulle*. Chaucer appears in a doctrinal aside:

> 'Purs is the ercedekenes helle,' seyde he.
> But wel I woot he lyed right in dede;

---

[1] A 634–57
*Questio quid iuris* the question is, what is the law on this point?

Of cursyng oghte ech gilty man drede,
For curs wol slee right as assoillyng savith . . .[1]

Yet even in these lines Chaucer preserves his detachment; for they have the balanced justice of the terrible supplication that our debts be forgiven as we forgive our debtors.[2]

Dante would probably, though not certainly, have placed the *Pardoner* in the eighth circle of Hell; and Chaucer's fraudulent seller of indulgences very nearly places himself there later in the pilgrimage. But for the moment he is a *castrato* riding Canterbury way, and singing a duet called *Come hither, love, to me* with the exceptionally powerful bass of the Summoner:

> Ful loude he soong 'Com hider, love, to me!'
> This Somonour bar to hym a stif burdoun,
> Was never trompe of half so greet a soun . . .
> A voys he hadde as smal as hath a goot.
> No berd hadde he, ne nevere sholde have;
> As smothe it was as it were late shave.
> I trowe he were a geldyng or a mare.
> But of his craft, fro Berwyk unto Ware,
> Ne was ther swich another pardoner . . .[3]

Chaucer resists opportunities for extravagant farce, such as we can see in the tenth story of the sixth day in the *Decameron*. There we find Boccaccio's Frà Cipolla, with his parrot's feather, announcing that he has a relic which fell from the wings of the Angel Gabriel after the Annunciation; and when two members of his audience substitute for the feather a few coals, these are associated, in a long oration, with St. Lawrence. Frà Cipolla is a simple rogue, a figure of fun, and if anyone is held up to ridicule in

---

[1] A 658–61
*Assoillyng* removal of the sentence of excommunication (*curs*) by the Archdeacon of the court; or sacramental absolution
John de Bromyard held the following opinion of the ecclesiastical courts of the time: 'By means of a little money given to the summoners or the ecclesiastical judges, who ought to be punished along with them with an equal punishment, adulterers and fornicators are always able to persist' (G. R. OWST, *Literature and Pulpit in Medieval England* p. 252). For Jean de Meun's treatment of the same theme, see the *Romaunt of the Rose* 7009ff. In relation to contemporary records, Chaucer's *Somonour* seems to be a caricature given verisimilitude.
[2] Compare the *Parson's Tale* I 1043
[3] A 672ff
Part of the register of John de Grandison, Bishop of Exeter, shows that it was sometimes through the connivance of archdeacons' officials that false pardoners were able to trade. There is also a hint of a perverted relation between the two characters in Chaucer (compare MURIEL BOWDEN, *A Commentary on the General Prologue* p. 274).

Boccaccio's story, it is the gullible mob. Chaucer finds nothing uproarious in the greater evil:

> For in his male he hadde a pilwe-beer,
> Which that he seyde was Oure Lady veyl;
> He seyde he hadde a gobet of the seyl
> That Seint Peter hadde, whan that he wente
> Upon the see, til Jhesu Crist hym hente.
> He hadde a croys of latoun ful of stones,
> And in a glas he hadde pigges bones.
> But with thise relikes, whan that he fond
> A povre person dwellynge upon lond,
> Upon a day he gat hym moore moneye
> Than that the person gat in monthes tweye.
> And thus, with feyned flaterye and japes,
> He made the person and the peple his apes.
> But trewely to tellen atte laste,
> He was in chirche a noble ecclesiaste.
> Wel koude he rede a lessoun or a storie,
> But alderbest he song an offertorie;
> For wel he wiste, whan that song was songe,
> He moste preche and wel affile his tonge
> To wynne silver, as he ful wel koude;
> Therefore he song the murierly and loude.[1]

Even here there is a hint of a line or two of Jean de Meun's personification of hypocrisy, which is more frequently in evidence in the Pardoner's own prologue; but we remember the goat-voice and the *glarynge eyen* when False-Seeming is forgotten. Chaucer, I think, with his less positive method, his method of comedy, is nearer to the seriousness of Dante's 'Jovial Friars' (though Dante could do better) than to Boccaccio or to Jean de Meun. I do not intend a comparison; but there are two lines in the episode of the *Inferno* which, for my own purposes, might have been printed before this chapter. They occur at the point at which Dante is interrupted at the beginning of a personal judgement. The place and cause of the interruption Chaucer could not have described: and I believe he did not require to do so.

---

[1] A 694–714
*Male* bag    *Pilwe-beer* pillow-case    *Latoun* latten-metal
*Person* parson    *Japes . . . apes* compare *Romaunt of the Rose* 6835–6 (quoted above, p. 163)    *Murierly* more pleasantly

*Io cominciai: 'O frati, i vostri mali—'*
*ma più non dissi . . .*[1]

In the last leaves of the *Prologue*, which include *Oure Hooste*, Chaucer was never more at ease with his reader; it is an ease which he has deserved. And I have not tried to tidy his pretty kettle of fish. But in the following pages, when it is not certain what precisely is Chaucer's admired disorder, I shall sometimes admire it in what order I please.

[1] *Inferno* XXIII 109–10
'I began: "O friars, your evil—" but said no more.'      Caiaphas appears, crucified
into the earth by three stakes.

# IX

. . . *Jacometta fell on her knees, and declared she was honest though poor—an exclamation which I dare say, Messer Geoffreddo, you have often heard in Italy: it being the preface to every act of roguery and lubricity, unless from a knight or knight's lady. The Princess of Policastro was ignorant of this, and so was Jacometta when she used it.*

LANDOR: *Imaginary Conversations*
'Chaucer, Boccaccio, and Petrarca'

*As hyt ys yknowe hough meny people buth in this ylond, ther buth also of so meny people longages and tonges . . . and som useth strange wlaffyng, chyteryng, harryng, and garryng grisbittyng . . .*

JOHN OF TREVISA 1387
translating HIGDEN's *Polychronicon LIX*

# KNIGHT AND LADY: CHURL AND LEMAN

THE *KNIGHT'S TALE*, IN COMPARISON WITH OTHER TALES, has been overpraised, or praised for the wrong reasons; and for this, Dryden is probably to be held responsible. There are passages in the poem which contain some of the most brilliant and effective verse written in medieval English, and there are other passages which suggest, to my mind, an inventory dreamt by the Chaucer who was Clerk of Works. I am not sure what W. P. Ker meant by calling this narrative a 'complete and perfect version of a medieval romance'. But I can understand, though I am not at present to defend or refute, an Italian view expressed by Signor Torraca,[1] that Chaucer has botched the adaptation of Boccaccio. And English critics should at least be aware of Signor Torraca's opinion.

I have wondered whether Dryden had his tongue in his cheek when he called Chaucer's handling of *Il Teseide* a 'Noble poem . . . of the Epique kind', and whether later critics took the phrase more literally than he meant it.[2] One can even imagine that there are glimmerings of mock-epic in his version. But Dryden, in *Palamon and Arcite*, entirely misjudged the intention at two important points. Theseus, coming upon his former prisoners

---

[1] F. TORRACA, *Scritti vari* (Milan, 1928). And H. M. Cummings in *The Indebtedness of Chaucer's Works to the Italian Works of Boccaccio*, University of Cincinnati Studies, Volume X, Part II (Cincinnati, 1916) pp. 135–7, had illustrated the superiority of the *Teseide*.

[2] The *Knight's Tale* appears to have been 'noble' since *The Two Noble Kinsmen*, and according to its latest interpreter at the time of writing 'it is predominantly noble, predominantly tragic . . .' (WILLIAM FROST, *Review of English Studies*, October 1949). Dryden's influential judgement (1700) is repeated, doubtfully, by Pope (1711), who called the piece 'an attempt towards an epic poem', and emphatically by Dart (1721) and by Joseph Warton (1782), who was concerned to set the 'serious and sublime' against 'the common notion . . . that Chaucer's vein of poetry was chiefly turned to the light and the ridiculous'. Hallam (1837) mentions the tale with *Troilus and Criseyde* as chief 'amongst the pathetic poems'. Johnson's laconic judgement in the Life of Dryden (1779), that 'the story of *Palamon and Arcite*' contains 'an action unsuitable to the times in which it is placed' is a reasonable verdict on the premise of Dryden's classification of the poem, and might be considered a *reductio ad absurdum*. On the other hand, an unknown writer *circa* 1785 states the independent view that the poem is, as he puts it, 'of a mixt nature'; and Lounsbury, in 1891, was obviously aware of this point.

fighting for Emily, is persuaded to mercy by the women of his
entourage, and speaks as follows:

'. . .
Who may been a fool, but if he love?
Bihoold, for Goddes sake that sit above,
Se how they blede! be they noght wel arrayed?
Thus hath hir lord, the god of love, ypayed
Hir wages and hir fees for hir servyse!
And yet they wenen for to been ful wyse
That serven love, for aught that may bifalle.
But this is yet the beste game of alle,
That she for whom they have this jolitee
Kan hem therfore as muche thank as me.
She woot namoore of al this hoote fare,
By God, than woot a cokkow or an hare!
But all moot ben assayed, hoot and coold;
A man moot ben a fool, or yong or oold—
I woot it by myself ful yore agon,
For in my time a servant was I oon . . .'[1]

Here is Dryden's impression of the Duke:

The Proverb holds, That to be wise and love,
Is hardly granted to the Gods above.
See how the Madmen bleed: Behold the Gains
With which their Master, Love, rewards their Pains:
For sev'n long Years, on Duty ev'ry Day,
Lo their Obedience, and their Monarch's Pay:
Yet, as in Duty bound, they serve him on,
And ask the Fools, they think it wisely done:
Nor Ease nor Wealth nor Life itself regard,
For 'tis their Maxim, Love is Love's Reward.
This is not all; the Fair, for whom they strove
Nor knew before, nor could suspect their Love,
Nor thought when she beheld the Fight from far,
Her Beauty was th' Occasion of the War.
But sure a gen'ral Doom on Man is past,
And all are Fools and Lovers, first or last:
This both by others and my self I know,
For I have serv'd their Sovereign, long ago . . .[2]

In Chaucer, the speech emerges from the surrounding flatness of
character with the humour of an experienced Officer in Command

[1] A 1799–814
[2] DRYDEN, *Palamon and Arcite: or, the Knight's Tale from Chaucer* II 364–81.

indulging a sudden access of hearty sympathy and worldly wisdom as he condones a serious breach of discipline.[1] For Want of Words in the Beginning of our Language, lacking the Modern Art of Fortifying, our father of *English* Poetry—our perpetual Fountain of good Sense—could not here achieve the full Epic vacancy of his translator. The Gothic must be stiffened, sharpened, and furnished for an age preparing to be Augustan.

The second instance is Arcite's dying speech; but it is unnecessary to expose Dryden by quoting his version entire. This is Chaucer:

> 'Nat may the woful spirit in myn herte
> Declare o point of alle my sorwes smerte
> To yow, my lady, that I love moost;
> But I biquethe the servyce of my goost
> To yow aboven every creature,
> Syn that my lyf may no lenger dure . . .
> What is this world? what asketh men to have?
> Now with his love, now in his colde grave
> Allone withouten any compaignye.
> Fare wel, my sweete foo, myn Emelye!
> And softe taak me in youre armes tweye,
> For love of God, and herkneth what I seye . . .
> As in this world right now ne knowe I non
> So worthy to ben loved as Palamon,
> That serveth yow, and wol doon al his lyf.
> And if that evere ye shul ben a wyf,
> Foryet nat Palamon, the gentil man.'
> And with that word his speche faille gan,
> For from his feet up to his brest was come
> The coold of deeth, that hadde hym overcome . . .
> But on his lady yet caste he his eye;
> His laste word was, 'Mercy, Emelye!'
> His spirit chaunged hous and wente ther,
> As I cam nevere, I kan nat tellen wher.[2]

And here is Dryden's paraphrase of the last two lines:

> The soul of *Arcite* went, where Heathens go,
> Who better live than we, though less they know.[3]

---

[1] Chaucer's *perspective* in disposing the materials of romance is admirably described by Professor Renwick: W. L. RENWICK and HAROLD ORTON, *The Beginnings of English Literature to Skelton* 1509 (London: Cresset Press, 1939) pp. 89–90.
[2] A 2765ff.
[3] *Op. cit.*, III 852–3

The difference between Chaucer's episode and Dryden's is the difference between high comedy and low epic. Chaucer is exhibiting, in a refined degree, the comedian's use of sentiment.[1] The gravity that he deliberately reserved is in the death-scene of Troilus; and on that occasion, Troilus is the only person who is amused. There the reader will remember the very passage from the *Teseide* that was kept out of the *Knight's Tale*.

Having given summary verdict upon the two most important episodes of this particular piece of Dryden's, I do not imagine that I have disposed of Dryden the critic, or even Dryden the translator, of Chaucer. His version of the *Nun's Priest's Tale* is the best modernization of a poem of Chaucer's that I can remember, and the famous Preface to *Fables Ancient and Modern* is a rambling, careless, brilliant piece of writing which has probably been the most influential document in the history of Chaucer criticism. We may smile when he says of Chaucer 'I found I had a Soul congenial to his'; yet it is true that Dryden possessed some engine which was occasionally in tune. It was not a soul; but it was enough to enable the leading man of letters of the Restoration to pay homage to the great master in medieval English.

In spite of Professor Tatlock and Professor Patch, the *Knight's Tale* is still taken too solemnly—or, if you prefer, Chaucer is not taken seriously enough. The first of the *Canterbury Tales* is read apart from the second and the third, so that its exaggerations are not seen in comic relation to the contrary exaggerations of the Miller and the Reeve. One should read the *Parliament of Birds* before the first Canterbury fragment. In the *Knight's Tale* a distinguished poet tells a high-falutin' story about knights and ladies, courtly love and jousting, improbable nobility and romanticized military exercises; a mixture of elaborate rhetoric and racy speech, of truth and nonsense; a *tour de force* which would amuse all the people some of the time, and impress some

---

[1] That acute critic of Chaucer, the late Professor Walter Raleigh, had in mind the opposite interpretation of this passage when, in illustration of the view that the poet sometimes displayed 'literary bad manners', he said: 'Even at a funeral he must insinuate his jest . . . Chaucer will arouse deep feelings of pathos and sympathy, and in the atmosphere thus created, he will let off a little crackling penny jest, from pure love of mischief' (*On Writing and Writers*, ed. GEORGE GORDON; London: Arnold, 1926, 1927, p. 109). Sir Walter Raleigh, like Sir Walter Scott, appears to have shared the customary view of eighteenth-century critics of the poem; but they both admitted—and blamed Chaucer for the fact—that certain verses did not suit the theory.

of the people all the time.  The narrative displays certain ideal
knightly virtues and implies a whole dignified, processional order
of society which Chaucer genuinely admired;[1] but he was not
interested in the persons, except, at moments, in Theseus.  Emily
is a wisp of a heroine.  Palamon is a cardboard knight; Arcite
is occasionally vigorous but finally incredible; and their rivalry
is followed by the rivalry of Absolon and Nicholas.  I assume
that the author of *Troilus and Criseyde* was aware of these things,
and that he intended them to be so.  The real knightly virtues
are those that remain when the laughter is finished and the
cardboard pushed back in the wings; when Nicholas and Absolon,
and the two Cambridge undergraduates, and Perkin Reveller,
have fallen through the trapdoor into the cellarage.  It is
thus possible to appreciate the verse without bothering very
much about the persons, who may look slightly absurd even
while you are moved by the poetry they utter.  What is distinctive about the tale is a bold combination of mockery and pathos,
of mock-epic and genuine rhetorical dignity, of lovers and buckets
and gods and butchers: a strangely congruous combination which
shocked Chaucer's worthy late eighteenth-century editor, and
Sir Walter Scott,[2] and which is never entirely burlesque.  Lovers
and buckets were connected by a perfectly natural idiom of
speech,

> Into a studie he fil sodeynly,
> As doon thise loveres in hir queynte geres,
> Now in the crope, now doun in the breres,
> Now up, now doun, as boket in a welle.[3]

Gods could be made more interesting by stellifying them, and
the medieval mind readily assumed that a star might even have
some influence upon the life of a butcher.

---

[1] See CHARLES MUSCATINE, 'Form, Texture and Meaning in Chaucer's *Knight's Tale*',
*Publications of the Modern Language Association of America* LXV 911–29 (1950), a paper
received when my book was in the press.  I should agree also with Mr. Muscatine
that this order is emphasized by an awareness of the threat of chaos, and that in
what he rightly calls our 'poetic pageant' the poetry of *disaster* is the most serious.

[2] In *Works of John Dryden*, Vol. I (1808), pp. 39–40, quoted by C. F. E. Spurgeon
(*op. cit.*): a comparison between the *Knight's Tale* and Dryden's version which may be
contrasted with Mr. Mark van Doren's perceptive account in *The Poetry of John Dryden*
(Cambridge: Minority Press, 1931) pp. 232–4. Scott regarded as 'degrading' and 'dis-
gusting' the circumstances in the description of the temple of Mars which do not fit
the category of Noble Epic, and which Dryden—in the words of Sir Walter—
'judiciously omitted or softened'.

[3] A 1530–3
*Queynte geres* curiously changeable moods        *Crope* tree-top

I have found a similar quality in parts of the *Legend of Good Women*; and there are parallels between the two, such as the accelerated narrative manner, and the rhymed rum-ram-ruf running commentary on joust or sea-fight; there are also slight but unmistakable resemblances of phrasing. And I think that if we silence the echo of Dryden's words, the *Knight's Tale* may be regarded as a criticism of the Renaissance epic, of what W. P. Ker called, apropos of *Il Teseide*, 'the idea of an epic without any filling in it'.[1] Chaucer drastically reduced the figure of Boccaccio's composition, and provided his own stuffing from experience, including the experience of other books. The result is not a 'perfect narrative poem, but *the smylere with the knyf under the cloke*[2] is not the only perfect line in it. A verse is lifted with elegant coolness from Dante's vision on emerging from the Inferno, and finds itself introducing the love-lorn Arcite:

> Lo bel pianeta che ad amar conforta
> faceva tutto rider l'oriente

> The bisy larke, messager of day,
> Salueth in hir song the morwe gray,
> And firy Phebus riseth up so bright
> That al the orient laugheth of the light;
> And with his stremes dryeth in the greves
> The silver dropes hangynge on the leves.
> And Arcite, that in the court roial
> With Theseus is squier principal,
> Is risen . . .[3]

Chaucer's comic effect was later vulgarized in prose by Fielding and Dickens. And Palamon, learning of the return of his rival,

> thoughte that thurgh his herte
> He felte a coold swerd sodeynliche glyde . . .[4]

But this looks much more intense than one's impression of the whole tale. There is also the attitude of amused *gentillesse*, the attitude to the attitude of Theseus towards tearful women:

> And eek his herte hadde compassioun
> Of wommen, for they wepen evere in oon . . .

[1] *Form and Style in Poetry* ed. R. W. CHAMBERS (London: Macmillan, 1928) p. 74
[2] A 1999
[3] *Purgatorio* I 19–20
Knight's Tale 1491–9      *Greves* branches
[4] A 1574–5

wommen have swich sorwe,
Whan that hir housbondes ben from hem ago,
That for the moore part they sorwen so,
Or ellis fallen in swich maladye,
That at the laste certeinly they dye.[1]

There is the well-known passage about the temple of Mars,
which I shall not quote; there is Saturn's speech; and there is
the suggestion, which will carry us through some of the tedious
inventory of ducal extravagance, that the tournament is all a
show for the mob to gape at.—'It will be considered negligent of
me', says the author, 'if I forget to tell the expenditure':

I trowe men wolde deme it necligence
If I foryete to tellen the dispence
Of Theseus, that gooth so bisily
To maken up the lystes roially . . .[2]

The Duke gave *mete and wages* to a host of people to do this and
that; and the other, too, cost a pretty penny (*of gold a fother*).
Then again, consider the shocking price of the artist's paint:
*with many a floryn he the hewes boghte*. But all this was nothing to
a man like Theseus. When, at great expense, the decorations
were finished, *him lyked wonder wel.*—And Chaucer, we must
admit, has an eye for a crowd:

'Why woldestow be deed,' thise wommen crye,
'And haddest gold ynough, and Emelye?'[3]

This couplet was characteristically caught and thrown by
Alexander Pope, in an epistolary reference to the death of Lord
Orrery's dog:

Ah Bounce! Ah gentle beast, why wouldst thou die
When thou hadst meat enough, and Orrery?[4]

Surely Pope was more than doubtful about Dryden's view of the
*Knight's Tale.*

At the same time, I am not convinced that such entertainment
entirely redeems the dullness. One should not advise a reader
approaching the *Canterbury Tales* for the first reading to omit the

[1] A 1770–1; 2822–6
*Evere in oon* incessantly
[2] A 1881–4
[3] A 2835–6
[4] Letter dated April 10, 1744

first story: but he is unlikely to find that a detailed study of medieval astrology and medieval tournaments is always animating. In the *Nun's Priest's Tale* Chaucer joked about Geoffrey de Vinsauf the thirteenth-century theorist of poetics, but quoted him soberly enough in *Troilus and Criseyde*: and the author of the *Poetria Nova* put his finger on a medieval weakness. He insisted on considerations of form.[1] Whether Chaucer took Geoffrey de Vinsauf seriously or not, in *Canterbury Tales* the warning was often ignored. And the reason is, of course, that their author had in mind other purposes besides perfecting a single piece for a student of the manuscript who has never heard a tale told. The court was not on the way to Canterbury; but the *Knight's Tale* must flatter the taste of the *gentils*, yet not too grossly. It is possible to see in Theseus, who is less gentle than his original Teseo,[2] an aggressive side of the narrator's character, an impulse to cruelty which the *parfit knight*, perhaps with difficulty, controlled. A man may tell a story for different reasons. He may wish to amuse his audience, or to edify them; he may also wish to exhibit or to disguise something of himself; and he may not succeed. Chaucer has an opportunity of adding another dimension thus to his portraits in the *Prologue*.

What has been written between tales generally receives the attention it deserves; and I assume that anyone who has read to this point is willing to look for jokes himself, provided that original research is not required to unearth them. The drunken Miller with difficulty keeps his mount after the Knight's highly respectable peroration, promises a *legende and a lyf*, and performs a *fabliau* which contains some of Chaucer's finest descriptive verse. Arcite would have been content to live and die, *paramour*, for an apparition; Absolon kisses the wrong end of the object and has had enough of it. The difference, as the Elizabethans perceived, is an illustration not of obscenity but *decorum*.[3]

[1] J. W. H. ATKINS, *English Literary Criticism: The Medieval Phase* (Cambridge, 1943) p. 99.
[2] See H. J. WEBB, 'A Reinterpretation of Chaucer's Theseus', *Review of English Studies*, October 1947.
[3] 'How much had hee swarved from Decorum, if hee had made his Miller, his Cooke, and his Carpenter, to have told such honest and good [*i.e.*, decent and correct] tales, as hee made his Knight, his Squire, his Lawyer, and Scholler tell?' (Beaumont 1597). Compare the extracts given by C. F. E. Spurgeon from Hanmer (1576), Sir John Harington (1591), Speght (1598). And Jusserand aptly observed of Chaucer in *Le Théâtre en Angleterre* . . . (Paris, 1878): *il croit que les honnêtes gens peuvent, sans grand mal, rire aux discours licencieux d'un meunier ivre; Madame de Sévigné était de son avis.*

Nothing that I know in English can so plainly expose the debility of the modern 'music-hall' or 'variety' as a piece like this of the Miller's. In place of the music-hall snigger, the roaring end to the tale itself; and in place of the anæmic sentiment of the dance lyric and monologue, Spring freshness and reality:

> She was ful moore blisful on to see
> Than is the newe pere-jonette tree,
> And softer than the wolle is of a wether.
> And by hir girdel heeng a purs of lether,
> Tasseled with silk, and perled with latoun.
> In al this world, to seken up and doun,
> There nys no man so wys that koude thenche
> So gay a popelote or swich a wenche.
> Ful brighter was the shynyng of hir hewe
> Than in the tour the noble yforged newe.
> But of hir song, it was as loude and yerne
> As any swalwe sittynge on a berne.
> Therto she koude skippe and make game,
> As any kid or calf folwynge his dame.
> Hir mouth was sweete as bragot or the meeth,
> Or hoord of apples leyd in hey or heeth.
> Wynsynge she was, as is a joly colt,
> Long as a mast, and upright as a bolt . . .[1]

But the comparison is impertinent. Chaucer did not descend to the *fabliau*; he raised it. There is nothing like the portrait of Alison in the *fabliaux*; it is English-grown; it is superb verse. For the moment everything about the Miller is forgotten, except his golden thumb; unless we are reminded by the Carpenter's boy Robin, that *strong carl for the nones* whose presence suggests that once upon a time the Miller himself was the Reeve's knave, and witnessed the events he describes.[2] And the remaining portraits are by no means negligible. Nicholas, that *deerne* lover, differs from the Clerk on pilgrimage as from the saintly singer of the Prioress. He is an undergraduate of mystifying charm, dabbling in astrology, sweet as a root of liquorice, with a hidden life of the senses not quite for certain swallowed in sensuality. In

[1] A 3247–64
*Pere-jonette* early-ripe pear    *Latoun* latten-metal
*Noble* the fine gold coin of the period, minted in the Tower
*Thenche* imagine        *Yerne* lively    *Berne* barn
*Bragot* a drink made of honey and ale        *Meeth* mead        *Wynsynge* skittish
[2] R. A. PRATT, *Modern Language Notes* January 1944

the heat of the chase he finds time to sing. An unsatisfactory student, but he is inconveniently alive: his life fills his room, as when he sang:

And *Angelus ad Virginem* he song . . .[1]

And if he used the music preserved in the *Dublin Troper*, and today in the *Oxford Book of Carols*, then we can understand with what lovely looks he contemplated virginity. In the end Nicholas presents a slightly different appearance, but the *Angelus ad Virginem* remains. It remains a song of love. Such a song, in the flesh, must always be a point of vantage for rising or descent, and that is the reason why Richard Rolle would distinguish his *canor*, which is the silent spiritual song of the mystic. It is not a reason why we should be suspicious of the melody heard, or nervous of the intention of singing it.

*Punch* regularly attempts a parody of the characters of the *Prologue*, but *Punch* is forestalled: Chaucer parodied himself in the second half of his description of Absolon. And Absolon, and Alison, are both in one way or another golden as the Miller's thumb: all, or nearly all, of the *fabliau* is transmuted. It is a splendid exhibition of the artist smiling at everyone, including himself, and giving the best he can, as he pretends to be doing his worst. And the art is so advanced that it has deceived certain recent critics rediscovering the tale. It sets Mr. Bateson off in pursuit of a 'yeoman democracy' of Merry England,[2] and Mr. Graves imagining 'criminal sympathies' in the mind of Chaucer; both inclining to forget that Alison and her young men are poetic inventions, and that a *community* of Alisons and Nicholases would be as inconceivable, and intolerable, as a society of Falstaffs. Mr. Graves indeed is so confused that we must pause to straighten him out. 'In the *Canterbury Tales*', he says, 'the official and unofficial literatures of his period occur side by side'. This is a promising start. A little later, we read, of Chaucer:

---

[1] A 3216
*Angelus ad Virginem* is an Annunciation sequence of which the Latin words, a fourteenth-century English translation, and tune, have all survived. It is complete in the early fourteenth-century MS Arundel 248 in the British Museum, as in the *Dublin Troper* of *circa* 1360.

[2] F. W. BATESON: *English Poetry: A Critical Introduction* (London, New York: Longmans, 1950) pp. 131ff. Mr. Bateson writes excellently upon the rapid change of English speech in the first thirty-five years of Chaucer's life; but *to saven his estaat of yomanrye* he must tell us very much more about the 'new' rural culture of fourteenth-century England, upon what grounds the Franklin may be counted a rustic 'democrat', and why, according to his 'fundamental sympathies', Chaucer was not more eager to display the Yeoman in *Canterbury Tales*.

At the finish he lets the prize for the best story be awarded to the Knight; but, by reporting the Miller's and the Reeve's contributions with the same force and skill as the Knight's and Parson's, he reveals how strong his criminal sympathies are. He himself, when asked by the Host for a contribution to the story telling, begins a popular burlesque on chivalry, *Sir Thopas*.[1]

Here are two sentences containing two errors of fact, and an indefinite premise leading to a dubious conclusion. So far as I know, Chaucer left the *Canterbury Tales* unfinished, and never reached the prize-giving. *Sir Thopas* is not so much a 'popular burlesque on chivalry' as a burlesque on popular chivalry: a very different thing. And even if we can grant that Chaucer used the 'same force and skill' in the Miller's and Reeve's tales as in the Knight's and Parson's—which will take some granting —we might draw the conclusion, with the same force and skill as Mr. Graves, that Chaucer is revealing the strength of the 'criminal sympathies' of other people, or of nobody at all. We are told also, as Mr. Graves continues, that 'the cutting-short of *Sir Thopas* is Chaucer's critical verdict that courteous-gentle and churlish-lewd are two worlds, and must keep their distance'. But Chaucer's 'critical verdict', if we can here speak of criticism, is something much more subtle than this. It is that 'courteous-gentle' and 'churlish-lewd' are supposed to be two worlds, but that their inhabitants show themselves oddly unable to tell which is which. The gentles are not always courteous, and the churls not always ignorant, and neither can be relied upon to see, or admit, when its own amusements are being ridiculed, if ever so delicately. So there is no sign that the Knight hears any overtones of comedy in his own tale, and the Host certainly does not laugh at *Sir Thopas*. The word 'decorum' is given meaning.

To introduce the *fabliau* into English,[2] and immediately after the *Knight's Tale*, was a stroke of a master: it extended the range of cultivated poetry so that comedy could expand beyond all 'worlds' to the infinite. This is the effect that is achieved in the *Nun's Priest's Tale* and anticipated, at another stage, at the end of the Miller's: and I can understand when Dr. Tillyard

[1] ROBERT GRAVES, *The Common Asphodel* (London: Hamish Hamilton, 1949) pp. 258–9

[2] See W. W. LAWRENCE, *Chaucer and the Canterbury Tales* (New York, Columbia University Press, 1950: O.U.P.) pp. 67–8

experiences at this climax 'feelings akin to those of religious wonder'.[1] The 'blasphemies' of the tale are so ordered to laughter that any hypocrisy which remains in us shrivels into the fear of God. And this result is entirely a matter of quality of mind, in a poet working upon what would appear to be the most intractable material.

Chaucer probably used a lost French version of the story; but there seems to be a distant echo, as if from the other end of the building, of some fifteenth-century Italian ribaldry[2] in which a friar participates after the divine service.

> And thus lith Alison and Nicholas,
> In bisynesse of mýrthe and in solas,
> Til that the belle of laudes gan to rynge,
> And freres in the chauncel gonne synge.[3]

And that is a transition more coolly brilliant than any comedian of the cinema would dare to attempt.

We are told that nobody is seriously offended by the tale except the Reeve, who *by-cause he was of carpenteris craft* growls, reproaches himself, and becomes a querulous old man pondering on desire outliving performance. The grumbling turns to moralizing, which is impressively done:

> ‿Foure gleedes have we, which I shal devyse—
> Avauntyng, liyng, anger, coveitise;
> Thise foure sparkles longen unto eelde.
> Oure olde lemes mowe wel been unweelde,
> But wyl ne shal nat faillen, that is sooth.
> And yet ik have alwey a coltes tooth,
> As many a yeer as it is passed henne
> Syn that my tappe of lif bigan to renne.
> For sikerly, whan I was bore, anon
> Deeth drough the tappe of lyf and leet it gon;
> And ever sithe hath so the tappe yronne
> Til that almoost al empty is the tonne.
> The streem of lyf now droppeth on the chymbe.
> The sely tonge may wel rynge and chymbe

---

[1] E. M. W. TILLYARD, *Poetry Direct and Oblique* (London: Chatto, revised edition 1945) p. 92
  And since Dr. Tillyard is specially interested in the effect of the *plot*, I may add here that only four of the ten stories listed by Mr. Stith Thompson in *Sources and Analogues* pp. 107–23 have anything resembling this conclusion.
[2] *Sources and Analogues* pp. 108–11
[3] A 3653–6

Of wrecchednesse that passed is ful yoore;
With olde folk, save dotage, is namoore!'[1]

The Host is not deceived; nor is he deceived later by the Pardoner's eloquence. In spite of that, the prologue of the Reeve is remarkable, not because it has the irony of the *Pardoner's Tale* (it has not), but because it expresses an emotion which is rarely expressed to this degree in Chaucer, and which is more frequent, and more intense, in Langland. There are points of comparison and points of difference between the Reeve's whole speech and the lines concerning Envy in Passus V of *Piers Plowman*; the resemblance is not close and is almost certainly accidental. But I cannot recall a stretch of verse of similar length in which Chaucer comes nearer, in his own way, to the feel of the poetry of his great English contemporary. There are passages in which he is nearer to the *rum ram ruf* of verse, but that is not what I mean; nor is it enough to say, here he approaches Langland's high and sullen art. Chaucer is producing choleric temperament and sense of persecution in a particular character, and behind this mask there is power in his *sermoning*. There is the essence of the best pagan reflection on the common theme, in a form that may be assimilated to Christianity. Irony is caught in words so flexible that they cannot be translated; in *sely*, which has no single equivalent in modern English. The tongue of a guilelessly happy man, says the poetry, is also the tongue of a bell ringing of sorrows long past, and nothing more remains for old age but to hear what the bell tolls.

The Oxford story is better than the Cambridge, but for that Oxford cannot be held responsible. They are both versions of folktale widely current in Europe at the time, probably adapted from French originals; but the Norfolk Reeve is given skill in north-country talk, and tells a tale not only against the Miller but also, I think, against a neighbouring county. His pair of poor scholars who come to the university from *fer in the north I kan nat telle where* are pinned down, by sheer linguistic accuracy, in England beyond the Tees; so that Professor Tolkien, conducting an examination of a text established from seven principal

---

[1] A 3883-98
*Gleedes* glowing coals     *Longen unto eelde* belong to old age     *Lemes* limbs
*Mowe* may     *Unweelde* weak     *Wyl* desire     *Yet* still: the surviving
northern use     *Chymbe* rim of the cask     *Sely* blessed, innocent, poor
     Mr. G. R. Coffman has traced the literary tradition of these lines in an article called 'Old Age from Horace to Chaucer', *Speculum*, July 1934.

manuscripts,[1] found himself able to award the author 'at least' 127 marks, out of a total of some 142, for correct dialect. This, the Professor observed, is a very notable result. What is more, the poet's errors are largely concentrated at a point where he either grew tired, or allowed burlesque to fade into farce. Whether or not Chaucer knew a distinguished Northumbrian family of the name of Strother, as it has been suggested, and entertained with mimicry an audience who also knew them, there are two points about the entertainment which are specially important to a critic. One is the writing of something much more authentic than what passes for northern speech on the London stage today, by a writer consciously observant of the word, who urged copyists to preserve his diction. The other point is that a polite idiom was fresh grown, a standard of comparison which alone would make possible the joke in the *Reeve's Tale*, and with which Chaucer could form highly civilized verse out of the ease and intimacy of his native tongue. The full, prized *variety* of the Canterbury pilgrimage is only seen through contrasts of forms of speech and of patterns of language which our poet had both the curiosity and the moment of time to enjoy. And without this enjoyment neither Robin the Miller nor Oswald the Reeve, or Nicholas or Absolon or Aleyn or John, would have got on the page at all.

Oswald begins with a description no doubt supposed to be a caricature of Robin, but much less extraordinary than the original. This is not very surprising, for there comes a point in the *Prologue* when we begin to realize that certain persons might escape notice in a distorting mirror. The story of *Le Meunier et les II Clers*, as Mrs. Dempster has shown, is a piece of straightforward medieval slapstick which Chaucer could have picked up in Artois, on the Calais road;[2] with a climax recalling the story of Hercules and Faunus, which Gower retold from Ovid.[3] Simkin the miller has the comic social pride of the Five Guildsmen, and a display of physique and armoury nearly as formidable as the flourish of that knight of similar stock, Sir Thopas:

> Ay by his belt he baar a long panade,
> And of a swerd ful trenchant was the blade.
> A joly poppere baar he in his pouche;

---

[1] J. R. R. TOLKIEN, 'Chaucer as a Philologist: the *Reeve's Tale*', *Transactions of the Philological Society* (London, 1934) pp. 1–70: an example of the kind of study of the *mots de la tribu* which is of interest also to a reader of literature.
[2] *Sources and Analogues* p. 127
[3] *Confessio Amantis* V 6807ff.

Ther was no man, for peril, dorste hym touche.
A Sheffeld thwitel baar he in his hose . . .

A wyf he hadde, comen of noble kyn;
The person of the toun hir fader was.
With hire he yaf ful many a panne of bras,
For that Symkyn sholde in his blood allye.
She was yfostred in a nonnerye;
For Symkyn wolde no wyf, as he sayde,
But she were wel ynorissed and a mayde,
To saven his estaat of yomanrye.
And she was proud, and peert as is a pye.
    A ful fair sighte was it upon hem two;
On halydayes biforn hire wolde he go
With his typet wounde aboute his heed,
And she cam after in a gyte of reed;
And Symkyn hadde hosen of the same.
    Ther dorste no wight clepen hire but 'dame';
Was noon so hardy that wente by the weye
That with hire dorste rage or ones pleye,
But if he wolde be slayn of Symkyn
With panade, or with knyf, or boidekyn.[1]

One of the best specimens of this idiom follows when the ille-
gitimate *dame* is said to be *as digne as water in a dich*. I do not
propose to comment upon the story itself, which begins as the
miller abandons his polite dishonesty (*he stal but curteisly*) and
undertakes a course of immoderate theft. It is enough to say
that Chaucer's ear is keen for the voice of the people, including
the voice of the human animal at night-time. The Reeve's is
not an overwhelming reply; and, except perhaps to the mind of
a public censor, the *Miller's Tale* is in every respect superior.

    The expansion of Chaucer's terse sketch of the Cook, and the
fragment of the *Cook's Tale* itself, are taken direct from London
life. A career of Perkin Reveller the idle apprentice was
published daily, in Chaucer's lifetime, at the pillory on Cornhill.[2]
Of the two pages of talk with and by Hodge of Ware, contradictory images remain; of fat geese and fly-blown meat, of New-
gate revels, of a prentice *gaillard as goldfinch in the shawe*; and a
rotten apple. Chaucer goes as far as the door of the brothel, and
then turns. He has had enough, for the time being, of low life.

[1] A 3929–33; 3942–60
*Panade* cutlass        *Poppere* dagger        *Thwitel* large knife
*Bras* still, of course, stock northern dialect for 'money'        *Rage* wanton
[2] *Sources and Analogues* p. 154

# X

*. . . if good lyfe do not insue and folow upon our readynge to the example of others we myghte as well spende that tyme in reading of prophane hystories, of cantorburye tales, or a fit of Roben Hode.*

HUGH LATIMER, preaching in 1549

# TRAGICAL-COMICAL-HISTORICAL-
# MARTYROLOGICAL

IF J. M. MANLY INDEED FOUND THE ORIGINAL MAN OF LAW, Chaucer no doubt amused himself and others in his circle when he placed the advertisement of his own work in the hands of the wretched Pynchbek. This very man, I understand, had signed a writ summonsing Chaucer for a small debt; and here (perhaps) he is, praising the poems of Chaucer, rolling in money, and holding forth—after Innocent III—on the evils of poverty. There is also the well-known supposition that in the lines condemning tales of incest, the Man of Law was hazarding a Puff Oblique at the expense of Chaucer's 'rival', Gower. But for the pursuit of such speculation my wit is short; *ye may well understonde.*

Some readers have found the Man of Law's prologue oddly contrived, though passages in the same strain occur on the slightest provocation in the *Romance of the Rose*—and the speech of the Man of Law could hardly be more appropriate to his description in the *Prologue*:

> Discreet he was and of greet reverence—
> He semed swich, his wordes weren so wise.[1]

The rich justice delivers himself 'like a Pope' on the advantages of being at least a rich merchant, such as the merchant from whom he heard the tale; and with rich merchants it begins. Not only did Chaucer apparently translate the ascetic treatise *De Contemptu Mundi* of Innocent III, for the good of his soul or of the souls of others; he also successfully incorporated in the *Tale of the Man of Law* itself extracts like those which answer the drunkenness of the Miller and the lust of the churls' tales. Here, in fact, is a *legende and a lyf*, as the Miller tipsily foretold.

Yet it is self-sufficient; there is in any case no certain connexion in the manuscripts between this tale and another; and so I shall

[1] A 312-3

pause for a moment to anticipate the similar story of the Clerk's. That is also about a spiritual principle, and about the struggles of a soul to abide by it. As Professor Raleigh once said, Griselde of the *Clerk's Tale* is not a patient woman; she is Patience. And in the same way the Man of Law's Constance is Constancy or Fortitude. The Man of Law's performance is more episodic, more various, than the Clerk's, and the episodes have richer associations of folktale. In the *Clerk's Tale* Chaucer keeps more strictly to his theme and, incidentally, to his sources. Of this apparent restriction to the letter there is an example when the Marquis of Saluzzo prepares to wed Griselde:

> Grisilde of this, God woot, ful innocent,
> That for hire shapen was al this array,
> To fecchen water at a welle is went,
> And cometh hoom as soone as ever she may;
> For wel she hadde herd seyd that thilke day
> The markys sholde wedde; and if she myghte,
> She wolde fayn han seyn som of that sighte.[1]

I see no hint in these lines of the interesting possibilities suggested by Professor Manly, who proposed that the same well in the primitive version was an entrance to the other world, a Well at the World's End. If the carrying of water bears significance beyond Griselde's peasant life, it has biblical associations of a kind certainly present elsewhere:

> But hye God somtyme sende kan
> His grace into a litel oxes stalle . . .

> The markys cam, and gan hire for to calle;
> And she set doun hir water pot anon,
> Biside the thresshfold, in an oxes stalle . . .[2]

So far as we know, Chaucer could not have found a stable either in his Petrarch or in *Le Livre Griseldis*.

The tale of Griselde contains very few verses which have power to fix themselves in the memory; the narrative is never to that extent at high tension. Yet it accumulates an emotion which is very impressive indeed. One can test this, to one's own satis-

---

[1] E 274–80
[2] E 206–7: 289–91
For the *oxes stalle*, the French text printed by Professor Severs has only *un petit hoste et mainnaige*, and the Latin *pauperum tuguria* (*Sources and Analogues* pp. 302–3).

faction, by marking certain lines that stand out as they come in the story, and then reading those lines alone some time later. Re-read in this way, they do not give the quality of the whole poem, they do not recall the development to a climax; they refuse to be samples. We have often been told that it is not possible, or at least not fair, to quote from Chaucer. But it is certainly possible, and more than fair, to quote from the *Tale of the Man of Law*. What we recollect of it is not the pattern, still less the details, of the story; but a range of the highest points of the verse. Everyone who has read this tale with some attention to its poetry will have been held by the lines which describe, through remembered glimpses of a condemned man in the crowd, the helplessness of Constance at her trial. They have just a hint of that contrary stanza of the *Troilus* in which he who was to die is suddenly rescued, and finds himself in the arms of his lady.

> Have ye nat seyn somtyme a pale face
> Among a prees, of hym that hath be lad
> Toward his deeth, wher as hym gat no grace
> And swich a colour in his face hath had
> Men myghte knowe his face that was bistad
> Amonges alle the faces in that route?
> So stant Custance, and looketh hire aboute.[1]

The repetition of a single word conveys appearance and re-appearance of the pallor of the man as he is led to execution. It is a remarkable expression of terror, and probably the most fitting and frequent quotation from Chaucer in our period of World War. But Chaucer was not greatly interested in the expression of terror, or in any intensity which might upset the equilibrium of the intelligence. For once he would show that he could produce a good line in melodrama, even a sequence and a 'cut' that would satisfy a twentieth-century amateur of the cinema. And in the whole tale Chaucer was doing, on a higher level, what a good film director tries to do with commonplace material; for, however fine the remote origins of the story may be, Trivet's telling is undistinguished; and Chaucer added to it some of his best exhibition verses. Such are (a flower of evil) the close of the speech of the *sowdanesse*, and the farewell of Constance to her father—above all, her address to the Cross.

---

[1] B 645–51: compare *Troilus and Criseyde* III 1240–6

'O cleere, o welful auter, hooly croys,
Red of the Lambes blood ful of pitee,
That wessh the world fro the olde iniquitee,
Me fro the feend and fro his clawes kepe,
That day that I shal drenchen in the depe.

Victorious tree, proteccioun of trewe,
That oonly worthy were for to bere
The Kyng of Hevene with his woundes newe,
The white Lamb, that hurt was with the spere,
Flemere of feendes out of hym and here
On which thy lymes feithfully extenden,
Me kepe, and yif me myght my lyf t'amenden.'[1]

This is the clarity of the medieval religious vision; the Chaucerian *cleere* is hardly translatable in modern English. This is a fulfilment of the promise of his version of Guillaume de Deguilleville praising the Virgin. At the ninth line the verse is incandescent. Constance echoes the liturgy; and throughout the story—even through its crudities of plot—she in some way represents the Church Militant.[2] The tale is told with an excess of rhetorical skill that might be expected from a lawyer who has been raised to the poetic stage of a Chaucerian pilgrimage: otherwise it no more appears to fit its narrator than the story of Appius and Virginia appears to fit the Physician.[3]

Both the *Clerk's Tale* and the *Tale of the Man of Law* may be seen, I think, as a medieval prognostic of Shakespeare's later plays. If we allow for the fact that Shakespeare was writing for the theatre, composing verse which had to make its effect in action, it is not so very difficult to associate Constance and Imogen, to compare the closing scenes of *Pericles* and the *Winter's Tale* with the reconciliation of Walter and Griselde, or the recognition

---

[1] B 451-62
*Cleere* shining, pure (Latin *clarus*)     *Welful auter* blessed altar
*Flemere of feendes* . . . banishing evil from man or woman over whom, by faith, through the sign of the cross, thy limbs are spread . . .
[2] Edith Rickert proposed (*Chaucer's World*, p. 325) that the *Man of Law's Tale* was written for the exiled princess Constance, daughter of Don Pedro of the *Monk's Tale* (B 3565ff.), the pious 'Queen of Castile' who in 1371 landed at Plymouth as the bride of John of Gaunt. Her character and fortunes could certainly have been suggestive to Chaucer: as an actual figure may be to a painter of Apocalypse. R. M. Smith, in *Journal of English and Germanic Philology* October 1948, thinks that he deliberately covered his tracks.
[3] Paul F. Beichner, *Speculum* January 1948, observes in B 204-31 a knowledge of canon law: but a poet wishing to dramatize a character can draw on more than information.

of Maurice. That which was lost, we say at the end, is now found: and I do not know another writer who has given so much of the joy of the finding. Chaucer set it down; Shakespeare orchestrated it.

I am not certain that our author intended the *Shipman's Tale* to follow the *Tale of the Man of Law*; and it is usually supposed that he changed his mind about the assignment of the story itself, which seems to have been written at first for the Wife of Bath. In our text, we have the Shipman comically imitating a woman's voice:

> The sely housbonde, algate he moot paye,
> He moot us clothe, and he moot us arraye,
> Al for his owene worshipe richely,
> In which array we dauncen jolily.
> And if that he noght may, par aventure,
> Or ellis list no swich dispence endure,
> But thynketh it is wasted and ylost,
> Thanne moot another payen for oure cost,
> Or lene us gold, and that is perilous.[1]

The sequence here begun now offers a *fabliau*, a miracle of Our Lady, a parody, a 'little thing in prose', a verse compendium, and a sophisticated fable. As I have already suggested, the group was probably devised to exhibit the variety of the forms themselves, and to mask what we expect them to lay bare: the hearts of the narrators. I do not believe that the tale told by the Prioress is to be taken as so much material for the analyst of Madame Eglentyne; and even if the Host is supposed to forget his manners to the extent of giving the Nun's Priest a brisk dig in the ribs,[2] one of the many qualities of that masterpiece the *Nun's Priest's Tale* is that it leaves us beautifully and finally and even Socratically persuaded that we cannot entirely know the Nun's Priest. As for the poet himself, there are two most effective methods of disguise at a fancy-dress ball, and Chaucer for this very different occasion has tried both of them. One is to wear as little as possible, and the other is to put on layers of stuff to the limit of endurance.

[1] B 1201–9
*Algate* in any event
[2] Manly suggested that Chaucer cancelled the epilogue to the *Nun's Priest's Tale* when he had used similar material for the Host's words to the Monk. I hope that Manly was right.

Of the remaining *Canterbury Tales*, three are about duped husbands and faithless wives; and of these the *Merchant's Tale* is worth more than the other two put together. The Manciple's digressions, his ironical apologies to the ladies, are amusing; his tale is perfunctory paraphrase of Ovid. But the Shipman's is a successful trifle, no more and no less appropriate to his *joly body* than to half a dozen others who have sent a conscience as luggage in advance to Canterbury. The folktale of the Lover's Gift Regained survives in anecdote to our own day, and in medieval times there were two Italian versions, among a few others which I have seen. In Boccaccio a merchant's wife, in Sercambi a banker's, each demands a sum of florins from a German soldier, who borrows the money from the husband and repays it to the wife, stating what he is doing in the presence of a witness. Boccaccio is terser than Sercambi, but both tell the story briefly to emphasize the neatness of the plot. Of that, Chaucer's audience was no doubt already aware; for the life of his verse dialogue, of his characterization, could amuse even those who found the plot a stale joke. In Sercambi and Boccaccio the wife exhibits Simple Cupidity and is simply outwitted: the Wife of St. Denis is not so simple and, within the frame of the story, is confirmed in her wickedness. She is a vain, feline coquette— hardly comparable with the Wife of Bath, but reminiscent of the wife of the jealous husband ridiculed by Friend in the *Romance of the Rose*. They are all out of the medieval game of anti-feminism, three marionettes and embellished scarecrows, given more or less life and size and reality according to the inclination of the writer. In the same way, Dan John is out of medieval anti-clericalism.

The *Canterbury Tales* have, among other comedies, the comedy of the Provocative Episode, which leaves us to imagine a victim reacting according to his nature. Only those who feel, or admit, attack will reply; such are the Reeve and the Summoner; from whom we do not expect the beautiful delaying tactics of the Clerk in answer to the Wife of Bath. The *Shipman's Tale* would be less entertaining if the Monk and the Merchant were excused from attendance, and we are to assume that above the sound of medieval traffic Hubert the limiter can hear the Wife of Bath, and the Squire can hear the Merchant. The Friar has no wish to fall out with any wife, even the Wife of Bath. The Knight's son is too well-bred a fish to bite.

When Madame Eglentyne tells her tale she comes to speak for the religious consciousness of the folk. She becomes as anonymous as her story, which expresses cruelty, and also tenderness and adoration honouring the Mother and Child. Now the fourteenth century was a period of astonishing spiritual vitality, in mysticism the classical moment of Christendom. Richard Rolle and Walter Hilton and Lady Julian of Norwich and the author of the *Cloud of Unknowing* in England, John Tauler and the Friends of God, Gerard Groote and Blessed Henry Suso and John Ruysbroeck *doctor ecstaticus*, and St. Brigid of Sweden and St. Catherine of Siena abroad, are all to be set against the Pardoner and his kind; and St. Vincent Ferrer, the great Dominican preacher, converted Jews instead of killing them. But the *Prioress's Tale* is not a presentation of exceptional religious consciousness; it is an exceptional presentation of the mind of the people.

The story was used as a pulpit *exemplum*, as a popular miracle of the Virgin. And though he apparently followed a more detailed narrative, Chaucer might have heard it at a Childermas service, *ex ore infantium*, from a boy bishop. In the folksong *Little Sir William* something of the kind can be heard from the modern concert platform today. And there is a parallel between the treatment that might be given to a folksong by a very distinguished composer, and Chaucer's handling of a popular story. He respected the folk imagination; he purified it; he expressed it as it had never been expressed before. At the same time, he did not change the 'wrong notes', even for a lady who was anxious to be correct. The traditional rumour of Jewish murders of Christian children is unjust; but it is there, and much older than stories of the miraculous power of Our Lady. One disapproves of it. One also disapproves of the alteration of a musical mode. The *Prioress's Tale* has its own melody, and to listen to a recital in something like the authentic pronunciation is an unforgettable experience.[1] The poetry is gentle and strong,

[1] It is a pity that the B.B.C. and the recording companies do not give more frequent opportunities of hearing Chaucer well read. At the time of writing, the British Council has just sponsored the issue of records of which three sides will play a modernization of Chaucer, and the fourth side an honest attempt at Chaucer himself. It is not merely that the proportions are wrong: the recording of translations of Chaucer is quite unnecessary. And it is one of the eccentricities of the B.B.C. to broadcast versions in modern English of a major English poet on a wavelength that rises to French and German poetry in the original.

painful and healing; it balances on a knife-edge the gracious image of the Maiden and Mother.

> This litel child, as he cam to and fro,
> Ful murily wolde he synge and crie
> *O Alma Redemptoris* evermo.
> The swetnesse hath his herte perced so
> Of Cristes mooder, that to hire to preye
> He kan nat stynte of syngyng by the weye.[1]

It can even bear a suggestion of jugglery without ceasing to be miraculous:

> This abbot, which that was an hooly man,
> As monkes been, or elles oghte be,
> This yonge child to conjure he bigan,
> And seyde, 'O deere child, I halse thee,
> In vertu of the hooly Trinitee,
> Tel me what is thy cause for to synge,
> Sith that thy throte is kut, to my semynge?'

> 'My throte is kut unto my nekke boon,'
> Seyde this child, 'and, as by wey of kynde,
> I sholde have dyed, ye, longe tyme agon.
> But Jesu Crist, as ye in bookes fynde,
> Wol that his glorie laste and be in mynde,
> And for the worship of his Mooder deere
> Yet may I synge *O Alma* loude and cleere.

> 'This welle of mercy, Cristes mooder sweete,
> I loved alwey, as after my konnynge;
> And whan that I my lyf sholde forlete,
> To me she cam, and bad me for to synge
> This anthem verraily in my deyynge,
> As ye han herd; and whan that I hadde songe,
> Me thoughte she leyde a greyn upon my tonge.

> 'Wherfore I synge, and synge moot certeyn,
> In honour of that blisful Mayden free,
> Til fro my tonge of-taken is the greyn;

[1] B 1742-7

Al - - - - - - - - ma__ Red-emp-
-tó - ris__ Má - ter quae per - vi - a__ caé - li por -
-ta má - - nes Et stel - la má - ris,
su - cúr - re ca - dén - ti súr - ge -re qui cú - rat__
pó -pu - lo: Tu__ quae ge - nu - í - sti, na - tu -
- ra mi - rán - - te, tu - um san - ctum Ge - ni - to - rem:
Vir - go__ pri - - us ac po - sté - ri - us,
Ga - bri - é - lis ab__ ó - re__ sú - mens íl -
- lud__ A - ve, pec - ca - tó - rum mi - se - ré - re.

And after that thus seyde she to me:
"My litel child, now wol I fecche thee,
Whan that the greyn is fro thy tonge ytake;
Be nat agast, I wol thee nat forsake".'

This hooly monk, this abbot, hym meene I,
His tonge out caughte, and took awey the greyn,
And he yaf up the goost ful softely.
And whan this abbot hadde this wonder seyn,
His salte teeris trikled doun as reyn . . .[1]

This has a wonderful effect in sobering the company; until
the Host turns with resolute heartiness upon Chaucer, whose
thoughts are elsewhere. (*He semeth elvish by his countenaunce*.)
And Chaucer gives him what he 'asks for': a parody of what
might have been the Host's favourite reading matter—if he read
at all. So the poet prepares himself to be one of the party, as
if he remembered that all the world, and not part of it, is a stage.

*Sir Thopas*, that miniature *Don Quixote*,[2] ridicules romances
popular among middle-class folk, the 'bestsellers' of the day, of
which Chaucer may have seen a score in some miscellany. The
originals are forgotten except by those interested in the history
of literature, but *Sir Thopas* is still entertaining. Yet to enjoy
the whole of this burlesque of bourgeois knight-errantry requires
a detailed study, by those who think it worth the trouble; and
anyone who writes even briefly upon its *drasty ryming* must
acknowledge the excellent essay by Mrs. Loomis.[3]

According to Francesco Barberino the topaz was worn by
young girls as a charm against luxury; and in fact the chaste
Flemish[4] knight himself was, in the words that Watriquet de
Couvin used in praise of his noble lord, *la topase des haus hommes*.
Like that knight of minstrelsy, *Sir Gy*, he came of *fer countree*, a
Hero Auntrous who looked, at moments, like a woman, a child,
a dwarf (in *Sir Libeux*) and a tradesman; and yet was of irresistible
fascination:

---

[1] B 1832–64
*Halse* implore        *By wey of kynde* in the natural course        *Forlete* give up
[2] Bishop Hurd (1765) described Thopas as 'Don Quixote in little'.
[3] LAURA HIBBARD LOOMIS, 'Sir Thopas', *Sources and Analogues* pp. 486–559
[4] It seems unlikely that Chaucer's 'primary object' was, as Manly suggested, 'to
produce a satire of the countrymen of Sir Thopas', though the bourgeois knights of
Flanders were not respected by the aristocracy of England and France.

> Ful many a mayde, bright in bour,
> They moorne for hym paramour,
> Whan hem were bet to slepe . . .[1]

After a hard ride he falls asleep, dreams of the Unseen, and loves the Unknown. It is, however, necessary to fight a giant called *Sir Elephant*[2]—though the combat may be postponed. But, in the course of some preliminary matter, Chaucer is interrupted, and the *bataille* is never reached. We have only the *chivalry*.

The reader who cannot be persuaded to examine the romances themselves—*Sir Guy of Warwick*, *Libeaus Desconus*, *Thomas of Erceldoune* and the rest—may look with amusement through the choice quotations of Mrs. Loomis; who will also inform him that *Sir Thopas* is in a line of English burlesque which begins with the thirteenth-century *Land of Cockaygne*. One might suggest that the line includes Edward Lear, who arrived before his time in the following verses:

> Ther spryngen herbes grete and smale,
> The lycorys and the cetewale,
> And many a clowe-gylofre;
> And notemuge to putte in ale,
> Wheither it be moyste or stale,
> Or for to leye in cofre.

> The briddes synge, it is no nay,
> The sparhauk and the papynjay,
> That joye it was to heere;
> The thrustelcok made eek her lay,
> The wodedowve upon the spray
> She sang ful loude and cleere.[3]

In the Lear nonsense of this, Chaucer has not only caught the rhythm of, say, *Sir Beves of Hamtoun*; he has improved upon it; as Lear, at his best, could improve upon the rhythms of his day. I give the quotation for another reason; for in it, Chaucer is parodying Guillaume de Lorris perhaps, Geoffrey Chaucer certainly.[4]

---

[1] B 1932-4
*Paramour* with the passionate devotion of the romances
[2] 'Into the one word *Olifaunt*, Chaucer condensed the usual prolix descriptions in the romances'—Mrs. Loomis, *op. cit.*, p. 530n.
[3] B 1950-61
[4] Compare *Romaunt of the Rose* 1359ff., and similar lists, such as *Parliament of Birds* 337ff.; prologue to the *Legend of Good Women* 139-40 B(F) and *Troilus* II 920 (*that joye it was to heere; sang ful loude*); *Clerk's Tale* E 817, 1139 (*it is no nay*). The same catalogue of spices and birds could be found in the romance *King Alisaunder*: it ridicules a worn convention rather than any one author.

Hymself drank water of the well,
As dide the knyght sire Percyvell . . .[1]

So Sir Thopas. But for the metre, one might add *as did the peples in the former age*.[2]

Yet anyone who knows the distinction and ease of Chaucer's habitual mode of address will be most struck by the exquisite imperatives of the tale. They appear too good to be true, but are in fact true minstrelsy:

Yet listeth, lordes, to my tale
Murier than the nightyngale
*Sir Thopas*

Lordinges, herkneth to me tale
Is merier than the nightingale
*Beves of Hamtoun*

NOW holde youre mouth, *par charitee*
*Sir Thopas*

Litheth, and lesteneth and holdeth your tonge.[3]
*Gamelyn*

And one may imagine that the Host, who does not appreciate the joke, has digested the Auchinleck *Guy of Warwick* so well as to use its phrasing unconsciously.[4] He is a little over-anxious to proclaim his disapproval of such things.

'Namoore of this, for Goddes dignitee,'
Quod oure Hooste, 'for thou makest me
So wery of thy verray lewednesse
That, also wisly God my soule blesse,
Myne eres aken of thy drasty speche.
Now swich a rym the devel I biteche!
This may wel be rym dogerel,' quod he.
'Why so?' quod I, 'why wiltow lette me
Moore of my tale than another man,
Syn that it is the beste rym I kan?'
'By God,' quod he, 'for pleynly, at a word,
Thy drasty rymyng is nat worth a toord!
Thou doost noght elles but despendest tyme.

[1] B 2105–6
[2] *Former Age* 2, 8
[3] B 2023–4; 2081
The quotations from the romances are given in *Sources and Analogues* pp. 498, 515.
[4] As Mrs. Loomis suggests in *Essays and Studies in Honour of Carleton Brown* (New York, 1940).

Sire, at o word, thou shalt no lenger ryme.
Lat see wher thou kanst tellen aught in geeste,
Or telle in prose somwhat, at the leeste,
In which ther be som murthe or som doctryne.'
'Gladly,' quod I, 'by Goddes sweete pyne!
I wol yow telle a litel thyng in prose
That oghte like yow, as I suppose—
Or elles, certes, ye been too daungerous.
It is a moral tale vertuous . . .'[1]

The *Tale of Melibeus* can be taken as a huge joke—but only by the modern reader who skips it; and no one, at a first reading of the *Canterbury Tales*, will do more. The piece is dated. Yet it was a *tour de force* on the part of Albertano de Brescia, and a considerable labour of translation on the part of Chaucer. It was a composition which Chaucer regarded with a certain degree of seriousness.

The tale may be plausibly read as—in the words of Pandarus— something *bitwixen game and ernest*. Prudence herself has to be heard to be believed, and is then immediately doubted. When she is beaten, and her daughter receives five wounds, she herself remains unmoved, and calmly applies to the sorrowful father Melibeus a sentence of Ovid about bereaved mothers. She is even capable of answering attacks of the opposite sex with cool reason and a gently aphoristic spray.

Whanne dame Prudence, ful debonairly and with greet pacience, hadde herd al that hir housbonde liked for to seye, thanne axed she of hym licence for to speke, and seyde in this wise: 'My lord,' quod she, '. . . where as ye seyn that alle wommen been wikke; save youre grace, certes ye despisen alle wommen in this wyse, and "he that al despiseth, al displeseth," as seith the book. And Senec saith . . . And though that Salomon seith that he ne foond nevere womman good, it folweth nat therfore that alle wommen ben wikke. For though that he ne foond no good womman, certes, many another man hath founden many a womman ful good and trewe. Or elles, per aventure, the entente of Salomon was this, that, as in sovereyn bounte, he foond no womman; this is to seyn, that ther is no wight that hath sovereyn bountee save God allone . . . For ther nys no

[1] B 2109-30
*Lewednesse* ignorance    *Drasty* filthy    *Swich a rym* . . . to hell with such rhyming
*Daungerous* hard to please

creature so good that hym ne wanteth somwhat of the perfeccioun of God, that is his makere . . .'[1]

The impossible perfection of her scholarly temper, her logic, is a delight, at least to the hen-pecked Harry Bailly: it is, we might suppose, fun. Possibly Chaucer added a word or two to emphasize his amusement—his enjoyment in carrying the personification of a single virtue as far as it would go:

'. . . Now, sire, as to the point that Tullius clepeth "causes", which that is the last point, thou shalt understonde that the wrong that thou hast receyved hath certeine causes, whiche that Clerkes clepen *Oriens* and *Efficiens*, and *Causa longinqua* and *Causa propinqua*, this is to seyn, the fer cause and the ny cause. The fer cause is almyghty God, that is cause of alle thynges. The neer cause is thy thre enemys. The cause accidental was hate. The cause material been the fyve woundes of thy doghter. The cause formal is the manere of hir werkynge that broghten laddres and cloumben in at thy wyndowes. The cause final was for to sle thy doghter . . .'[2]

It is all, perhaps, a little more in earnest than the didacticism of Pandarus. And did not Mackail remind us that some jokes are too funny to excite laughter?

But I do not believe that this argument alone will sustain the reader for more than two pages. Only resolute determination, together with an interest in the habits of the medieval mind, will carry him through. And one can attain historical perspective by reflecting that most of the books which now tell us how to Live Successfully will be as dead in a few centuries as *Melibeus*. The piece was edifying; as it is still, if you can endure it; and edification was popular. Maxims and proverbs abounded, and here was an ingenious arrangement of them, with a leading message: take no revenge—forgive in order that you may be forgiven by the infinite mercy of God. There were other things to enjoy, also: a clever handling of the conventional satire against women; a wise man's answer to the young warmongers; Prudence's distrust of a majority vote; and the vindication of law. Much of

---

[1] B 2254ff.
[2] B 2583–91
It is recognized that the *Tale of Melibeus* is a close translation of *Le Livre de Melibee et de Dame Prudence*; and of the Latin terms here introduced only *efficiens* is found in any French MS.

this would be thought 'provocative' and most of it salutary, in the particular restlessness of late fourteenth-century politics. The French manuscript was chosen, in fact, with a publisher's flair. At this distance, once we have admitted the importance of the first cardinal virtue, *Melibeus* is a museum of medieval commonplace. Yet even a museum can remind us of ideas that have lived, and will live again, in fresh air. The middle ages believed that the world was the creation of a spirit; they sought beyond appearance for reality; they had the allegorical habit of mind. But the 'allegory' of the *Tale of Melibeus* does not deserve the name. It merely suggests that among those who could afford to buy medieval manuscripts, some were very easily persuaded that they were getting double value for their money. The opening of the tale is no more than excuse for the discussion of vengeance that follows.

A yong man called Melibeus, myghty and riche, bigat upon his wyf, that called was Prudence, a doghter which that called was Sophie.

Upon a day bifel that he for his desport is went into the feeldes hym to pleye. His wyf and eek his doghter hath he left inwith his hous, of which the dores weren faste yshette. Three of his olde foes han it espyed, and setten laddres to the walles of his hous, and by windowes been entred, and betten his wyf, and wounded his doghter with fyve mortal woundes in fyve sondry places—this is to seyn, in hir feet, in hire handes, in hir erys, in hir nose, and in hire mouth—and leften hire for deed, and wenten awey.[1]

*Fyve mortal woundes* promise some allegorical development, which is later attempted in a most imprudent speech of Prudence:

'. . . Now, sire, if men wolde axe me why that God suffred men to do yow this vileynye, certes, I kan nat wel answere, as for no soothfastnesse . . . Nathelees, by certeyne presumpciouns and conjectynges, I holde and bileeve that God, which that is ful of justice and of rightwisnesse, hath suffred this bityde by just cause resonable.

Thy name is Melibee, this is to seyn, "a man that drynketh hony". Thou hast ydronke so muchel hony of sweete temporeel richesses, and delices and honours of this world, that thou art dronken, and hast forgeten Jhesu Crist thy creatour . . . Thou hast doon synne agayn oure Lord Crist;

[1] B 2157–62

for certes, the three enemys of mankynde, that is to seyn, the flessh, the feend, and the world, thou hast suffred hem entre in to thyn herte wilfully by the windowes of thy body, and hast nat defended thyself suffisantly agayns hire assautes and hire temptaciouns, so that they han wounded thy soule in fyve places; this is to seyn, the deedly synnes that been entred into thy herte by thy fyve wittes . . .'[1]

What is this peace that the lady has counselled? If the opponents are the World, the Flesh and the Devil, it would seem advisable to side with the Church Militant. If we regard the 'allegory', the question is How far will prudence take a man in resisting evil? At one point the answer appears to be that Prudence would make a compact with Satan. But all is right in the end. Prudence would make peace with God, and then the World, the Flesh and the Devil will submit. Now if the allegory is anything more than an ill-advised digression, it brings out—as it thus rattles over the points and lurches into the right track— the acuteness of the problem: the distinction between mercy and laxity: or between the two senses of the 'toleration' with which Chaucer himself has been ambiguously credited. I believe that when he read *Le Livre de Melibee et de Dame Prudence* he saw that it was an artistic failure too instructive to miss. Unsteadily balancing the literal and the allegorical, it tottered beneath the weight of a genuine moral difficulty. Moderation, understanding and goodwill were urgently needed in practical affairs, and here was a pamphlet to advertise them. At the same time, to the intelligent man, it raised the question of persons who might suffer the defect of these qualities. 'Strive not', says the *ballade* of Truth; and Prudence agrees. But Prudence is blood-less, Chaucer a living heart.

It is one thing for the World, the Flesh and the Devil to sur-render to Melibeus—if they indeed do so—but for the Monk to submit to the Host is more complicated and amusing. The company has just been told that Fortune is an unreliable lady, but the middle ages were never tired of hearing that, or any, general advice. Now, as if to recall the ironically genial con-versation of the *Prologue*, the Monk has the honour of performing after the poet. But whereas Chaucer had succeeded in getting

[1] B 2595ff.
*Soothfastnesse* certainty

Dan Piers to talk, the ribaldry of our Host freezes the hunter back into *My lord the Monk*: and according to the illustrator of MS Gg 4.27 in the University Library of Cambridge, he is frozen into a gloriously sinister stage tragedian. Everything conspires against Dan Piers. The Host addresses him as Dan John, which was the name of the contemptible young puppy that the Shipman had drawn (the sort of scrawl one would expect from an ill-bred pirate)—and even the Prioress had raised an eyebrow:

> This abbot, which that was an hooly man,
> As monkes been, or elles oghte be . . .

Yet after all this provocation the Monk merely calls to mind his sermon-notes, and tells a series of *exempla* like the anecdotes with which Reason in Jean de Meun tried to persuade the Lover that life is not a bed of roses, or like the *De Casibus Virorum et Feminarum* of Boccaccio. There were points about Queen Zenobia, and even Nero, which Dan Piers could have found attractive; if *hunters ben nat hooly men*, here at least was an admirable huntress, and a male who dressed supremely well. But on the whole he did penance, and with a very good attempt at dignity. The Pardoner was a far more successful preacher; the Monk was certainly a better man.

A modern reader also may regard the tale as minor penance, and the immediate reward will be an English version of Ugolino. Perhaps Chaucer thought in the same way: certainly most of his verse synopses were so much practice in a stanza which he used elsewhere only for half a dozen short poems. One could assume a dramatic purpose behind the deadness, and a suggestion (from the Monk) that only an ignoramus would make a song about a stock example. But the Monk did what was expected of him in the way of rhetorical emphasis, and I think he brought the series to an adequate, even beautiful, close. The Knight then blew off what was meant to be an interruption in the name of the whole company, but he was evidently sleepier than the Host. What happens is that the Knight gives a comic representation of Theseus arresting a duel, and of a fourth-rate criticism of a Third Programme failure:

> 'Hoo!' quod the Knyght, 'good sire, namoore of this! .
> That ye han seyd is right ynough, ywis,
> And muche moore; for litel hevynesse

Is right ynough to muche folk, I gesse.
I seye for me, it is a greet disese,
Wheras men han been in greet welthe and ese,
To heeren of hire sodeyn fal, allas!
And the contrarie is joye and greet solas,
As whan a man hath been in povre estaat,
And clymbeth up and wexeth fortunat,
And there abideth in prosperitee.
Swich thyng is gladsom, as it thynketh me,
And of swich thyng were goodly for to telle.'[1]

Or if we have read the French original, and find the end of the
Croesus story abrupt,[2] we may always suppose that Chaucer
was dramatizing the exhaustion of his Monk's patience, as we
may suppose he tried to dramatize the exhaustion of his own in
the legends of Good Women. Such an assumption, at any rate,
makes either series more tolerable reading. The joke is not then
that a fat monk tells a boring story and sends everyone to sleep,
but that the Monk has done his best with some partly impressive
and wholly improving material which might have convinced the
company, if only he himself had been capable of conviction.
Unfortunately he fails in the real thing as in the counterfeit, and
is just about as far from the one as from the other.

*De Hugelino* is poetic performance; with the exception of one
or two lines and one or two stanzas, the rest of the tale is poetic
exercise. The characteristic of its stanza is a point of emphasis
at the central couplet, which in the brilliant envoy to Bukton on
marriage Chaucer used effectively for the turn of an argument:

> My maister Bukton: whan of Crist our kyng
> Was axed what is trouth or sothfastnesse,
> He nat a word answerde to that axing—
> As who saith, 'No man is al trewe', I gesse.
> And therfore, though I highte to expresse
> The sorwe and wo that is in mariage,
> I dar not writen of it no wikkednesse,
> Lest I myself falle eft in swich dotage.

> I wol nat seyn how that yt is the cheyne
> Of Sathanas, on which he gnaweth evere;

---

[1] B 3957–69
My view could not of course be held of those manuscripts of the tale in which the
'modern instances' come last.

[2] Dean Spruill Fansler, in *Chaucer and the Roman de la Rose* p. 28, suggests that the
author was tired of *swich ensaumples*.

But I dar seyn, were he out of his peyne,
As by his wille he wolde be bounde nevere.
But thilke doted fool that eft hath levere
Ycheyned be than out of prison crepe,
God lete him never fro his wo dissevere,
Ne no man him bewayle, though he wepe!

But yet, lest thow do worse, take a wyf;
Bet ys to wedde than brenne in worse wise.
But thow shal have sorwe on thy flessh, thy lyf,
And ben thy wives thral, as seyn these wise;
And yf that hooly writ may nat suffyse,
Experience shal thee teche, so may happe,
That thee were lever to be take in Frise
Than eft to falle of weddynge in the trappe.

*Envoy*
This lytel writ, proverbes, or figure
I sende yow, take kepe of yt, I rede;
Unwys is he that kan no wele endure.
If thow be siker, put thee nat in drede.
The Wyf of Bathe I praye yow that ye rede
Of this matere that we have on honde.
God graunte yow your lyf frely to lede
In fredam; for ful hard is to be bonde.[1]

*Fortune*, which exploits the witty argumentative possibilities of the stanza with more elaboration and less wisdom, is certainly dead; *Lenvoy de Chaucer a Bukton* is still kicking. But the octave in Chaucer is more often a mould than a rhythmic pattern, and it seemed impossible for him to attain in this form, in English, the superb *sostenuto* from stanza to stanza which he achieved with the narrative rhyme royal. Dunbar perhaps had more success with it. Chaucer probably learnt from experience, or from Deschamps, that some additional means of sustaining rhythm was required, such as the refrain in the fine *ballade* to Rosemounde. *The Former Age*, like *Rosemounde*, links an assortment of images; but in spite of a vigorous line or two, it fails. The verse form remains a file of miscellaneous notes on *felix nimium prior etas*. The *ABC*[2] does very beautifully what it was designed to do: it presents in the order of the alphabet a discipline of meditation

---

[1] *Highte* promised     *Eft* again     *Hath levere* would rather
*Brenne* burn.     According to Froissart, capture *in Frise* (Friesland) meant death.
*Unwys is he that kan no wele endure* let well alone     *Siker* sure
[2] There is a sympathetic account of this poem in *A Lost Language* by SISTER MADELEVA, C.S.C. (New York: Sheed and Ward, 1951), pp. 11–17.

upon the Virgin Mary. The so-called *Compleynt of Venus* is a *curiositee* following the rhyme scheme and some of the matter of a poem by Oton de Granson.

Chaucer realized, I think, that Dante's *terza rima* was not one of the most rewarding patterns for his own language, and after an attempt he put it aside, as if awaiting a new approach five and six centuries later.[1] He would have been interested in Shelley's finest poem, and even in certain recent experiments. But in the Ugolino story he comes nearer than we at once notice to Dante's verse; and yet not too near. His octave is like seven lines of *terza rima* with an extra rhyme in the middle; it stands at a tactful distance. And to set Chaucer's brief version beside the terror and intensity of the episode in the *Inferno* is unfair. But there is a sublimity about Chaucer's compassion for suffering childhood, a quality composed through living with stone and glass and illuminated manuscript of the infant Christ.

> And on a day bifel that in that hour
> What that his mete wont was to be broght,
> The gayler shette the dores of the tour.
> He herde it wel; but he spake right noght,
> And in his herte anon ther fil a thoght
> That they for hunger wolde doon hym dyen.
> 'Allas!' quod he, 'allas, that I was wroght!'
> Therwith the teeris fillen from his eyen.

> His yonge sone, that three yeer was of age,
> Unto hym seyde, 'Fader, why do ye wepe?
> Whanne wol the gayler bryngen oure potage?
> Is ther no morsel breed that ye do kepe?
> I am so hungry that I may nat slepe.
> Now wolde God that I myghte slepen evere!
> Thanne sholde nat hunger in my wombe crepe;
> Ther is nothyng but breed that me were levere.'

> Thus day by day this child bigan to crye,
> Til in his fadres barme adoun it lay,
> And seyde, 'Farewel, fader, I moot dye!'
> And kiste his fader, and deyde the same day.
> And whan the woful fader deed it say,
> For wo his armes two he gan to byte,
> And seyde, 'Allas, Fortune, and weylaway!
> Thy false wheel my wo al may I wyte.'

---

[1] Wyatt also attempted it, more persistently, a little over a century after Chaucer: but not with triumphant success.

> His children wende that it for hunger was
> That he his armes gnow, and nat for wo,
> And seyde, 'Fader, do nat so, allas!
> But rather ete the flessh upon us two.
> Oure flessh thou yaf us, take oure flessh us fro,
> And ete ynough'—right thus they to hym seyde;
> And after that, withinne a day or two,
> They leyde hem in his lappe adoun and deyde.[1]

So the Monk, like the Prioress, is granted a moment of genuine religious emotion. In comparison, the *Nero* is passable narrative and the *De Rege Antiocho Illustri* turns to homiletic spellbinding.[2] Elsewhere, it appears more than once that the poet would have been happier with a seven-line verse; we mark a stanza filled out with eloquence.

> Who shal me yeven teeris to compleyne
> The deeth of gentillesse and of franchise,
> That al the world weelded in his demeyne,
> And yet hym thoughte it myghte nat suffise?
> So ful was his corage of heigh emprise.
> Allas! who shal me helpe to endite
> False Fortune, and poyson to despise,
> The whiche two of al this wo I wyte?[3]

Looking through the rest of the tale for poetry, I find phrases: like *Adam in the field of Damyssene*, or Hercules setting a pillar *at bothe the worldes endes.*

Sir John's story of the Cock and the Fox is in medieval tradition of bestiary and follows a portion of the 'epic' of Reynard; yet it is not simply a fable, and *daun Russel* is not Reynard.[4] It is the literary equivalent of a jig fugue, or of a *quodlibet.* And here Chaucer comes nearest to expressing in a single tale the variety and comedy of the whole Canterbury sequence.

The most important thing that Dryden missed in his lively, inaccurate adaptation was the *sweete preest.* At one point in his transcript the nun's confessor even turns Restoration gallant:

---

[1] B 3613–44
*Barme* lap       *Wyte* lay to your charge
  [2] I except the fine paraphrase of II *Maccabees* ix 8 and 10 in B 3774–7.
  [3] *De Alexandro* B 3853–60
*Wyte* blame
  [4] In spite of Dryden: *The Cock and the Fox: or, the Tale of the Nun's Priest* 48off.

Silence in times of Suff'ring is the best,
'Tis dang'rous to disturb a Hornet's Nest.
In other Authors you may find enough,
But all they say of Dames is idle Stuff.
Legends of lying Wits together bound,
The Wife of *Bath* would throw 'em to the Ground:
These are the words of Chanticleer, not mine,
I honour Dames, and think their Sex divine.[1]

Chaucer, on the other hand, holds us with the voice, the versatility of tone, of the admirable father who can attempt anything from mimicry to morality and lyricism to mock-heroic, and prefer nothing to the *heighe blisse* of God. If Sir John is a preacher on holiday, telling *exempla* and letting the sermon look after itself, his gaiety is a gift of the divine wisdom.

And the verse, for Chaucer, is simply the clearest means of expressing his range of tone, a convenient stave for melodic speech. Dryden makes the couplet a smart vehicle for wit. Thus Chaucer is improved:

If, spurning up the Ground, he sprung a Corn,
The Tribute in his Bill to her was born.
But oh! what Joy it was to hear him sing
In Summer, when the Day began to spring,
Stretching his Neck, and warbling in his Throat,
*Solus cum Sola*, then was all his Note.
For in the Days of Yore, the Birds of Parts
Were bred to Speak, and Sing, and learn the Lib'ral Arts.[2]

Chaunticleer, in Restoration costume, is a pantomime actor with a throaty delivery, and a satirical eye for Man like Dryden's for Achitophel:

Thus numb'ring Times, and Seasons in his Breast,
His second crowing the third Hour confess'd.
Then turning, said to Partlet, See, my Dear,
How lavish Nature has adorn'd the Year;
How the pale Primrose, and blue Violet spring,
And Birds essay their Throats disus'd to sing:
All these are ours; and I with pleasure see
Man strutting on two Legs, and aping me!
An unfledg'd Creature, of a lumpish frame,
Indew'd with fewer Particles of Flame:

[1] Dryden, *op. cit.*, 565–72
[2] 85–92

Our Dame sits couring o'er the Kitchen-fire,
I draw fresh Air, and Nature's Works admire:
And ev'n this Day, in more delight abound,
Than, since I was an Egg, I ever found.[1]

This is good Dryden, generously expanded from four lines of the original. For an example, in a sentence, of what Chaucer can do, we must go back a little; but not very far.

Whan that the month in which the world bigan,
That highte March, whan God first maked man,
Was compleet, and passed were also,
Syn March bigan, thritty dayes and two,
Bifel that Chauntecleer in al his pryde,
His sevene wyves walkynge by his syde,
Caste up his eyen to the brighte sonne,
That in the signe of Taurus hadde yronne
Twenty degrees and oon, and somwhat moore,
And knew by kynde, and by noon oother loore,
That it was pryme; and crew with blisful stevene.[2]

Into a single period, and without any suggestion of forcing, he has combined the Creation, Chaunticleer the born Astronomer Royal, the Royal Lover and Organ Voice, proud Chaunticleer seven times sinful, and the sound of Chaunticleer the golden spangled Hamburg. And in the whole tale there is the same easy mastery of the most diverse ideas: the sobriety of the respectable poor—the burlesque of time and pomp—the elegant fowls as strutting humans, complacently informed—the scholarly husband —O Venus!—the announcement of a moral, or at least a soveregn notabilitee (some dignified platitude from Geoffrey de Vinsauf). From a certain position, a cock may look as funny as a man with a little learning; a revolt of murderous peasants is not entirely dissimilar from an uproar in an English farmyard; which in turn may suggest that the end of the world has come. If for a moment you can look at these things from above, they all (even Talbot and Gerland and Malkin with a distaff in her hand) matter; and none of them matters, in isolation, at all; none is self-sufficient. And in Chaucer you can look, and for more than a moment. There is plenty of time, without violence or distraction of language, during which the mind is gently raised,

[1] 453–66
[2] B 4377–87
*Stevene* voice

and surrounded by a grace of comedy. 'This is easy', we say,
'—easy mastery; the verse, for Chaucer, is simply—' But
simplification is the hardest thing in the world: the last reward
of any discipline, including poetics. How many major poets
achieve it?

The Nun's Priest has amused us by re-arranging many modes
of being, action, and expression, and without confounding them;
without sentimentality or cynicism. This may be observed by
comparison with the late George Orwell's *Animal Farm*. The
Nun's Priest's fable is a masterpiece of mock-heroic verse, written
out of medieval learning, the sermon-books, and oral tradition.
It is even a very intelligent demonstration, six centuries in
advance, of how far surrealism can go without incoherence.
And yet Mr. Orwell, having to rely upon Swift, children's fairy-
tales, and the newspapers, wrote a very neat little piece.

# XI

*Alle thing that is and hath beynge is oon, and thilke same oon is good . . .*
*Alle thing that fayleth to ben good, it stinteth for to be . . . Yif thou seest*
*a wyght that be transformed into vices, thow ne mayst nat wene that he*
*be a man. For if he be ardaunt in avaryce . . . thou shalt seyn that he is*
*lik to the wolf.*

*Boece IV pr. 3*


*So it happeth oft, they that were more worthy to bee hanged damneth*
*them that be lesse worthy; as a clerk telleth of Socrates the philosopher.*
*Saith he, 'Upon a day a man asked of him why he laughed. And he saide,*
*For I see great theeves leaden a little theefe to hanging'.*

RICHARD WIMBLEDON, preaching at Paul's Cross, 1388

# EVIL AND THE PHYSICIAN

I MUST REMIND THE READER THAT I DO NOT KNOW ANY DECISIVE argument for accepting the order of Skeat's edition of the *Canterbury Tales*, and that the Physician and Pardoner come before the Shipman in nearly all surviving manuscripts. At the same time there is no agreed opinion about the reliance to be placed upon any of them. So this is a convenient moment, when the Wife of Bath may very well insist on a hearing, to point out that according to Dr. Lawrence preparations have already been made for her performance. There is one kind of wedding breakfast in the Host's words after *Melibeus*, and another in the *Nun's Priest's Tale*; and the realities of marriage are on the way.[1] This again assumes a certain order, which is the order I am assuming myself. And without necessarily contradicting Dr. Lawrence, we can perceive another pattern. I have sometimes thought that the *Tale of the Man of Law* and the groups begun by the Shipman and the Physician form a sequence in which Chaucer conceived a range of possibilities of ironic relationship between tale and teller; a sequence culminating in a clash between the Pardoner and his story, and a perilous cadence, the kiss of Pardoner and Host. Whether or not this is so, our present fragment has sufficient interest in itself. What we have now is a doctor of the body followed by a more remarkable doctor of the soul.

The *Physician's Tale* is a curtain-raiser, possibly a reminder that we are reading a compilation of pieces written at different periods. But if Chaucer picked up an old draft, he contrived with it a new surprise. He produced something unexpectedly orthodox through the mask of one whose study was but little on the Bible. The pilgrims no doubt expected the Pardoner to

---

[1] W. W. LAWRENCE, *Chaucer and the Canterbury Tales* pp. 121ff., 136. On this particular view of the *Nun's Priest's Tale* Dr. Lawrence refers to articles which could be taken to supplement my last few pages.

essay morality; they were not prepared for the Physician to be moral too.

At one point the voice of Chaucer is unmistakably heard admonishing those who have in charge the education of young gentlewomen: and there is even a very distant rumour of the tone of the witty letter to Bukton:

> And ye maistresses, in youre olde lyf,
> That lordes doghtres han in governaunce,
> Ne taketh of my wordes no displesaunce.
> Thenketh that ye been set in governynges
> Of lordes doghtres, oonly for two thynges:
> Outher for ye han kept youre honestee,
> Or elles ye han falle in freletee,
> And knowen wel ynough the olde daunce,
> And han forsaken fully swich meschaunce
> For evermo; therfore, for Cristes sake,
> To teche hem vertu looke that ye ne slake . . .
> And taketh kep of that that I shal seyn:
> Of alle tresons sovereyn pestilence
> Is whan a wight bitrayseth innocence.[1]

This shrewd aside is the best thing in the tale. As for the teller: John of Salisbury spoke of physicians who 'attribute too much to Nature, cast aside the Author of Nature';[2] and what was surprising was not that the Physician should imagine Nature's pride in her production of the beautiful and virtuous Virginia, but that he should carefully add a couplet in memory of the Creator:

> 'For He that is the formere principal
> Hath maked me his vicaire general.'[3]

And when the maiden is so beautifully and improvingly characterized in terms reminiscent of the Blessed Virgin in St. Ambrose of Milan, the Host might well praise the performer for being *lyk a prelat*.

Jean de Meun told the story simply as an illustration of the corruption of justice, and the only thing I find in Chaucer's version of the tale that obviously fits the reputation of a physician is the professionally brisk manner of piling the corpses. This

---

[1] C 72ff.
*Swich meschaunce* such wickedness
[2] *Policraticus* II 29, quoted by W. C. Curry
[3] C 19-20
*Formere principal* principal Author of Forms. Nature is speaking.

would have been appreciated at least by the medieval preacher John of Mirfield, who gave as one of the most coveted medical qualifications of his time 'boldness in killing'.[1] And from this point of view the justice of the *Physician's Tale* is surgical rather than poetic.

The *Pardoner's Tale* has been reviewed, advertised and modernized at intervals; it has been adapted for the theatre and for broadcasting; sound morals have been quoted from it; and it has more than once been called the greatest short story in existence. Not even the Pardoner could have improved upon such publicity. And the Pardoner's idea of heaven is something like the American system of wireless telegraphy, only bigger: the negation of the end of the medieval contemplative life. This, above all, the hermit fled from.

We are to reckon with the most vigorous son of False-Seeming; and a paradox expressed in Jean de Meun seems to have fascinated Chaucer, and suggested the chief ironic point of his prologue and tale. It is not simply that, as the Venerable Bede observed, a talent for story-telling has made more effective preachers than has literacy. The point is here:

> For ofte good predicacioun
> Cometh of evel entencioun
> > *Romaunt of the Rose*

> For certes, many a predicacioun
> Comth ofte tyme of yvel entencioun . . .[2]
> > *Pardoner's prologue*

Chaucer develops a hint, a contradiction, from Jean de Meun into a great study in the problem of evil. So William Blake perceived, when he wrote of the quæstor: 'This man is sent in every age for a rod and a scourge, and for a blight, for a trial of men, to divide the classes of men; he is in the most holy sanctuary, and has also his great use'. Perhaps there is more than was intended in the second part of this sentence; in any event, it is very well said. There is a terrible irony of circumstance in the Pardoner's words:

---

[1] G. R. OWST, *Literature and Pulpit in Medieval England*, pp. 350–1
[2] *Romaunt* 5763–4; *Pardoner's prologue* C 407–8
*Predicacioun* sermon

229

EVIL AND THE PHYSICIAN

But though myself be gilty in that synne,
Yet kan I maken oother folk to twynne
From avarice, and soore to repente.
But that is nat my principal entente.[1]

And it was Blake also who recommended the young reader to study the character of the Wife of Bath: 'it is useful as a scarecrow'. What Blake was getting at, what is in Chaucer, is what a contemporary of Chaucer's has said, and a contemporary of ours has repeated:

Sin is Behovely, but
All shall be well, and
All manner of thing shall be well.[2]

That is where the medieval poet and the medieval visionary meet. And it is the ground upon which we can reach them both.

The *gentils* ask for morality: they shall have it, in a first-class sermon with a masterly *exemplum*, condemning the Pardoner's own vices. But, before and after, the 'Age's Knave' will reveal himself, as the Wife of Bath is to reveal herself, without reserve and without—or almost without—shame. The tavern of his story is there on the Canterbury road, and he drinks before he tells of the drinking of the rioters. The goat voice is strained to address the crowd, the neck outstretched. You come to recognize the trick of speech:

' "Goode men", I seye, "taak of my wordes keep . . .
. . . Taak kep eek what I telle . . .
Goode men and wommen, o thyng warne I yow:
If any wight be in this chirche now
That hath doon synne horrible, that he
Dar nat, for shame, of it yshryven be,
Or any womman, be she yong or old,
That hath ymaad hir housbonde cokewold,
Swich folk shal have no power ne no grace
To offren to my relikes in this place.

<hr>

[1] C 429–32
*Twynne* depart
[2] T. S. ELIOT, *Little Gidding* III
*Synne is behovabil, but al shal be wel & al shal be wel & al manner of thyng shal be wele.*
Julian of Norwich, *Revelations of Divine Love*, ed. GRACE WARRACK (London: Methuen, 1901, 1945) p. 56n, British Museum MS Sloane 2499 f. 18.

And whoso fyndeth hym out of swich blame,
He wol come up and offre in Goddes name,
And I assoille him by the auctoritee
Which that by bulle ygraunted was to me."
—By this gaude have I wonne, yeer by yeer,
An hundred mark sith I was pardoner.'[1]

He is dramatized, and his tale. He is himself a brilliant performer, himself a walking *exemplum*.[2] And Chaucer's critical
faculty was very sharp indeed when he gave to the Pardoner one
of the most hypnotic lines of poetry he ever wrote; for the Pardoner
can hypnotize his audience merely by speaking

Of olde stories longe tyme agoon.

In 1910, the distinguished French critic M. Émile Legouis
remarked in this performance a rare instance of indignation on
the part of Chaucer.[3]   Except the Pardoner's, we were to understand, the 'satirical' tales are those in which the poet is observing
someone else on the offensive: here he is on the offensive himself.
There is no perspective; an abstraction of hypocrisy fills the
frame.

'Thus spitte I out my venym under hewe
Of hoolynesse, to seme hooly and trewe. . . .'

But if we place these lines in their context—M. Legouis, I think,
did not—False-Seeming comes alive; the Pardoner has loosened
his tongue with liquor.

'I stonde lyk a clerk in my pulpet,
And whan the lewed peple is doun yset,
I preche so as ye han herd bifoore,
And telle an hundred false japes moore.
Thanne peyne I me to strecche forth the nekke,
And est and west upon the peple I bekke,
As dooth a dowve sittynge on a berne.
Myne handes and my tonge goon so yerne
That it is joye to see my bisynesse.
Of avarice and of swich cursednesse

---

[1] C 352, 360, 377–90
*Assoille* absolve        *Gaude* trick
[2] In *Sources and Analogues* pp. 411–4 Mrs. Dempster quotes a preacher's illustrative
anecdote exposing the very trick by which the Pardoner claims to have extorted an
income estimated at twenty times the annual salary of a chaplain.
[3] English readers may find the passage in ÉMILE LEGOUIS, *Geoffrey Chaucer*, translated
by L. Lailavoix (London: Dent, New York: Dutton, 1913) pp. 154–5.

Is al my prechyng, for to make hem free
To yeven hir pens, and namely unto me.
For myn entente is nat but for to wynne,
And nothyng for correccioun of synne.
I rekke nevere, whan that they been beryed,
Though that hir soules goon a-blakeberyed.
For certes, many a predicacioun
Comth ofte tyme of yvel entencioun;
Som for plesance of folk and flaterye,
To been avaunced by ypocrisye,
And som for veyne glorie, and som for hate.
For whan I dar noon oother weyes debate,
Thanne wol I stynge hym with my tonge smerte
In prechyng, so that he shal nat asterte
To been defamed falsly, if that he
Hath trespased to my bretheren or to me.
For though I telle noght his propre name,
Men shal wel knowe that it is the same,
By signes, and by othere circumstances.
Thus quyte I folk that doon us displesances;
Thus spitte I out my venym under hewe
Of hoolynesse, to seme hooly and trewe.'[1]

I have tried to interpret his view; and it seems to me that M. Legouis acutely stated a half-truth, which is not truth. For the treatment of the Pardoner is a test of *sincerity*, a distinction between serenity and indifference; and of indifference M. Legouis implied his disapproval. Chaucer, we know, did not scream at the smaller sins. Nor did he smile at the possibility of damnation.

Yet at a first reading the Pardoner's prologue appears a crude piece of soliloquizing, as if originally written as an exercise in the manner of Jean de Meun and later furbished for the *Canterbury Tales*. I do not mean that the convention is difficult to accept: one can easily allow the Pardoner to lay his cards on the table. But need he lay them down so often? Corny ale in the story is not so repetitive as it seems here. I believe that the prologue can only be defended against this stricture on the grounds that it was not meant to be judged from the manuscript or printed page. It was necessary to establish a certain chord in the mind of the listener, a chord that he could hear, now and again, all

---

[1] C 391–422
*Bekke* nod      *Yerne* eagerly      *Namely* especially      *Plesance* pleasing
*Asterte* escape

through the Pardoner's performance. So Chaucer kept deliberately close to Jean de Meun: repetition and emphasis were required—even something a little melodramatic. For we are to have his boldest experiment in a technique which interested him very much, which I can only call the technique of the modifying context. I mean by this the attempt to change or determine in a particular way the effect of a word or line, a passage or poem, by placing it in a certain relation. It is no longer, in this case, a matter of ironical play upon the term *worthy*, or such a line as *he was in chirche a noble ecclesiaste*; it is a question of exposing to the same treatment a great and good sermon, a great and good narrative poem; and anyone who has read *Troilus and Criseyde* with understanding will have his own theory of relativity from Chaucer. It is a stroke which could only be brought off by a comedian of genius, and a master of his art. For the *Pardoner's Tale* is not merely a sermon in an age of sermons: it is a sermon composed by a poet who was in a sense a dramatic poet. And the dramatic conflict is between, not two persons, but a person and a poem. What is to be decided, in the event, is whether the Pardoner can endure his own eloquence, or whether his own words will swallow him up; and if this is to be a dramatic conflict, we must believe, all the time, that the eloquence is given to this particular person, that this particular person is performing. Only a combination of brilliant mechanics and a sound nervous system in the Pardoner could make this probable. He must have the trained competence of a dentist who can effect a successful extraction, and forget his own carious teeth.

On the superb tale itself there is no need for interpretative commentary. I wish only to add one note to what can be found in the latest annotated editions at the time of writing; and it concerns the most impressive episode in the poem, an episode which will remain, however it is expounded, the most mysterious, macabre, in 'plain' Chaucer. The three rioters have set out in search of Death, who is addressed by the proudest of the three:

'Why artow al forwrapped save thy face?
Why lyvestow so longe in so greet age?'
This olde man gan looke in his visage,
And seyde thus, 'For I ne kan nat fynde
A man, though that I walked into Ynde,
Neither in citee ne in no village,

233

That wolde chaunge his youthe for myn age;
And therfore moot I han myn age stille,
As longe tyme as it is Goddes wille.
 Ne Deeth, allas! ne wol nat han my lyf.
Thus walke I, lyk a restelees kaityf;
And on the ground, which is my moodres gate,
I knokke with my staf, bothe erly and late,
And seye "Leeve mooder, leet me in!
Lo how I vanysshe, flessh, and blood, and skyn!
Allas! whan shul my bones been at reste?
Mooder, with yow wolde I chaunge my cheste
That in my chambre longe tyme hath be,
Ye for an heyre clowt to wrappe me!"
But yet to me she wol nat do that grace,
For which ful pale and welked is my face.
 But, sires, to yow it is no curteisye
To speken to an old man vileynye,
But he trespasse in word, or elles in dede.
In Hooly Writ ye may yourself wel rede:
"Agayns an old man, hoor upon his heed,
Ye sholde arise"; wherfore I yeve yow reed,
Ne dooth unto an oold man noon harm now,
Namoore than that ye wolde men did to yow
In age, if that ye so longe abyde.
And God be with yow, where ye go or ryde!
I moot go thider as I have to go.'
 'Nay olde cherl, by God, thou shalt nat so,'
Seyde this oother hasardour anon;
'Thou partest nat so lightly, by Seint John!
Thou spak right now of thilke traytour Deeth,
That in this contree alle oure freendes sleeth.
Have heer my trouthe, as thou art his espye,
Telle where he is, or thou shalt it abye,
By God, and by the hooly sacrement!
For soothly thou art oon of his assent
To sleen us yonge folk, thou false theef!'
 'Now, sires,' quod he, 'if that yow be so leef
To fynde Deeth, turne up this croked wey,
For in that grove I lafte hym, by my fey,
Under a tree, and there he wole abyde;
Noght for youre boost he wole him no thyng hyde.
See ye that ook? Right there ye shal hyme fynde.
God save yow, that boghte agayn mankynde,
And yow amende!' Thus seyde this olde man;
And everich of thise riotoures ran

Til they came to the tree, and ther they founde
Of floryns fyne of gold ycoyned rounde
Wel ny an eighte busshels, as hem thoughte.
No lenger thanne after Deeth they soughte . . .[1]

Miss M. P. Hamilton has observed[2] that in the fourteenth-century poem *Of Thre Messagers of Death*, Death's spies are Sickness, Disaster, and Elde; and that these three correspond to the plague at the beginning of the *Pardoner's Tale*, the violent deaths at the end, and the Old Man who meets the rioters. The idea of Old Age as a messenger of Death had appeared to me the most reasonable interpretation of Chaucer's line, before I heard of the poem to which Miss Hamilton refers; but if only one interpretation were conceivable, I believe that the passage would be less powerful than it is.

Ne Deeth, allas! ne wol nat han my lyf

This line loses in potency if on the strength of an editorial note we close our minds to the possibility that Death himself may be speaking. And I do not see why the Wandering Jew should be wholly rejected either.[3] A Chaucerian character is capable of uniting more than two diverse figures. The story is a folktale of ancient source in the Jātakas of Buddha; and though we do not know in precisely what form this came to Chaucer, it would not be surprising if the Hermit of the *novella* had developed in Chaucer's century, and still more in Chaucer's mind.

My last quotation was the heart of the tale; the next is the peroration of the sermon, which leads to the dramatic climax.

'Now goode men, God foryeve yow youre trespas,
And ware yow fro the synne of avarice!
Myn hooly pardoun may yow alle warice,
So that ye offre nobles or sterlynges,
Or elles silver broches, spoones, rynges.

[1] C 718–72
*Kaityf* (captive) wretch    Mr. H. W. Heckstall-Smith draws my attention to the *cattivo coro degli angeli* of *Inferno* III 37–8; and it seems to me that here Chaucer's Old Man recalls Dante's restless Trimmers, *la setta dei cattivi* who 'have no hope of death'.
    *Welked* withered          *Agayns* before          *Hasardour* gamester
    Manly and Rickert note that the generally accepted grammatical emendation of *Til they came* 769 to *Til he cam* is probably not Chaucer's.
[2] *Studies in Philology* October 1939
[3] *Sources and Analogues* p. 436. The whole of Professor Tupper's chapter may be consulted for matter illustrating the origins of the tale.

Boweth youre heed under this hooly bulle!
Cometh up ye wyves, offreth of youre wolle!
Youre name I entre heer in my rolle anon;
Into the blisse of hevene shul ye gon.
I yow assoille, by myn heigh power,
Yow that wol offre, as clene and eek as cleer
As ye were born.—And lo, sires, thus I preche.
And Jhesu Crist, that is oure soules leche,
So graunte yow his pardoun to receyve,
For that is best; I wol yow nat deceyve.'[1]

Is this last line the Pardoner's one moment of hesitation, attrition? or is it the salesman's 'confidence' to a favoured audience? The tension is not released, between the Pardoner and the poem: the Pardoner remains, his words remain, and it is not, after all, time for the seven thunders. The air is cleared by nothing more terrifying than the explosion of Sir Host, as he is asked (*for he is moost envoluped in synne*) to be the first to contribute to the collection. The problem of evil, the problem of the existence of sin under divine power and goodness, has not been 'solved': Chaucer had translated Boethius, he was aware of the scholastic discussion of the subject from Augustine onwards, and wise enough to know that he could do no better in that line. The problem has been dramatized. It is all there: the offence, the moment of possible repentance, the impotence of evil, the Pardoner doing good in spite of himself. Sin is Behovely. *It must needs be that offences come; but woe to that man by whom the offence cometh.*

The quarrel between Host and Pardoner recalls that Socratic dialogue in the *Romance of the Rose* which is probably Jean de Meun's one stroke of genius, the moment when the lover rebukes Reason herself for indecent language. It recalls especially these lines of Reason:

Se je, quant mis les nons aus choses
Que si reprendre e blasmer oses,
Coilles reliques apelasse
E reliques coilles clamasse,
Tu, qui si m'en morz e depiques,
Me redeïsses de reliques
Que ce fust laiz moz e vilains.

---

[1] C 904–18
*Warice* heal    The Pardoner's audience, if they had thought about it, would not of course have supposed themselves *clene* and *cleer* at birth.    *Leche* physician

Coilles est beaus nons e si l'ains;
Si sont, par fei, coillon e vit;
Onc nus plus beaus guieres ne vit . . .[1]

which we may continue in English translation:

Now if I'd named
The cullions relics, nought ashamed
Thou'dst been thereat, but hadst been fired
With approbation, and admired
The word as something quite divine,
And in the church wouldst thou incline
Thine head before them set in gold
And silver, and wouldst doubtless hold
Thy breath whilst with adoring kiss
Thou knelt'st before them.[2]

I am not quite convinced of the *divinity* of Jean de Meun's Reason,
even though God *made hir aftir his ymage*, but I approve heartily
the good sense of a comment of Mr. C. S. Lewis's. 'The whole
scene',[3] he writes, 'implies a criticism of courtly love far more
damaging than the bludgeon work of Jean de Meun's satirical
passages . . . That the spirit of polite adultery should be genuinely
shocked by the unrepentant grossness of the divine Wisdom . . .
is a conception as profound as it is piquant'. And this is Chaucer's
sense also: *Crist spak hymself ful brode in hooly writ.*

Now the Host speaks of cullions and relics in a different tone
and context from Reason's, but his rage is also reasonable. The
very colours, which I will not trust to reproduction, of the picture
in MS Gg 4.27 of the Cambridge University Library approve it.
And if Sir Host is in fact unreasonably sunk in sin, Sir Pardoner
is much more deeply involved than the Lover. I think that
Chaucer remembered Reason, yet he is not writing allegory;
and if he owes anything here to Jean de Meun, it is only a rude
word. Chaucer's humour and, in this one episode, the humour
of Jean de Meun will both stand comparison with the humour of
Plato. But Chaucer's is as English as the hammer-beam roof by
his King's master carpenter.

---

[1] *Le Roman de la Rose* ed. LANGLOIS, 7109ff.
[2] *Romance of the Rose* tr. F. S. ELLIS, 7491ff.
[3] *Le Roman de la Rose* 5535ff.
The Allegory of Love p. 149

# XII

*I have heard of the Wife of Bath, I think in Shakespeare.*

SWIFT: letter to Gay, 20 November 1729

*Chaucer appears also to have been his favourite, for I observe among his papers a memorandum of the oaths used in the* Canterbury Tales, *classed with the personages by whom they are used.*

SCOTT: *Memoirs of Jonathan Swift D.D.* (1814)

*Oh, there is a precedent, legal tradition,*
*To sing one song when your song means another,*
'Et albirar ab lor bordon—'

EZRA POUND: *Near Perigord*

# OF WOE THAT IS IN MARRIAGE

WE KNOW THE WIFE OF BATH AS BROAD COMEDY, BUT IT IS easy to ignore another dimension. As in two mirrors set opposite each other, there is also a *depth*. Now the mirrors are the Wife of Bath and the source of whatever she is quoting, misquoting, or attacking at a given moment: they are Alice and, for example, Jerome. She may throw powerful anti-feminism in the teeth of her old husbands, when the old husbands in their drunkenness, she tells us, were guiltless; and what in fact we see is the Wife herself reflecting, perhaps, *Le Miroir de Mariage*. And the Wife of Bath is not one mirror, she is several. She is in the first place a much-married woman in spurs—or, in her own terms,

> I am al Venerien
> In feelynge, and myn herte is Marcien.[1]

The Pardoner, who is an expert, calls her a *noble prechour*, and if she fails to reach heaven it will certainly not be through ignorance. At the same time she is the sinful woman of the *Proverbs*, the preacher's horrible warning, Blake's scarecrow; though, in an age of vigorous homiletics, Chaucer need call her none of these things. So the light spring lilt of a coming fifth marriage has at least three vices that the Wife of Bath herself heard condemned in the pulpit, and a parting smack at the Lenten sermon:

> And so bifel that ones, in a Lente,—
> (So often tymes I to my gossyb wente,
> For evere yet I loved to be gay,
> And for to walke in March, Averill, and May,
> Fro hous to hous, to heere sondry talys)
> That Jankyn clerk, and my gossyb dame Alys,
> And I myself, into the feeldes wente.
> Myn housbonde was at Londoun al that Lente;

[1] D 609-10
According to her horoscope she was subject to Venus and Mars.

I hadde the bettre leyser for to pleye,
And for to see, and eek for to be seye
Of lusty folk.   What wiste I wher my grace
Was shapen for to be, or in what place?[1]

She is less simply evil than the Pardoner, and the ironies of her
prologue are more complicated—the irony of her prayers for the
soul of her last husband, or (at the beginning) the irony of her
pretended innocence of the meaning of Christ's words to the
woman of Samaria, Christ's words to herself,

> Biside a welle, Jhesus, God and man,
> Spak in repreeve of the Samaritan:
> 'Thou hast yhad fyve housbondes', quod he,
> 'And that ilke man that now hath thee
> Is noght thyn housbonde'; thus he seyde certeyn.
> What that he mente therby, I kan nat seyn;
> But that I axe, why that the fifthe man
> Was noon housbonde to the Samaritan?
> How many myghte she have in mariage?
> Yet herde I nevere tellen in myn age
> Upon this nombre diffinicioun.
> Men may devyne and glosen, up and doun,
> But wel I woot, expres, withoute lye,
> God bad us for to wexe and multiplye;
> That gentil text kan I wel understonde . . .[2]

Without her orthodox instruction, she might be a disciple of
Genius in the *Romance of the Rose*.   It seems she has followed his
exhortation to fertility.   The Pardoner who interrupts her
prologue is, in turn, like the vicious eunuch that Genius reviles,[3]
and his declared thoughts of marriage are a mockery of the cult
of Nature.   But the Wife of Bath constructs no rival religion,
being content to remain an imperfect Christian; and it is even
doubtful whether she has considered problems of birth-rate with
much enthusiasm.   Her real emotions are here:

> But, Lord Crist! whan that it remembreth me
> Upon my yowthe, and on my jolitee,
> It tikleth me about myn herte roote.

---

[1] D 543–54
*Gossyb* crony          *Pleye* take a holiday (a usage which still survives in northern
England)
 See G. R. OWST, *Literature and Pulpit in Medieval England* p. 388
[2] D 15–29
[3] *Le Roman de la Rose* ed. LANGLOIS, 20050ff.   Compare the *Prologue* A 691.

Unto this day it dooth˙myn herte boote
That I have had my world as in my tyme.
But age, allas! that al wole envenyme,
Hath me biraft my beautee and my pith.
Lat go, farwel! the devel go therwith!
The flour is goon, ther is namoore to telle;
The bren, as I best kan, now moste I selle;
But yet to be right myrie wol I fonde.
Now wol I tellen of my fourthe housbonde.

*Wife of Bath's prologue*

*Par Deu! si me plaist il encores*
*Quant je m'i sui bien pourpensee;*
*Mout me delite en ma pensee*
*E me resbaudissent li membre*
*Quant de mon bon tens me remembre*
*E de la joliete vie*
*Don mes cueurs a si grant envie;*
*Tout me rejovenist le cors*
*Quant j'i pens e quant jou recors;*
*Touz les biens dou monde me fait*
*Quant me souvient de tout le fait,*
*Qu'au meins ai je ma joie eüe,*
*Combien qu'il m'aient deceüe.*
*Jenne dame n'est pas oiseuse*
*Quant el meine vie joieuse,*
*Meïsmement cele qui pense*
*D'aquerre a faire sa despense . . .*[1]

Le Roman de la Rose

Chaucer is closer to certain details of the French than the following free translation would suggest:

Yet, when thereon I musing think,
Long draughts of joy supreme I drink
From memory's well.   Oh, dear delights!
Wherof the very thought excites
A thrill through every limb, as though
The merry life of long ago
I lived once more.   My body seems
Rejuvenate, as in sweet dreams
Sometimes appears.   Now, by the rood,
I swear it does me untold good

---

[1] *Wife of Bath's prologue* 469–80; *Le Roman de la Rose* ed. LANGLOIS, 12932–48
*Boote* good          *Fonde* try

To muse of youth's sweet joys, though I
By men was cozened cruelly:
No idle life a damsel leads
Who makes her pleasure serve her needs.

*Romance of the Rose* tr. F. S. Ellis 13639ff.

*I have had my world as in my tyme* is the speech of the Wife of Bath, untranslated and untranslatable, and very little to do with the *bon tens* and *touz les biens du monde* of La Vieille. The lines of Jean de Meun that Chaucer remembered are in comparison anæmic.

She continues:

I seye, I hadde in herte greet despit
That he of any oother had delit.
But he was quit, by God and by Seint Joce!
I made hym of the same wode a croce;
Nat of my body, in no foul manere,
But certeinly, I made folk swich cheere
That in his owene grece I made hym frye
For angre, and for verray jalousye.
By God! in erthe I was his purgatorie,
For which I hope his soule be in glorie . . .
He deyde when I cam fro Jerusalem,
And lith ygrave under the roode beem . . .[1]

To find verses that may be put beside the whole passage of Chaucer we must look beyond Jean de Meun, to *La Belle Heaul-mière* of Villon. And if the Wife of Bath's memories are on one side of *La Belle Heaulmière*, on the other side, lower down, we have Dunbar's *Of Manis Mortalitie*.

The whole appraisal of Alice's prologue is beyond me. It calls for a specialist in her subject, such as D. H. Lawrence; who, whatever his errors, saw that it is not the act of sex but 'sex in the head' that is evil. And on this point, so long as it remains unfalsified, he was in agreement both with Chaucer and with St. Thomas Aquinas, and even with Jean de Meun's Reason. What I have called the 'orthodox' view of sex in the *Romaunt of the Rose*, no matter how far it may castigate lust, praises pro-creation and the natural delight that impels it,[2] and blames

[1] D 481ff.
*Swich cheere* such 'eyes'
[2] *Romaunt of the Rose* 4845ff., 4865ff., 5077ff.
The different opinions of early fathers and medieval doctors may be found in C. S. LEWIS: *The Allegory of Love* pp. 14ff., and in ERNEST MESSENGER: *The Mystery of Sex and Marriage in Catholic Theology* (London: Sands, 1948), esp. Appendix II.

244

only that indulgence of desire which is against the order of intelligence. Now the possibilities of marriage, of generous love and mutual forbearance, we can wait for Chaucer to show. Meanwhile, the saint's good sense is too nearly angelic to be ignored:

It does not follow that the act in question is contrary to virtue, from the fact that a free act of mind and spirit cannot accompany the pleasure. For it is not contrary to virtue if we interrupt the act of reason to do something reasonable, or it would be sinful to go to sleep . . .
In the state of innocence nothing of this kind happened which was unregulated by reason, *not because delight of sense was less, as some say (for rather it was greater in proportion to the greater purity of nature and the greater sensibility of the body),* but because the force of desire did not throw itself so inordinately into such delight, being directed by reason, *whose place it is not to lessen pleasure but to prevent the force of desire gratifying it immoderately.* By 'immoderately' I mean beyond the bounds of reason, as a temperate person does not take less pleasure in food eaten in moderation than the glutton . . . *Therefore continence would not have been praiseworthy in the state of innocence . . .*[1]

But we cannot accuse Alice of living in Eden. And let us not forget her indebtedness to the Parson: or when we come to the *Parson's Tale* forget the new Woman of Samaria, deaf in one ear to Jerome. The fact that at least one quarter of her head was filled with exact theological knowledge is to the credit, not only of the Wife of Bath, but of the maligned Church of the late fourteenth century.

He that is without sin among you, let him first cast a stone. This might be the poet's text, when he has heard and respected the preacher. Chaucer was sure of two things: that human kind would multiply, and that grace would abound. And he was sure that both were right. As sure as of the Judgement.

During the reign of Queen Elizabeth there was published in ballad form the description of a journey of the Wife of Bath to heaven, and the replies of that lady to the Biblical persons who refused her admittance. The copies were burnt; the printers and balladmonger fined.[2] I have not rescued a singed sample

---

[1] *Summa Theologica* II–II Q.cliii a.2; I Q.xcviii *ad*3. The italics are mine.
[2] Stationers' Registers, '25 Junij' 1600: quoted by C. F. E. Spurgeon

of the sheet, and I am prepared to admit that it may have given a very debased semblance, almost certainly lacking the doctrinal equipment of the original. But, however unworthy, an up-to-date Grand-daughter of Bath has turned up, as popular entertainment, long after the death of Chaucer; and she has thereupon, in Shakespeare's day, been muzzled. Shakespeare had to do without a freedom. It was a freedom, certainly, which might be abused. It might also be used, by a great artist.

Chaucer possessed too, but in common with Shakespeare, the freedom to employ *any* selection of language really used by men, and not merely the restricted selection which Wordsworth had in mind when he wrote his phrase. I do not mean alteration of the spoken order of words, nor am I suggesting that the value of writers may be estimated by the comparative range of their vocabularies. But the Summoner would not be the Summoner if his two anecdotes were set down differently; and I doubt— *Le Dis de la Vescie a Prestre* has only a very general resemblance to the *Summoner's Tale*—whether they would have been set down at all if Chaucer had not been interested in the speech of the people. 'If we are to understand Chaucer', said Professor Walter Raleigh, 'it must be by reference to a tribe of story-tellers, songsters, traffickers in popular lore and moral maxims who . . . have almost passed, except by inference, from our ken.'[1] And the statement of Professor Walter Raleigh has not been disproved by modern scholarship. *Not only the worde but verely the thynge*: the author of the fifteenth-century *Book of Curtesye* was right—and, *curtesye* or no, Chaucer got the 'thing' down on paper straight from the *reverberacioun* of air impinging on his ear-drums.

The next three pieces, then, are with special propriety called tales, to be quoted, to be read aloud, and left to speak for themselves. The tellers have little or nothing to say, but have their own way of saying it: so the Friar and the Summoner are licensed to intrude with the shortest disturbance from me. At present the Wife of Bath is continuing the exposure of her sex, and has just recalled, innocently, in a digression, her fifth husband's version of the story of Midas:

> Heere may ye see, thogh we a tyme abyde,
> Yet out it moot; we kan no conseil hyde.[2]

[1] WALTER RALEIGH: *On Writing and Writers* p. 117
[2] D 979–80
In Ovid the story is told of the barber of Midas, not of his wife.

Now she comfortably identifies herself with the Loathly Lady, who upon gaining sovereignty over her husband can turn beautiful at will, and who can preach the doctrine of *gentillesse* to other people. The hot-blooded Summoner speaks as intently against anger, through the mouth of his soft-voiced Friar. The more impressive sermon, on *gentillesse*, is an elaboration indebted to Dante of Chaucer's *ballade* on the same subject, the moral *ballade* with the fine verse,

Vyce may wel be heir to old richesse.

Gower's *Tale of Florent*, a ballad called the *Marriage of Sir Gawaine*, and the romance of the *Weddynge of Sir Gawen and Dame Ragnell* have all been compared to the Wife's tale; but Chaucer alone keeps the transformation of the hag until the very end. And to accommodate his Lady of Bath, he makes the Loathly Lady as human as possible. *Fayerye* is sophisticated:

In th'olde dayes of the Kyng Arthour,
Of which that Britons speken greet honour,
Al was this land fulfild of fayerye.
The elf-queene, with hir joly compaignye,
Daunced ful ofte in many a grene mede—
This was the olde opinion, as I rede
(I speke of manye hundred yeres ago).
But now kan no man see none elves mo.
For now the grete charitee and prayeres
Of lymytours and othere hooly freres,
That serchen every lond and every streem,
As thikke as motes in the sonne-beem,
Blessynge halles, chambres, kichenes, boures,
Citees, burghes, castels, hye toures,
Thropes, bernes, shipnes, dayeryes—
This maketh that ther been no fayeryes.
For ther as wont to walken was an elf,
Ther walketh now the lymytour hymself
In undermeles and in morwenynges,
And seyth his matyns and his hooly thynges
As he gooth in his lymytacioun.
Wommen may go saufly up and doun
In every bussh or under every tree;
Ther is noon oother incubus but he,
And he ne wol doon hem but dishonour.[1]

[1] D 857–81
*Lymytours* friars licensed to beg within a definite limit    *Thropes* thorps, hamlets
*Shipnes* stables    *Undermeles* the hours of prayer of terce, sext, none, vespers?

This is folk-lore for Alice.

But the Friar, in spite of his promise, is not attending; pondering his attack on the Summoner, he has apparently heard only one word. And that was towards the end.

> 'Dame', quod he, 'God yeve yow right good lyf!
> Ye han heer touched, also moot I thee,
> In scole-matere greet difficultee.
> Ye han seyd muche thyng right wel, I seye;
> But, dame, heere as we ryde by the weye,
> Us nedeth nat to speken but of game,
> And lete auctoritees, on Goddes name,
> To prechyng and to scole eek of clergye . . .'[1]

Our 'marriage group' is the most quarrelsome and ill-mannered of all. Pilgrims interrupt one another, and there is an interlude for the principal dispute. Angry prologues promise hard hitting, but Chaucer insists on a game of skill, and the Summoner has to do his best to be delicate. The Friar is better at this, and can afford to give away a point:

> This somonour clappeth at the wydwes gate.
> 'Com out', quod he, 'thou olde virytrate!
> I trowe thou hast som frere or preest with thee.'[2]

It is a question which will show the greater refinement of satire; and when the Summoner comes forward with unexpectedly brilliant mimicry, the Friar's victory is by no means certain. Each, of course, exposes himself—and the Friar is throwing at the Summoner a stock preacher's anecdote, an excellent *narratio jocosa*.[3] The Friar's *somnour* meets an unusual yeoman from the north,

> 'Brother', quod he, 'where is now youre dwellyng,
> Another day if that I sholde yow seche?'
> This yeman hym answerde in softe speche,
>     'Brother', quod he, 'fer in the north contree,
> Where-as I hope som tyme I shal thee see . . .'[4]

The North Country, we gather, is an infernal region: and its fiend has an interesting resemblance to the Pardoner.

---

[1] D 1270-7
*Also moot I thee* as I may thrive      *Scole-matere* scholastic questions
[2] D 1581-3
*Virytrate* hag
[3] G. R. OWST, *Literature and Pulpit in Medieval England* pp. 162-3
[4] D 1410-4

'For somtyme we been Goddes instrumentz,
And meenes to doon his comandementz,
Whan that hym list, upon his creatures,
In divers art and in diverse figures . . .
And somtyme be we suffred for to seke
Upon a man, and doon his soule unreste,
And nat his body, and al is for the beste.
Whan he withstandeth oure temptacioun,
It is a cause of his savacioun,
Al be it that it was nat oure entente
He sholde be sauf, but that we wolde hym hente . . .'[1]

*Friar's Tale*

'But though myself be gilty in that synne,
Yet kan I maken oother folk to twynne
From avarice, and soore to repente.
But that is nat my principal entente . . .'

*Pardoner's prologue*

Here is the problem of evil again, treated in comedy: the problem of the complicated interaction of evil and good, and of the mystery of good rising out of evil. Laughter in Chaucer clears the mind not for vacancy, but for thought undistracted by emotion.

This is to recall, for a moment, the greater seriousness of the *Pardoner's Tale*. We must have a more representative passage from the Friar:

And right at the entryng of the townes ende,
To which this somonour shoop hym for to wende,
They saugh a cart that charged was with hey,
Which that a cartere droof forth in his wey.
Deep was the wey, for which the carte stood;
This cartere smoot, and cryde as he were wood,
'Hayt, Brok! hayt, Scot! what spare ye for the stones?
The feend', quod he, 'yow fecche, body and bones,
As ferforthly as evere were ye foled,
So muche wo as I have with yow tholed!
The devel have al, bothe hors and cart and hey!'
This somonour seyde, 'Heere shal we have a pley';
And neer the feend he drough, as noght ne were,
Ful prively, and rowned in his ere:
'Herkne, my brother, herkne, by thy feith!

[1] D 1483ff.
*Seke upon* attack, harass        *Hente* seize

Herestow nat how that the cartere seith?
Hent it anon, for he hath yeve it thee,
Both hey and cart, and eek his caples three.'
    'Nay', quod the devel, 'God woot, never a deel!
It is nat his entente, trust me weel.
Axe hym thyself, if thou nat trowest me;
Or elles stynt a while and thou shalt see.'
    This cartere thakketh his hors upon the croupe,
And they bigonne to drawen and to stoupe.
'Heyt! now,' quod he, 'ther Jhesu Crist yow blesse,
And al his handwerk, bothe moore and lesse!
That was wel twight, myn owene lyard boy.
I pray God save thee, and Seinte Loy!
Now is my cart out of the slow, pardee!'
    'Lo, brother,' quod the feend, 'what tolde I thee?
Heere may ye see, myn owene deere brother,
The carl spak oo thing, but he thoghte another.'[1]

The point of this little story, in Chaucer's context, is that the *entente* of the Summoner, or the Pardoner, or the teller of the tale, is much more seriously at fault than the language of a carter stuck in the mud. No one would make high claims for such a passage. I quote it in full as the nearest to an authenticated illustration of Chaucer *hearing a tale told*. One might guess that he had an auditory memory of a line like *both hey and cart and eek his caples three* and had not seen it in writing, though this would be impossible to prove. But we can say that the only known parallel to the episode survived until recent years in oral tradition.[2]

After the Summoner's reply, the trivialities of the interlude over, at last we have the Clerk's delayed, delicate and over-whelming answer to the Wife of Bath. On this I had something to say when we came to the *Man of Law's Tale*. Now I should like to look a little more closely at Chaucer's *poetics*, and to propose a fresh interpretation of his poem. For I believe that the *Clerk's Tale* has been underestimated, because incompletely understood.

It is as interesting to compare passages of Petrarch's Latin and the French redaction with the poetry that Chaucer made out of them, as it is to consider those lines of *Antony and Cleopatra*

---

[1] D 1537–68

| *Ferforthly* thoroughly | | *Tholed* endured | | *Rowned* whispered |
| *Caples* cart-horses | *Thakketh* smacks | | *Twight* pulled | *Lyard* grey |

[2] *Sources and Analogues* pp. 269, 274

in which Shakespeare closely followed North's *Plutarch*; and the methods of two great poets could hardly be more unlike. Chaucer's style is so restrained, so chaste, that no quotation can convey an idea of the whole tale. The lines I shall give are not intended to represent it, and should be read in their context.

> *sed virilis senilisque animus virgineo latebat in pectore*

> *toutesfoiz courage meur et ancien estoit muciez et enclos en sa virginite*

> Yet in the brest of hire virginitee
> Ther was enclosed rype and sad corage[1]

Here Chaucer could not have translated the French much more literally within his metre; but the difference is that lingering emphasis of rhyme and rhythm which makes certain words shine with clarity. The next version is only slightly less literal:

> *s'il n'eust sceu qu'elle amast parfaitement ses enffans, il l'eust tenue pour suspette et mauvaise femme, et eust crue celle fermete et constance venir de couraige d'aucune crueuse voulenté*

> . . . if that he
> Ne hadde soothly knowen therbifoore
> That parfitly hir children loved she,
> He wolde have wend that of som subtiltee,
> And of malice, or of cruel corage,
> That she hadde suffred this with sad visage.

> But wel he knew that next hymself, certayn,
> She loved hir children best in every wyse[2]

The alteration, the prominence given to the term *subtiltee*, emphasize sinister possibilities; just as, in a larger context,

---

[1] E 219–20
*Sad* sober, constant   *Corage* heart, spirit   The Latin quotation may be translated, literally, 'but the spirit of manhood and of age lay hidden in her maiden bosom'; and the French, 'yet the spirit of ripeness and of old age was hidden and enclosed in her virginity'.
   The French and Latin extracts are taken from *Epistolæ Seniles*, Book XVII, Letter III, and from *Le Livre Griseldis* respectively, in the texts given by J. B. Severs in *Sources and Analogues*. Dr. Severs has also published a study under the title *The Literary Relationships of Chaucer's Clerkes Tale* (New Haven, 1942).
[2] E 688–95
The French reads 'if he had not known that she perfectly loved her children, he would have held her a suspicious and evil woman, and have believed this steadiness and constancy to come from some cruel will'.

Chaucer finds the persons opposed to Griselde more evil and, without any trace of overemphasis, underlines the contrasts of character.

*reverenter atque humiliter*

*humblement et en tres grant reverence*

And she set doun hir water pot anon,
Biside the thresshfold, in an oxes stalle,
And doun upon hir knees she gan to falle,
And with sad contenance kneleth stille,
Til she had herd what was the lordes wille.[1]

This is clearly imagination of objects and acts which *mean more* than the general phrasing of the prose. Through a long tradition of folktale Psyche has become, in these lines, the maid for whom her lord prepared a marriage-feast, the maid recalling the Virgin, recalling Christ, in humility and suffering; but obedient, in the first place, to a power which is not divine. The power is to be—though how should Griselde know?—a cruelty in itself wholly unjustified, yet in the event proving, through divine grace,[2] the strength of a single virtue. We may set down this Oxenford logic: that a single virtue is an abstraction, but Griselde personifies a single virtue, therefore Griselde is an unnatural mother. Yet if there is one line that we can quote to suggest the poetic quality of the *Clerk's Tale*, it is

O tendre, o deere, o yonge children myne . . .

Chaucer, against the laws of probability, has given Griselde the essence of the human feeling. That is how a mother would speak if she could speak poetry. A single virtue is difficult, true; grant the possibility, and the virtue of Griselde appears inexhaustible.

What I have so far said is about less than half of the *Clerk's Tale*: it is to show the poetry of the persuasiveness of the Clerk, which is a kind of dramatic poetry. In terms of the liberal arts, with which the narrator was familiar, the tale is a superb piece of Rhetoric and Music; but its Dialectic is quite untenable, as Petrarch himself, and Chaucer's Clerk, were aware.

---

[1] E 290–4
The Latin has only 'reverently and humbly'; the French, 'humbly and with very great reverence'.
[2] E 395: *God hath swich favour sent hire of his grace* . . .

This story it has seemed good to me to weave anew, in another tongue, not so much that it might stir the matrons of our times to imitate the patience of this wife—who seems to me scarcely imitable—as that it might stir all those who read it to imitate the woman's steadfastness, at least; so that they may have the resolution to perform for God what this woman performed for her husband. For He cannot be tempted with evil, as saith James the Apostle, and He himself tempts no man. Nevertheless, He often proves us and suffers us to be vexed with many a grievous scourge; not that He may know our spirit, for that He knew ere we were made, but that our own frailty may be made known to us through notable private signs.

> This storie is seyd, nat for that wyves sholde
> Folwen Grisilde as in humylitee,
> For it were importable, though they wolde;
> But for that every wight, in his degree,
> Sholde be constant in adversitee
> As was Grisilde; therfore Petrak writeth
> This storie, which with heigh stile he enditeth.
>
> For, sith a womman was so pacient
> Unto a mortal man, wel moore us oghte
> Receyven al in gree that God us sent;
> For greet skile is, he preeve that he wroghte.
> But he ne tempteth no man that he boghte,
> As seith Seint Jame, if ye his pistel rede;
> He preveth folk al day, it is no drede,
>
> And suffreth us, as for oure exercise,
> With sharpe scourges of adversitee
> Ful ofte to be bete in sondry wise;
> Nat for to knowe oure wyl; for certes he,
> Er we were born, knew al oure freletee;
> And for oure beste is al his governaunce.
> Lat us thanne lyve in vertuous suffraunce.[1]

Only if the husband represents a supernatural power, as in the earliest versions of the tale, is Griselde's behaviour logically

---

[1] E 1142–62
*Importable* intolerable　　　*In gree* in good part　　　*For greet skile is, he preeve that he wroghte* for it is very reasonable that he should prove (test) that which he created　　　*Suffraunce* longsuffering
I have quoted from R. D. French's translation of Petrarch's Latin. The original is given as a marginal gloss in several MSS: see *The Text of the Canterbury Tales* ed. MANLY and RICKERT III pp. 507–8.

justified. The Wife of Bath had enough sense not to make a god of a husband, and was quite capable of perceiving the fallacy of Griselde's submission to Walter as to a creator of life who has the right to destroy. She was also capable of recognizing, at least for argument's sake, what was to be admired in such humility. Both Alice and the Clerk, whatever their intentions, have shown the evil of domination in marriage, and the *ernestful matere* of the *Clerk's Tale*, in the end, is high comedy.

> But o word, lordynges, herkneth er I go:
> It were ful hard to fynde now-a-dayes
> In al a toun Grisildis three or two;
> For if that they were put to swiche assayes,
> The gold of hem hath now so badde alayes
> With bras, that thogh the coyne be fair at eye,
> It wolde rather breste a-two than plye.

> For which heere, for the Wyves love of Bathe—
> Whos lyf and al hire secte God mayntene
> In heigh maistrie, and elles were it scathe—
> I wol with lusty herte, fressh and grene,
> Seyn yow a song to glade yow, I wene;
> And lat us stynte of ernestful matere.
> Herkneth my song, that seith in this manere:

> *Lenvoy de Chaucer*

> Grisilde is deed, and eek hire pacience,
> And bothe atones buryed in Ytaille;
> For which I crie in open audience,
> No wedded man so hardy be t'assaille
> His wyves pacience in trust to fynde
> Grisildis, for in certein he shal faille.

> O noble wyves, ful of heigh prudence,
> Lat noon humylitee youre tonge naille,
> Ne lat no clerk have cause or diligence
> To write of yow a storie of swich mervaille
> As of Grisildis pacient and kynde,
> Lest Chichevache yow swelwe in hire entraille!

> Folweth Ekko, that holdeth no silence,
> But evere answereth at the countretaille.
> Beth nat bidaffed for your innocence,
> But sharply taak on yow the governaille.
> Emprenteth wel this lessoun in youre mynde,
> For commune profit sith it may availle.

Ye archewyves, stondeth at defense,
Syn ye be strong as is a greet camaille;
Ne suffreth nat that men yow doon offense.
And sklendre wyves, fieble as in bataille,
Beth egre as is a tygre yond in Ynde;
Ay clappeth as a mille, I yow consaille.

Ne dreed hem nat, doth hem no reverence
For though thyn housbonde armed be in maille,
The arwes of thy crabbed eloquence
Shal perce his brest, and eek his aventaille.
In jalousie I rede eek thou hym bynde,
And thou shalt make hym couche as doth a quaille.

If thou be fair, ther folk been in presence
Shewe thou thy visage and thyn apparaille;
If thou be foul, be free of thy dispence;
To gete thee freendes ay do thy travaille;
Be ay of chiere as light as leef on lynde,
And lat hym care, and wepe, and wrynge, and waille![1]

In composing this passage Chaucer may have remembered again the simpler ridicule of Jean de Meun: the jealous husband telling of Penelope and Lucretia, and observing that such women were nowhere to be found.[2]   The master of logic coming forward with his song in honour of the Wife of Bath is one of the most amusing spectacles on pilgrimage; and it is an affront to a great comedian of Christendom to ask whether Chaucer really intended his *envoy* for the Clerk.   The scribe's heading is not to be taken.

Thus Chaucer presents his 'drama': less *in* verse than *through* verse, so that we can look beyond the immediate persuasion, and the emotion of the moment.   I do not say that he is writing poetry for us to 'see through'—that would be too obvious to suit the Oxford scholar.   The simple feeling is there, of reverence for Griselde; unblurred; but complicated without confusion, to a degree which may place the modern reader, for a time, out of his depth.   The poetry is not cancelled by the comedy, and the comic *envoy* is no less poetic than the tale.   And when I consider the poetry I am reminded that Wordsworth was a reader of Chaucer, and indeed was almost forestalled by the calmness of

[1] E 1163–212
*Alayes* alloys          *Scathe* misfortune          *Chichevache* a fabulous cow who kept lean on a diet of patient wives, while her mate Bicorne grew fat on humble husbands
*At the countretaille* in retort          *Bidaffed* fooled          *Clappeth* chatter
[2] *Le Roman de la Rose* ed. LANGLOIS, 8608ff.

the Clerk. For Wordsworth's finest work is essentially a firm desire for the single quality that is already there, in a large and various relation to many very different qualities, in Chaucer; the quality of *still rootedness*.

> And richely his doghter maryed he
> Unto a lord, oon of the worthieste
> Of al Ytaille; and than in pees and reste
> His wyves fader in his court he kepeth,
> Til that the soule out of his body crepeth.[1]

The great technicians of art—among whom are Chaucer, and the composer Guillaume de Machaut, and Bach—assimilate, discover, re-discover so much that they seem to anticipate later developments almost casually. A substantial amount of English poetry is already in the following lines of three works of a single author of the fourteenth century:

> If no love is, O God, what fele I so?
> And if love is, what thing and which is he?
> If love be good, from whennes cometh my woo?
> If it be wikke, a wonder thynketh me,
> When every torment and adversite
> That cometh of hym, may to me savory thinke;
> For ay thurst I, the more that ich it drynke.[2]

> What? is this al the joye and al the feste?
> Is this youre reed? Is this my blisful cas?
> Is this the verray mede of youre byheeste?
> Is al this paynted proces seyd, allas!
> Right for this fyn?[3]

> ye ben verrayly
> The maistresse of my wit, and nothing I.[4]

[1] E 1130–4
I refer particularly to the last line, which is not taken from the Latin or French source. The same metaphor occurs in E 121: *In crepeth age alwey, as stille as stoon* . . . Compare Wordsworth's *Evening Walk* 354, *The Old Cumberland Beggar* 59–61, *The Excursion* VII 707–9. Dr. D. J. Enright draws my attention also to a likeness between Griselda and the Wordsworthian maiden.
[2] *Troilus* I 400–6 : extending Petrarch's Sonnet LXXXVIII 1–4 *S'Amoz non è* . . . *Savory thinke* seem delightful
On Chaucer's discovery of Italian song two centuries before the Elizabethans, compare the observation of Thomas Watson (1582), quoted by C. F. E. Spurgeon in *Five Hundred Years of Chaucer Criticism and Allusion*.
[3] See, for comment, pp. 79ff.
[4] *Legend of Good Women* B(F) 87–8
Except by travelling to the year 1600, Chaucer could not have got nearer, in two lines, to Donne's very habit of phrase.

For hooly chirches good moot been despended
On hooly chirches blood, that is descended.
Therfore he wolde his hooly blood honoure,
Though that he hooly chirche sholde devoure.[1]

For lyk the moone ay wexe ye and wane,
Ay ful of clappyng, deere ynogh a jane.[2]

Upon that oother syde Damyan
Bicomen is the sorwefulleste man
That evere was . . .[3]

Have ye nat seyn somtyme a pale face
Among a prees, of hym that hath be lad
Toward his deeth, wher as hym gat no grace
And swich a colour in his face hath had
Men myghte knowe his face that was bistad
Amonges alle the faces in that route?[4]

Upon this subject there has perhaps been a literary competition
which I have escaped; and these are only a few passages marked
by the way in reading Chaucer. But the Master might have
shuffled them, and handed out trump cards of the next five and
a half centuries of our verse.

[1] *Canterbury Tales* A 3983–6
Dryden might have appropriated this, with little change of diction, and no change of
syntax, for *Absalom and Achitophel*.
[2] *Canterbury Tales* E 998–9: a couplet of Pope's discovered?
*Deere ynogh a jane* not worth a groat
[3] *Canterbury Tales* E 2097–9
Pope, adapting these lines in nominally the same metre, wrote:
> No less impatience vex'd her amorous Squire,
> Wild with delay, and burning with desire.
> > *January and May* 494–5
But how was he to know that Chaucer had *in comedy* hit on Wordsworthian pathos?
[4] The whole stanza is quoted on p. 203
I have from Mr. Eliot, in a letter dated 23 October 1951, this statement: 'I am
certainly struck by the quotation, and while I cannot say that these are not lines
which embedded themselves in my mind long ago, I have certainly not made any
deliberate use of them.'

# XIII

*To what may be seen by the mind's eye (de entibus imaginabilibus) we can grant a true existence, before the beginning of the act of imagination, and after the end . . . thus the chimera exists. If anyone dreams he is a cardinal, a cardinal he will be (sic erit) ; we can only object that he has not been so in appearance . . . Realities are various . . .*

NICHOLAS OF AUTRECOURT: *Satis exigit ordo executionis* (c. 1350)
Bodleian MS Canonici misc. 43

*Clerkys that canne the scyens seven*
*Seye that curtasy came fro heven*
*When Gabryell owre lady grette,*
*And Elyzabeth with her mette.*
*All vertus be closyde in curtasy,*
*And alle vyces in vilany.*

Bodleian MS Ashmoleum 61
*The Young Children's Book*

# AND LAUNCELOT HE IS DEAD

THE MARRIAGE SEQUENCE CONTINUES, AND THE MERCHANT follows without intermission. And when I remember his tale, some time after reading it, my first impression is of a peculiar light, in which there then appear objects that had caught the eye: sharp bristles on a chin, skin shaking at the neck, an old man with his fresh young wife, and a silver *cliket* opening the gate of a garden of pleasure. It is not these things themselves that are now remarkable, but the light that plays on them. From the figure and make-believe of the story, they stand out in a way which permits neither illusion nor despair.

The disillusionment may be imputed to the Merchant, who has been married two months. He has just repeated the Clerk's last words, but in a very different tone:

> 'Wepyng and wayling, care and other sorwe
> I knowe ynogh, on even and a-morwe,'
> Quod the Marchant, 'and so doon other mo
> That wedded been; I trowe that it be so;
> For wel I woot it fareth so with me.
> I have a wyf, the worste that may be—
> For thogh the feend to hire ycoupled were,
> She wolde hym overmacche, I dar wel swere.
> What sholde I yow reherce in special
> Hir hye malice? She is a shrewe at al . . .'[1]

And the tone of his tale is to be different again, as he himself suggests upon invitation:

> 'Gladly,' quod he, 'but of myn owene soore,
> For sory herte, I telle may namoore.'[2]

The *Prologue* had sketched a character poker-faced in business practice, and therefore, in Chaucer's hands, a fit instrument for irony. And whether or not the tale was originally intended for the Monk, as J. M. Manly proposed, many of the introductory lines on wedlock, and all of the scriptural instances, burlesque

[1] E 1213–22
[2] E 1243–4

261

the tones of preaching. So, with mock solemnity, the essence of right marriage guidance comes out in full.

Now the *Merchant's Tale* is so excellently done that the difficulty in writing about it is to decide what to omit from quotation. One is left to compromise, and to be brief in comment. To make up for this one's readers will be forced, in sheer exasperation, to read Chaucer. We are introduced to a new and greater *senex amans*, to the Merchant's January dreaming of his own Eden.

> Whilom ther was dwellynge in Lumbardye
> A worthy knyght, that born was of Pavye,
> In which he lyved in greet prosperitee;
> And sixty yeer a wyflees man was hee,
> And folwed ay his bodily delyt
> On wommen, ther as was his appetyt,
> As doon thise fooles that been seculeer.
> And whan that he was passed sixty yeer,
> Were it for hoolynesse or for dotage,
> I kan nat seye, but swich a greet corage
> Hadde this knyght to been a wedded man
> That day and nyght he dooth al that he kan
> T'espien where he myghte wedded be . . .
> 'Noon oother lyf', seyde he, 'is worth a bene;
> For wedlock is so esy and so clene,
> That in this world it is a paradys.'
> Thus seyde this olde knyght, that was so wys.
>     And certainly, as sooth as God is kyng,
> To take a wyf it is a glorious thyng,
> And namely whan a man is oold and hoor;
> Thanne is a wyf the fruyt of his tresor . . .
> For who kan be so buxom as a wyf?
> Who is so trewe, and eek so ententyf
> To kepe hym, syk and hool, as is his make?
> For wele or wo she wole hym nat forsake . . .
>     A wyf is Goddes yifte verraily;
> Alle othere manere yiftes hardily,
> As londes, rentes, pasture, or commune,
> Or moebles, alle been yiftes of Fortune,
> That passen as a shadwe upon a wal.
> But drede nat, if pleynly speke I shal,
> A wyf wol laste, and in thyn hous endure,
> Wel lenger than thee list, paraventure.[1]

[1] E 1245ff.
*Corage* desire          *Namely* especially          *Buxom* obedient
*Moebles* movable goods

Equivocation and innuendo are here to enjoy, and also that exquisite, that sublimated pain with which the Merchant finds matrimony more durable than merchandise.

> A wyf! a, Seinte Marie, *benedicite!*
> How myghte a man han any adversitee
> That hath a wyf?   Certes, I kan nat seye.
> The blisse which that is bitwixe hem tweye
> Ther may no tonge telle, or herte thynke . . .
> She seith nat ones 'nay' whan he seith 'ye'.
> 'Do this', seith he; 'Al redy sire', seith she.[1]

And there is more play upon this theme: the storyteller ever glancing through a mask at the Wife of Bath.

> Suffre thy wyves tonge, as Catoun bit;
> She shal comande, and thou shalt suffren it,
> And yet she wole obeye of curteisye. . . .
> Housbonde and wyf, what so men jape or pleye,
> Of worldly folk holden the siker weye;
> They been so knyt ther may noon harm bityde,
> And namely upon the wyves syde.[2]

Old January thinks in terms of fish and flesh, and the two sins which the Parson calls *ny cousins* in him are one:

> 'But o thyng warne I yow, my freendes deere,
> I wol noon oold wyf han in no manere.
> She shal nat passe twenty yeer, certayn;
> Oold fissh and yong flessh wolde I have fayn;
> Bet is', quod he, 'a pyk than a pykerel,
> And bet than old boef is the tendre veel.'[3]

So much light shines on this luxury that we need not call in the Parson for more.   But Chaucer did not entirely dispense with him.   January employs the preachers in the same manner as the Wife of Bath handles her texts.

---

[1] E 1337ff.
[2] E 1377ff.
*Bit* bids          *Siker* safe
[3] Professor Lowes has observed resemblance between *Le Miroir de Mariage* and the *Merchant's Tale*, and the opening situation of Chaucer's poem may well have been suggested by the poem of Deschamps.   But hesitant young *Franc Vouloir* is very different from January; the passages quoted by Mrs. Dempster in *Sources and Analogues* were not closely followed; and the parallels to the whole speech from which these lines are taken (E 1415–68; *Miroir* 722–73) reveal no more than an ordinary sensual man with some worldly wisdom, and an aptitude for day-dreaming with apparent logic.

A man may do no synne with his wyf,
Ne hurte hymselven with his owene knyf;
*Merchant's Tale*

And for that many man weneth that he may nat synne,
for no likerousnesse that he dooth with his wyf, certes,
that opinion is false.   God woot, a man may sleen hymself
with his owene knyf . . .
*Parson's Tale*

Right thus the Apostel tolde it unto me;
And bad oure housbondes for to love us weel.
Al this sentence me liketh every deel . . .
*Wife of Bath's Tale*

Wives, submit yourselves unto your own husbands . . .
Husbands, love your wives . . .[1]
*Paul the Apostle to the Colossians*

January has listened to Placebo the servile court-flatterer, and
ignored Justinus; but he has not yet chosen a wife.

Heigh fantasye and curious bisynesse
Fro day to day gan in the soule impresse
Of Januarie aboute his mariage.
Many fair shap and many a fair visage
Ther passeth thurgh his herte nyght by nyght,
As whoso tooke a mirour polisshed bryght,
And sette it in a commune market-place,
Thanne sholde he see ful many a figure pace
By his mirour; and in the same wyse
Gan Januarie inwith his thoght devyse
Of maydens, whiche that dwelten hym bisyde.[2]

Ironic magniloquence turns this unaccustomed mental activity
to ridicule, and the delicate mirror of the courtly mind[3] now
reflects the rabble.   But only a theological fancy troubles the
would-be lover:

---

[1] E 1839–40; I 859; D 160–2; *Colossians* iii 18–9
*Likerousnesse* licentiousness
  The text from St. Paul is quoted in the *Parson's Tale* I 634; and the Parson does not
omit the first sentence.
  [2] E 1577–87
*Fantasye* imaginings          *Curious bisynesse* eager activity
  [3] Thus gan he make a mirour of his mynde,
  In which he saugh al holly hire figure . . .
*Troilus* I 365–6

'I have', quod he, 'herd seyd, ful yoore ago,
Ther may no man han parfite blisses two,
This is to seye, in erthe and eek in hevene.
For though he kepe hym fro the synnes sevene,
And eek from every branche of thilke tree,
Yet is ther so parfit felicitee
And so greet ese and lust in mariage,
That evere I am agast now in myn age
That I shal lede now so myrie a lyf,
So delicat, withouten wo and stryf,
That I shal han myn hevene in erthe heere.
For sith that verray hevene is boght so deere
With tribulacion and greet penaunce,
How sholde I thanne, that lyve in swich plesaunce
As alle wedded men doon with hire wyvys,
Come to the blisse ther Crist eterne on lyve ys?
This is my drede, and ye, my bretheren tweye,
Assoilleth me this question, I preye.'[1]

And Justinus is at hand to reply.

Dispeire yow noght, but have in youre memorie,
Paraunter she may be youre purgatorie!
She may be Goddes meene and Goddes whippe
Thanne shal youre soule up to hevene skippe
Swifter than dooth an arwe out of a bowe
I hope to God herafter shul ye knowe
That ther nys noon so greet felicitee
In mariage ne nevere mo shal be
That yow shal lette of youre salvacion
So that ye use as skile is and reson
The lustes of youre wyf attemprely
And that ye plese hire nat too amorously . . .
Beth nat agast herof my brother deere
But lat us waden out of this matere
The Wyf of Bathe if ye han understonde
Of mariage which we have on honde
Declared hath ful wel in litel space.[2]

I have left these lines almost unpointed, much as they might
have been written out in an early manuscript, to show (what
some modern poets have discovered) that our convenient system
of punctuation is at times a nuisance. Chaucer did not have to

---

[1] E 1637-54
The Parson, in I 389, refers to the 'branches' of each sin.
[2] E 1669ff.
*Meene* means, instrument      *Lette of* impede      *Lustes* delights

bother with the troubles of editors transcribing him. Who exactly is talking about the Wife of Bath? Geoffrey, or Justin, or the Merchant? Professor Manly and Miss Rickert were so plagued by indecision at this Chaucerian quirk that they threw up the sponge, and dreamed about the poet jotting down a marginal memorandum of the *envoy* he meant to write to Bukton.[1] Yet there is no great cause for alarm. Either the Merchant interrupts Justinus to refer to Alice, or Justin, like an actor, addresses the audience from the stage of the Merchant's, and the poet's, imagination. But the teller of the tale, whoever he is, identifies himself with the justice of Justinus; the Merchant, at this point, is Justinus; so Justinus, being the Merchant, is acquainted with the Wife of Bath. And this is more than an editorial puzzle. It is another piece of fourteenth-century freedom: like the second player, in the play within a play, appealing to an imaginary friend of his author in the stalls.

Chaucer's relation to the Merchant is less simple. It is not, for one thing, that Griselde is the 'ideal' and May the reality; for May is given as the Merchant's example, the example of a new misogamist, and Griselde, I have suggested, is almost a hypothetical case of Oxenford logic. Yet the Merchant is reticent about May as Chaucer, in the *Prologue*, is reticent about the Merchant: neither the poet nor his storyteller, that is to say, exhibits more curiosity than is proper to the object. And so Chaucer, for a moment of his own divine comedy, has raised a shady business man into the light. We know the ironist, but the satire remains anonymous.

> Forth comth the preest, with stole aboute his nekke,
> And bad hire be lyk Sarra and Rebekke . . .
> And made al siker ynogh with holynesse . . .

> Hoold thou thy pees, thou poete Marcian,
> That writest us that ilke weddyng murie
> Of hire Philologie and hym Mercurie,
> And of the songes that the Muses songe!
> Too smal is bothe thy penne, and eek thy tonge,
> For to descryven of this mariage.
> Whan tendre youthe hath wedded stoupyng age,
> Ther is swich myrthe that it may nat be writen.
> Assayeth it youreself, thanne may ye witen
> If that I lye or noon in this matiere.

[1] *The Text of the Canterbury Tales* ed. MANLY and RICKERT III p. 475

Mayus, that sit with so benygne a chiere,
Hire to biholde it semed fayerye . . .
This Januarie is ravysshed in a traunce
At every tyme he looked on hir face;
But in his herte he gan hire to manace
That he that nyght in armes wolde hire streyne
Harder than evere Parys dide Eleyne.[1]

The satire remains anonymous in two ways. As Chaucer forgot, or failed to discover, the name of the narrator, his Merchant; so we may well forget, or fail to discover, the names of all those who laughed at old lovers and young wives and told the Pear-tree Story. *Whan tendre youthe hath wedded stoupyng age* . . . joins Shakespearian song in comedy, and in two lines comedy rises to the upper air. And Chaucer would be the last to claim copyright even for his best bits. Let us have them:

And whan the bed was with the preest yblessed,
Out of the chambre hath every wight hym dressed;
And Januarie hath faste in armes take
His fresshe May, his paradys, his make.
He lulleth hire, he kisseth hire ful ofte
With thikke bristles of his berd unsofte,
Lyk to the skyn of houndfyssh, sharp as brere—
For he was shave al newe in his manere—
He rubbeth hire aboute hir tendre face,
And seyde . . .[2]

In the morning,[3]

He was al coltissh, ful of ragerye,
And ful of jargon as a flekked pye.
The slakke skyn aboute his nekke shaketh
Whil that he sang, so chaunteth he and craketh.

---

[1] E 1703ff., 1732ff.
*Hoold thou thy pees, thou poete* . . . a comic adaptation of the Dantesque phrase *Taccia . . . omai.* *Marcian* Martianus Capella, author of *De Nuptiis Philologiæ et Mercurii,* the allegory in which the middle ages could read of the Seven Liberal Arts.

[2] E 1819–28

[3] E 1847–54
*Jargon* chatter        *Pye* magpie
Here, from Boccaccio, writing about the time of Chaucer's birth, is Agape's picture of her old husband in the *Ameto*:
. . . la barba grossa e prolissa, nè più nè meno pugnente che le penne d'un istrice . . . E il sottile collo nè ossa nè vena nasconde, anzi tremante, spesso con tutto il capo muove le vizze parti . . .
. . . the coarse, long beard, no more and no less prickly than the quills of a porcupine . . . And the thin neck concealing neither bone nor vein, nay trembling, often moves flabbily with the whole head . . .
Quoted in *Sources and Analogues,* pp. 339–40

But God woot what that May thoughte in hir herte,
Whan she hym saugh up sittynge in his sherte,
In his nyght-cappe, and with his nekke lene;
She preyseth nat his pleyyng worth a bene.

The young Alexander Pope, who (in the words of Dr. Johnson) 'was tempted to try his own skill in giving Chaucer a more fashionable appearance', first reduced this quotation to a pair of pedestrian couplets, then with the cleverness of youth scored a point over his master in too slick an allusion to pregnancy:

The longing dame look'd up, and spy'd her Love
Full fairly perch'd among the boughs above.
She stopp'd and sighing: 'Oh good Gods,' she cry'd,
'What pangs, what sudden shoots distend my side?
Oh for that tempting fruit, so fresh, so green;
Help, for the love of heav'n's immortal Queen!'

*January and May*

This fresshe May, that is so bright and sheene,
Gan for to syke, and seyde, 'Allas, my syde!
Now sire,' quod she, 'for aught that may bityde,
I most han of the peres that I see,
Or I moot dye, so soore longeth me
To eten of the smale peres grene.
Help, for hir love that is of hevene queene!'[1]

*Merchant's Tale*

But before the pear-tree, there is something else, besides January in his nightcap, that Pope (even the mature Pope) could not have attempted. It is one of the most remarkable examples of poetic mutation in existence:

'Rys up, my wyf, my love, my lady free!
The turtles voys is herd, my dowve sweete;
The wynter is goon with alle his reynes weete.
Com forth now, with thyne eyen columbyn!
How fairer been thy brestes than is wyn!
The garden is enclosed al aboute;
Com forth, my white spouse! Out of doute
Thou haste me wounded in myn herte, O wyf!
No spot of thee ne knew I al my lyf.
Com forth, and lat us taken oure disport;
I chees thee for my wyf and my confort.'[2]

[1] E 2328-34
[2] E 2138-48
*Free* gracious

Chaucer has dissolved the hard images of the *Song of Solomon*[1]
to transparency, and placed them in what we have called a
modifying context. *A garden enclosed* that to the ancient lover
was *my sister, my spouse*—to the medieval interpreter, the Church—
is now the province of the *Romance of the Rose* and of Priapus, of
courtly love turned *fabliau*; and of the higher pantomime of
Pluto and Proserpina as king and queen of *fayerye*. The poet
had read a great deal about gardens, and Gardens, but is so
excellently clear and cool on the subject that no one is conscious
of a weight upon the mind.

January, now stricken blind, appeals to his wife's pity; but
the pity of May's *gentil* heart has run elsewhere, having climbed
the pear-tree where her young man is waiting. Most similar
versions of the story have, next, the sort of dialogue between St.
Peter and God that still survives in jest: in the *Merchant's Tale*
Pluto and Proserpina dispute at once like the divinities in the
*Knight's Tale* and the fowls of the Nun's Priest. The husband
insists on restoring January's sight (*I am a kyng, it sit me noght to
lye*),[2] and the wife will see that May is not at a loss for an answer
(*And alle wommen after, for hir sake*).—So Genius, in Jean de Meun,
found Venus and all women.

> And she ansered, 'Sir, what eyleth yow?
> Have pacience and resoun in youre mynde!
> I have yow holpe on bothe youre eyen blynde.
> Up peril of my soule, I shal nat lyen,
> As me was taught, to heele with youre eyen,
> Was no thyng bet, to make yow to see,
> Than strugle with a man upon a tree.
> God woot, I dide it in ful good entente.'
> 'Strugle!' quod he, 'ye, algate in it wente!
> God yeve yow bothe on shames deth to dyen!
> He swyved thee, I saugh it with myne eyen,
> And elles be I hanged by the hals!'
> 'Thanne is', quod she, 'my medicyne fals;
> For certeinly, if that ye mighte see,
> Ye wolde nat seyn thise wordes unto me.
> Ye han som glymsyng, and no parfit sighte.'
> 'I see', quod he, 'as wel as evere I myghte,
> Thonked be God! with bothe myne eyen two,
> And by my trouthe, me thoughte he dide thee so.'

---

[1] i 15; ii 10–2; iv 7–16
[2] E 2315
*It sit me noght* it does not befit me

'Ye maze, maze, goode sire,' quod she;
'This thank have I for I have maad yow see!
Allas', quod she, 'that evere I was so kynde!'
'Now, dame,' quod he, 'lat al passe out of mynde.
Com doun, my lief . . .'[1]

Thus Chaucer's Merchant on marriage, and on the love of squire
and lady. The comedy of January's *I saugh it with myne eyen . . .*
is not so very far from Molière:

*Je l'ai vu, dis-je, vu, de mes propres yeux vu,*
*Ce qu'on appelle vu . . .*[2]

And another point comes still nearer,

But certeynly, a yong thyng may men gye,
Right as men may warm wex with handes plye

*Comme un morceau de cire entre mes mains elle est,*
*Et je lui puis donner la forme qui me plaît*[3]

This is French from *Le Miroir de Mariage* to *L'École des Femmes*;
and Tartuffe might have been the Summoner's friar when *fort
dévotement il mangea deux perdrix.* In essentials comedy has not
changed between the Miller and the Merchant and the French
classical stage, and at its higher levels it always moves towards
tragedy, and stops short, as in Harpagon and Malvolio and
January. And not only can we think in this way of universal
high comedy, beyond social conditions at a particular time; we
can also find in Molière the perfect description of Chaucerian
balance. It is that gentle equilibrium which Cléante called *les
doux tempéraments*, a *dévotion humaine et traitable.*

In spite of a litter of manuscripts at this stage of the journey,
I cannot refuse to believe that the Host—who has more com-
plaints against his wife than he has courage to tell them all—

---

[1] E 2368-91
*Algate* anyhow        *Hals* neck        *Maze* are bewildered
   The replies of May to January's persistence (E 2380-410) seem to be distinctive:
in the stories quoted by Mrs. Dempster in *Sources and Analogues*, 341ff., the only amusing
elaboration is the wife's remark, in a Low German text, that she has tried seventy-
two treatments (*Deygher bôte hebbe yk wol lxxii ghemaket*) before finding a cure for her
husband. In a medieval Italian tale which Chaucer may have known, the husband
is at once satisfied with the wife's answer.
   [2] *Tartuffe* V iii: Orgon
   [3] E 1429-30: cf. *Le Miroir de Mariage* 730-3
*Gye* govern, guide
   *L'École des Femmes* III iii: Arnolphe

turns at the end of his tether to the *servisable* Squire for something on love.  It is not, after what has been said about *servisable* Damian, a complimentary request; but the Squire is too discreet to quarrel with his elders, and his only reply is to set against the conscienceless May not a virtuous wife (even that would be too outspoken) but a deserted yet still faithful female bird.

> A faucon peregryn thanne semed she
> Of fremde land . . .[1]

That, I believe, is the one echoing cadence of the most mispraised poem of Chaucer; and innocent young minds who might have been persuaded to peruse the *Squire's Tale* earnestly in the manner encouraged by Spenser and Milton owe their gratitude to Mr. Gardiner Stillwell for his criticism of the 'romantic' reading.[2]  Chaucer approximates the remote, Dr. Johnson failed to say, and familiarizes the wonderful—and that is why those who are looking for the wonderful and remote will, if they are honest, find this fragment of 'romance' disappointing.  It seems to me that the man who was once amused by oriental magic gifts and classical marvels, such as his Squire speaks about, had now heard more than enough of them from traders, sailors and preachers.[3]  For whatever reason, he is bored; and laughing in his sleeve at any incidental entertainment that can be found to lighten the labour of composition.  There are shocking rumours of Tartar diet: we may allude nonchalantly to the subject.  There is a strange knight (remark his elocution!).  There are goings-on at the court—only Launcelot could tell you, *and he is ded.*

Not all the jokes were to be appreciated by the Squire, though he is a very tame young man if he does not see some of them; but I am not sure that they were fully appreciated by his audience either, and I share Mr. Stillwell's impression that Chaucer was not always very certain what he was trying to do.  In a tale of which so much is ineffectual, and even carelessly composed, the lines that to my mind have the most life are delivered by the falcon upon her hypocritical tercelet.  There is something in

[1] F 428–9
*Fremde* foreign
[2] GARDINER STILLWELL, 'Chaucer in Tartary', *Review of English Studies* July 1948
I hopefully assume that those who direct 'innocent young minds' in reading selected books of Chaucer will not in fact ignore Mr. Stillwell.
[3] G. R. OWST, *Literature and Pulpit in Medieval England* p.187

them not of the best but the second-best of the *Legend of Good Women*.

'Anon this tigre, ful of doublenesse,
Fil on his knees with so devout humblesse,
With so heigh reverence and, as by his cheere,
So lyk a gentil lovere of manere,
So ravysshed, as it semed, for the joye,
That nevere Jason ne Parys of Troye—
Jason? certes, ne noon oother man
Syn Lameth was, that alderfirst bigan
To loven two, as writen folk biforn—
Ne nevere, syn the firste man was born,
Ne koude man by twenty thousand part
Countrefete the sophymes of his art;
Ne were worthy unbokele his galoche,
Ther doublenesse or feynyng sholde approche,
Ne so koude thanke a wight as he dide me!
His manere was an hevene for to see
Til any womman, were she never so wys;
So peynted he and kembe at point-devys
As wel his wordes as his contenaunce . . .
So on a day of me he took his leve,
So sorwefully eek that I wende verraily
That he had felt as muche harm as I . . .
As I best myghte, I hidde from hym my sorwe,
And took hym by the hond, Seint John to borwe,
And seyde thus: "Lo, I am youres al;
Beth swich as I to yow have been and shal."
What he answerde, it nedeth noght reherce;
Who can say bet than he, who kan do werse?
Whan he hath al wel seyd, thanne hath he doon.'[1]

Here, certainly, the Squire can be admired. Indeed if Sir Philip Sidney in his *Apology for Poetry* had known how to quote as well as to persuade, the Elizabethans, by merely digesting this extract, might have saved several years of waiting for a truly dramatic syntax.

According to Mr. Stillwell, Chaucer thought it 'better to abandon an attempt to force an entrance into fairyland than to get stuck in a magic casement'. I should add the opinion that

[1] F 543ff.
*Unbokele his galoche* an ironical use of the phrase of *John* i 27     *Til* to
*Kembe at point-devys* combed to perfection     *To borwe* as a pledge

Chaucer intended the Franklin's praise to be a blunderingly tactful interruption. The Squire had virtually promised a repetition of the kind of thing we had heard from the Knight— Cambiuskan was to be a conqueror, like Theseus; Algarsyf was to marry with the help of the magic steed of brass, as Palamon had won Emily by the intervention of Venus; and another tournament was in the wind. And so congratulations begin before the son has a chance to make a fool of himself and of his father. The Franklin's tone is both condescending and fulsome (we have all heard it as children); but I believe the intention to be wholly charitable.

> 'In feith, Squier, thow hast thee wel yquit
> And gentilly.   I preise wel thy wit,'
> Quod the Frankeleyn, 'considerynge thy yowthe,
> So feelyngly thou spekest, sire, I allow thee!
> As to my doom, ther is noon that is heere
> Of eloquence that shal be thy peere,
> If that thou lyve; God yeve thee good chaunce,
> And in vertu sende thee continuaunce!
> For of thy speche I have greet deyntee . . .'[1]

The young man was not to be expected, after all, to win the Canterbury competition, but had as it were 'passed' in English. And whatever he might make of his *éducation sentimentale*, his report has the words *'Gentillesse*—excellent'.


'Straw for youre gentillesse!' quod oure Hoost.

—This Courtesy that the Franklin has mentioned is more than the sum of the cardinal virtues; it is the highest reach of medieval civilization, and therefore untranslatable in the language of our time.   More of its meaning may be learnt from the Franklin himself, but not all: for it was a concept capable of infinite extension, so that the Parson could apply it even to his Christ.[2]

---

[1] F 673–81
*Doom* judgement          *Chaunce* luck          *Deyntee* estimation, delight
[2] I 154
There is a convenient note on the early senses of the word *gentleman.* in Sir Ernest Barker's *Traditions of Civility* (Cambridge, 1948) pp. 125–8, and a very perceptive paragraph on *curteisye* in Mr. John Speirs's *Chaucer the Maker* (London: Faber, 1951) pp. 21–2.

Yet if the Franklin is in the Chaucerian sense *Epicurus owene sone*—even if he is January's own brother—he has *manners*: and his tale is about them. If he was touched, as he listened to the Merchant, by a character partially after his own heart, he gives no sign. His famous digression on forbearance in marriage discourses on the high virtue of patience; and at the beginning one can see him throwing out a line for the Merchant to play with as he likes:

> In Armorik, that called is Britayne,
> Ther was a knyght that loved and dide his payne
> To serve a lady in his beste wise;
> And many a labour, many a greet emprise
> He for his lady wroghte, er she were wonne.
> For she was oon the faireste under sonne . . .
> But atte laste she, for his worthynesse,
> And namely for his meke obeysaunce,
> Hath swich a pitee caught of his penaunce
> That pryvely she fil of his accord
> To take hym for hir housbonde and hir lord—
> Of swich lordshipe as men han over hir wyves . . .[1]

The Franklin might in our own day be a comfortable don of an ancient college, careful to be wise and not too serious, and telling his story with mellow vinous satisfaction. He must be able, like the magician in the tale, to clap his hands and whisk away all the conjury; to leave behind simply an aroma in which all problems appear to be solved, including the problems of matrimony, and all difficulties of human character smoothed away. The *Franklin's Tale* was certainly written, or re-written, for the Franklin: it fits him exactly, even at the point where he can step into the part of his own sorcerer, and be unnecessarily sharp about the supper. *Thise amorous folk* and *this wyde world* are phrases with which he could make an impression. To the Franklin, though not to Boccaccio, the magic is all mumbo-jumbo, and therefore the third and last act of *curteisye* in the story is the more surprising. He can bring off his piece, and at the same time feel superior to it. Yet Chaucer, as it were under the mask of the Franklin and above his *lay*, is at least as serious as he is behind the *Knight's Tale*. The debate on marriage,

[1] F 729ff.

Professor Kittredge said, is soundly concluded.[1] *Maiestas et amor* do not agree; domination will not work. And there is also a very neat demonstration, in story, of a part of the problem of evil: the problem of the *raison d'être* of suffering. This is what troubles Dorigen as she looks down from the cliffs of Brittany to the black rocks, and searches the sea for her husband's ship; and she is ironically answered when the magic removal of the one danger she feared places her in a still more perplexing position. As Arcite said, *we woot nat what thing that we preyen heere*.[2] Palamon in prison is distressed at the punishment of the guiltless, while it is a *questione d'amore* whether his escaped cousin is not more miserable. We do not, I believe, feel in very painful sympathy with Palamon or Arcite or even Dorigen: so we are allowed to consider the relativity of evil without distraction of personal grief.

Excepting the Knight's special descriptive display, I am reminded of his performance by the verse of the Franklin; and not only when Chaucer is glancing back at *Il Teseide*. The speech of the *Franklin's Tale* is at its most eloquent in Aurelius:

'Lord Phebus, cast thy merciable eighe
On wrecche Aurelie, which that am but lorn. . . .
    Youre blisful suster, Lucina the sheene,
That of the see is chief goddesse and queene . . .
Ye knowen wel, lord, that right as hir desir
Is to be quyked and lighted of youre fir,
For which she folweth yow ful bisily,
Right so the see desireth naturelly
To folwen hire, as she that is goddesse
Bothe in the see and ryveres more and lesse.
Wherfore, lord Phebus, this is my requeste—
Do this miracle, or do myn herte breste—
That now next at this opposicion

---

[1] Though not so surprisingly as is sometimes assumed. The Franklin's reconciliation of *amour courtois* and marriage was, in theory, and in spite of Petrarch, a sufficiently recognized social development to be represented as familiar also to the Knight (A 3097ff.) and even to the Wife of Bath (D 1230–1, 1255–6). Compare GERVASE MATHEW, 'Marriage and *Amour Courtois* in Late XIVth Century England', *Essays Presented to Charles Williams* (Oxford, 1947) p. 131: and see also the *Owl and the Nightingale, Sir Gawain and the Green Knight*, and the *Book of the Knight of La Tour Landry*.
[2] A 1260
Although I cannot accept Mr. William Frost's point of view in his interpretation of the *Knight's Tale* (*Review of English Studies* October 1949) I must add that he has made interesting comments upon theodicy.

Which in the signe shal be of the Leon,
As preieth hire so greet a flood to brynge
That fyve fadme at the leeste it oversprynge
The hyeste rokke in Armorik Briteyne;
And lat this flood endure yeres tweyne.
Thanne certes to my lady may I seye,
"Holdeth youre heste, the rokkes been aweye."
     Lord Phebus, dooth this miracle for me.
Preye hire she go no faster cours than ye;
I seye, preyeth your suster that she go
No faster cours than ye thise yeres two.
Thanne shal she been evene atte the fulle alway,
And spryng flood laste bothe nyght and day . . .'[1]

The young man prays, in these last lines, very beautifully; but
not having heard the *Manciple's Tale*, is unaware that it is little
use appealing to Phoebus in the matter.   And of course there is
a less remote irony than this: for the rocks disappear, the Damsel
is to keep her Rash Promise, and Aurelius to come forward with
his generous renunciation.   The old plot is an opportunity for
rhetorical narrative not very different from the Knight's.   At the
end, after the husband, the lover and the magician have given
way one to another, it is as if the pieces are knocked down and the
game is over, and no one expects us to take the Franklin's question,
who was the most generous, as a serious point of casuistry.   In
the version of *Il Filocolo* which Chaucer probably knew, it is a
*questione d'amore* that Fiammetta finally answers in the husband's
favour, with the view that honour is more precious than wealth
or a lover's pleasure; but King Trivikramasena, who judged
the earliest known form of the story, plumped for the third person
—in those days a benevolent robber, with no magic.   The
Wife of Bath, I imagine, had her own opinion.

---

[1] F 1036ff.
*At this opposicion* at the opposition of the sun and moon, when the highest tides occur
*Holdeth youre heste* keep your promise

# XIV

Aquinas . . . insists that, though the monastic life in its perfection is the most directly supernatural life, nevertheless the most perfect, i.e., the most complete, the richest, life of the church would not be an organism composed of monks and nuns alone. The married state, in its perfection, requires representation also — and not merely as an ineluctable, regrettable necessity: no, but also as a necessary contributor of variety, tension, richness for the whole . . . The church, hurrah! remains unchangeably greater than any and every *spirituality of one direct dimension only.* Catholicism is no Pietism, however sublime.

BARON VON HÜGEL : Letter to Algar Thorold 15 September 1921

> *Now do you see, that something's to be done,*
> *Beside your beech-coal, and your corsive waters,*
> *Your crosslets, crucibles, and cucurbites?*

BEN JONSON : The Alchemist I i

# ODOUR OF SANCTITY,
## STENCH OF ALCHEMY

IN SOME EARLY COPIES THE NUN AND THE CANON'S YEOMAN follow the Nun's Priest; in others they speak before the Physician and Pardoner, and even before the Shipman and his companions. But if we remember the whereabouts of *Boughton under Blee*, and if the shadowy figure of the Second Nun can possess anything so substantial as an intention, it may be that she wishes to remind her fellow-pilgrims that they are not very far from the shrine of a Christian martyr. There is point, too, in having her after the *Nun's Priest's Tale* (as one might have grace after meat), for if her story is sufficiently distinct from the Prioress's, it will fit as one of a group of mixed tales not meant by the tellers to be tell-tale.

Here certainly—even apart from the order of the pilgrims' way—there is something to be said for the arrangement which Skeat followed, and however little the modern reader may find himself in sympathy, we must not omit to say it. To the medieval mind the *Second Nun's Tale* would be a valid appendix to the marriage sequence; and by the 'medieval mind' I mean the mind of the Parson, or the contemporary mind at one with the Parson.

> And certes, if that a wyf koude kepen hire al chaast by licence of hir housbonde, so that she yeve nevere noon occasion that he agilte, it were to hire a greet merite. Thise manere wommen that observen chastitee . . . been the vessel or the boyste of the blissed Magdelene, that fulfilleth hooly chirche of good odour.[1]

This might be chosen as a motto for our present piece; and such a doctrine, carried to an extreme, as in the *Golden Legend* from which the story is taken, is the kind of thing to which Jean de

[1] I 946–7
*Boyste* box

Meun's cult of Nature—or the cult of Jean de Meun's Genius—is logically opposed. The tale of St. Cecilia is not part of the marriage debate, but is possibly a pious addendum.

And yet I am doubtful about the word 'pious', for this version seems to me as far below the poetry of the Miracle of the Virgin as it could decently be. I have even wondered whether that is not to say too much in favour of certain lines on Cecilia's married life. In the mature Chaucerian stanza the narrative rhythm fits the verse rhythm; in the *Second Nun's Tale* they clutter. And for the verse cadence there is a misjudged application of brakes to a metre or a stanza out of control.[1] *And right as hym was taught by his lernynge* is a line which, in its undistinguished context,[2] suddenly revives the memory of a finer poem.

It has perhaps occurred to the reader at this point to relish an imagined irony: to conceive the possibility that, in spite of the poorness of her tale, the Second Nun had gone further in her life of prayer than the Prioress. Maybe we have a nun of real humility, saying, 'I know this is not great literature, but it is a good theme and I am doing my best': as it is just possible, in our day, for a person singing a weak hymn to sing it with genuine devotion, even though, if all things were perfect, he would not be singing a weak hymn. Even the doubt about the *presence* of the Second Nun[3] may be thought, in relation to the unquestionable shape of the Pardoner and Summoner, right. For the meek are hidden. But this is to pursue an interpretation based not upon the text but on the incompleteness of the text. I therefore abandon it, in order to speak for the defence after Professor Gerould; who writes, in a footnote,

> Persistent detractors of the Second Nun's Tale ought to be compelled by some Court of Poetry to recite aloud verse 140, for example, until the music of it is revealed to them.[4]

In a court of law, I am out of order, since my witness is still that the whole of the tale does not proceed beyond the sacristy. Yet I am thinking of Professor Gerould's 'court of poetry', in which

---

[1] It would be tedious to quote examples, but I refer to G 34–5, 45–6, 220; 284–7, 323–9, 358–64.
[2] G 184
[3] See N. E. ELIASON, 'Chaucer's Second Nun', *Modern Language Quarterly*, III 9–16 (1942).
[4] *Sources and Analogues* p. 669n.
The line that Professor Gerould enumerates is *Ay biddynge in hire orisons ful faste.* Persistent admirers might be given a longer imposition.

anything memorable should be given when it is most likely to be remembered. So I give it here.

> *Vergine madre, figlia del tuo figlio*
> *umile ed alta più che creatura . . .*
> Paradiso

> Thow Mayde and Mooder, doghter of thy Sone,
> Thow welle of mercy, synful soules cure,
> In whom that God for bountee chees to wone,
> Thow humble and heigh over every creature . . .
> *Second Nun's prologue*

> . . . 'I wondre, this tyme of the yeer,
> Whennes that soote savour cometh so
> Of rose and lilies that I smelle heer.
> For though I hadde hem in myne handes two,
> The savour myghte in me no depper go.
> The sweete smel that in myn herte I fynde
> Hath chaunged me al in another kynde.'[1]
> *Second Nun's Tale*

Chaucer has granted his Second Nun a fine translation of Dante; and I find nothing in the rest of her recital to compare with that superb last couplet of the stanza.

In the *Canon's Yeoman's Tale* there occurs the following description of alchemists:

> And everemoore, where that evere they goon,
> Men may hem knowe by smel of brymstoon:
> For al the world they stynken as a goot:
> Hir savour is so rammyssh and so hoot
> That though a man from hem a mile be,
> The savour wole infecte hym, trusteth me.[2]

The 'dramatic' contrast between Second Nun's Tale and Canon's Yeoman's is a difference of scent. And here we recall that hell,

---

[1] *Paradiso* XXXIII 1–2; G 36–9, 246–52 (Tiburtius speaks)
In B 1664–70 of the *Prioress's Tale*, Chaucer appears to have rewritten a later stanza of the Second Nun's prologue (G 50–6) and to have improved the first two lines.
The opening of the quotation from the tale follows closely the text of the *Legenda Aurea* cited in *Sources and Analogues*, p. 673, but the translation is less literal towards the end of the verse:
> *dixit: Miror, hoc tempore, roseus odor hic et liliorum unde respirat, nam si ipsas rosas uel lilia in manibus meis tenerem nec sic poterunt odoramenta tante mihi suauitatis infundere. Confiteor uobis, ita sum refectus ut putem me subito mutatum.*

[2] G 884–9

now appearing a hygienic eternity of distrust and terror of war, an air-conditioned nightmare, was to the imagination of an age of bad drains, sufficiently, a stench.

In more than one manuscript the sweating canon who overtakes the company at Boughton-under-Blean heads a group associated in various ways with sharp practice, including the Physician and Pardoner and Manciple. If this was not Chaucer's final intention, it is still less likely that the slight *Manciple's Tale* was meant to stand alone before the Parson's concluding sermon. The story of the Tell-tale Bird, as it is told here, looks like a left-over from the marriage-feast, and I shall leave it. The *Canon's Yeoman's Tale* appears to us the most remote in subject-matter of the whole collection, the most difficult for the un-instructed reader to follow; and Professor J. W. Spargo, in his valuable essay on the sources of the piece, admits that about the fourteenth-century prelude to chemistry very little is known even by the experts.[1] In that they are more fortunate than the teller of the tale, who apparently knew nothing. For us the chief thing is the vigour of Chaucer's verse, of the yeoman's speech, breaking through the cobwebs and burnt bones and the tomes of Geber and Arnold of Villa Nova so that, in our way, we admire it as much as Lord Coke, who valued the poet highly because his poem illustrated the Statute fifth Henry IV chapter 4 against alchemy.[2] We admire it because it perpetuates the topical. Chaucer's Canon apostate, in our day, is more efficient and more dangerous; and so is his Merchant. The evils of competition and applied science, after six centuries, are more completely out of control, draw larger numbers of people to destruction, and of this progress Chaucer observed the beginnings. A great deal may be learnt—I do not mean by literal inter-pretation—from Professor Spargo's remark that the art of

---

[1] *Sources and Analogues* pp. 685–6. It may be useful to place here a few definitions of technical terms upon which Professor Spargo is more informative than most of the editors:
*Cementyng* combining two solids at high temperature in such a way as to change the properties of one before the melting point
*Citrinacioun* transmuting to gold
*Enbibynge* moistening or soaking
*Mortifie* deaden. 'A widespread belief of the time was that . . . *quick*silver differed from silver . . . only in that the mercury was *alive*, i.e., in fluid state' (p. 688*n*).
*Watres albificacioun* fluids which transmute to silver
*Watres rubifyng* fluids which transmute to gold
[2] Cited by Emerson in *The Conduct of Life* (1860) and, from this source, by C. F. E. Spurgeon, *Five Hundred Years of Chaucer Criticism and Allusion*, under 1634, the date of Lord Coke's death.

*multiplicacioun* reviled by the Canon's Yeoman and condemned by decree of Pope John XXII is carried on constantly today in the making of fourteen-carat or eighteen-carat gold.

The verse of the tale has, in one notable passage at least, an alliterative sinew which suggests that Chaucer was alluding, and paying homage, to a lower level of culture than his own:

> Ye been as boold as is Bayard the blynde,
> That blondreth forth . . .[1]

I mean 'lower' in the way that the ground is lower than the head; both are required for equilibrium, and the soil for health. So Chaucer respected his Ploughman, but did not revere the mob. The Canon's Yeoman contributes to the literature of complaint, not of revolution:

> God sende every trewe man boote of his bale![2]

He is let loose within a selected field.

This raises, again, the matter of Chaucer's relation to his narrators. It is sometimes difficult, as we have seen, to define exactly the degree of his favour, and we have found this non-committal caution of his a wisdom, not a weakness.[3] There is satire in the *Canterbury Tales* but we cannot say, without careful qualification, that it is Chaucer's satire, for he discovered a way of exposing evil at the same time as he was neutralizing the aggressive impulse. That is one thing that makes him a great comedian of Christendom. This *secreta secretorum* he has comically bequeathed to the Canon's Yeoman, who accepts it with gratitude, and later drops it in the ditch:

> There is a chanoun of religioun
> Amonges us, wolde infecte al a toun,
> Though it as greet were as was Nynyvee,
> Rome, Alisaundre, Troye, and othere three . . .
> For in his termes he wol hym so wynde,
> And speke his wordes in so sly a kynde,
> Whanne he commune shal with any wight,
> That he wol make hym doten anonright,
> But it a feend be, as hymselven is . . .

---

[1] G 1413-4
'As bold as blind Bayard' (a horse) was proverbial.
[2] G 1481
*Boote of his bale* good out of evil, help in his trouble
[3] Contrast SIDNEY HAYES COX, 'Chaucer's Cheerful Cynicism', *Modern Language Notes* XXXVI 475-81 (1921).

But worshipful chanons religious,
Ne demeth nat that I sclaundre youre hous,
Although my tale of a chanoun be.
Of every ordre som shrewe is, pardee . . .
This tale was nat oonly toold for yow,
But eek for othere mo; ye woot wel how
That among Cristes apostelles twelve
Ther was no traytour but Judas hymselve . . .
This chanon was my lord, ye wolden weene?
Sir hoost, in feith, and by the hevenes queene,
It was another chanoun, and nat hee,
That kan an hundred foold moore subtiltee . . .

On his falshede fayn wolde I me wreke,
If I wiste how; but he is heere and there;
He is so variaunt, he abit nowhere.[1]

The suggestion of Chaucer's most eminent eighteenth-century editor[2] that 'some sudden resentment had determined Chaucer to interrupt the regular course of his work, in order to insert a Satire against the Alchemists' has been developed by scholarly speculation; even if it should prove true, it could be critically misleading. If you stick a pin into a poet, it may be some time, and a great deal may happen, before a line of poetry is produced. When M. Jusserand extracted the last few lines of the following passage from the *Manciple's Tale* to make comparisons with Swift and *Jonathan Wild*,[3] he was led to ignore the deliberate propriety of the whole passage to the speaker:

The wise Plato seith, as ye may rede,
The word moot nede accorde with the dede:
If men shal telle proprely a thyng,
The word moot cosyn be to the werkyng.
I am a boystous man, right thus seye I,
Ther nys no difference, trewely,
Bitwixe a wyf that is of heigh degree,
If of hir body dishonest she bee,
And a povre wench, oother than this—
If it so be they werke bothe amys—

---

[1] G 972ff., 1088ff., 1173ff.
*Shrewe* wicked person    The last line might be paraphrased 'he is so elusive, you can't pin him down'.
    There is another personal outburst in G 1273–5.
[2] Tyrwhitt, quoted by R. D. French, *A Chaucer Handbook* (New York, 2nd edition, 1947) p. 328
[3] *Histoire littéraire du peuple anglais* (Paris, 1894) I 341

But that the gentile, in estaat above,
She shal be cleped his lady, as in love;
And for that oother is a povre womman,
She shal be cleped his wenche or his lemman.
And, God it woot, myn owene deere brother,
Men leyn that oon as lowe as lith that oother.
   Right so bitwixe a titlelees tiraunt
And an outlawe, or a theef erraunt,
The same I seye, ther is no difference.
To Alisaundre was toold this sentence
That for the tirant is of gretter myght,
By force of meynee, for to sleen dounright
And brennen hous and hoom and make al playn,
Lo, therfore is he cleped a capitayn;
And for the outlawe hath but smal meynee,
And may nat doon so greet an harm as he,
Ne brynge a contree to so greet mescheef,
Men clepen hym an outlawe or a theef . . .[1]

Such defence of reason and morality is nearly as plausible as the Physician's, and more zealous than Reason herself. The text that Chaucer presents to the Manciple to support these keen reflections is the very text that he used in the *Prologue* to justify accurate reporting of statements that might give offence.

So whatever we may think of the unscrupulous purveyor, his digressions are effectively and logically related to certain passages in the Parson's sermon, which is the subject of a part of my last chapter. As for the farce of the Manciple's prologue, that would provide a preacher with a very great deal of first-rate material.

---

[1] H 207-34

| *Boystous* 'plain' | *Leyn* lay | *Lith* lies | *Meynee* military support |
| *Playn* flat | | | |

# XV

*And when comes vivification?*
*—After mortification.*

*The Alchemist II i*

*Though Mr. Humble's taste in the matter of food and drink must be considered a little ordinary, yet in his love of reading he was above the vulgar.   He hardly ever went out without taking one or other of the older English poets in his pockets.   And, as the day was Good Friday, he carried Chaucer. . . .*
*Mr. Humble gave one look at Jenny, and opened Chaucer.   'O gode god,' he read, loudly, 'ye women that been of so greet beautee, remembreth yow of the proverbe of Salomon, that seith: "he lykneth a fair womman, that is a fool of hir body, lyk to a ring of gold that were in the groyn of a sowe."   For right as a sowe wroteth in everich ordure, so wroteth she hir beautee in the stinkinge ordure of sinne.'*

T. F. POWYS: *Goat Green*

*. . . This is the way, and that thou keep the learning that I teach thee. Whatso thou hearest or seest or feelest that should let thee in the way, abide not with it wilfully, tarry not for it restfully, behold it not, like it not, dread it not; but ay go forth in thy way, and think that thou wouldest be at Jerusalem. . . . And also if men will tarry thee with tales and feed thee with lesings, to draw thee to mirths and to leave thy pilgrimage, make deaf ear and answer not again, and say naught else but that thou wouldest be at Jerusalem . . .*

WALTER HILTON: *Scale of Perfection* II 21

# THE SUM OF PENITENCE AND OF THE VICES

TRACTATES OF CHAUCERIAN PROSE AWAIT NEW JUDGEMENT, all of which (except *Melibeus*) I have successfully evaded till now. Here I am, driven to a corner, and pressed for a reckoning. They shall have it: let the other vices wait.

No sane person will look very long for the 'consolation of philosophy' in Chaucer's exercise. One studies *Boece*, if at all, not for wisdom but for information, to see how Dan Geoffrey was reading and thinking in the 'eighties. And one turns for relief to the Jacobean translator honoured in the Loeb Classical Library.

> Forwhi alle othere lyvynge beestes han of kynde to knowe nat hemself; but whan that men leeten the knowynge of hemself, it cometh hem of vice.[1]

Those who wish to read Boethius in English will prefer 'I.T.'

> For in other living creatures the ignorance of themselves is nature, but in men it is vice.[2]

For the *Consolation of Philosophy* is not on any account to be neglected. And what I think matters most to the reader of Chaucer is not the recognition of incidental allusions to Boethius, or even of a Boethian passage or poem, but the attempt of Boethius to form a theodicy. I mean that the greatest consolation, and today apparently the most difficult to accept, is the answer of Philosophy to the problem of evil: an answer for which the torture administered in sixth-century Pavia was nevertheless a sufficiently overwhelming test of experience. It is this: that the divine power is incapable of evil, which is therefore nothing: that *being* is good, and the contrary of goodness in the end a failure to *be*. 'Being and unity and goodness is all one', explains

---

[1] *Boece* II pr. v 172–6 (F. N. Robinson's numbering)
[2] The translation of 'I.T.', revised by H. F. Stewart, of the following text of Book II pr. v 88–9 in the *Consolation of Philosophy* (Loeb Classical Library: London and New York, 1918):
    *Nam ceteris animantibus sese ignorare naturæ est; hominibus uitio uenit.*

Chaucer: and that is the essence of the strength behind his comedy. The great comedian has his part of what he called 'tranquillity of soul', as well as the great mystic. And give Boethius, who was neither, his due. It is not only that he handed on to the middle ages, from Plato and Aristotle, an example of speculative thought. A martyr needs more to die for.

*Artow like an asse to the harpe?* the lady Philosophy is translated, in a fortunate moment—and Chaucer might himself have observed, during an interlude between two masterpieces, that his own art, the art of poetry, is not always very reviving. He found the same thought in his book. *Certeynly,* says Boethius, *thise ben faire thynges and enoynted with hony swetness of Rethorik and Musike; and oonly whil thei ben herd thei ben delycious.*[1] This is the kind of craft Chaucer could use in comedy, knowing very well what he was doing. Boethius himself was occasionally a poet; and his metres were translated in forty days of poetic exhaustion. Yet something comes through: enough to be interrupted, at times, by a gloss. They would be worth attempting again, by another who, like Chaucer, has no desire to rhyme them. However tired, he managed to write of thought *imaked a knyght of the clere sterre . . .*[2]

There remains the beginning of an elementary textbook on the astrolabe, most of which I leave to the antiquary. The manuscript was composed for a boy of ten years, *lyte Lowys my sone,* perhaps Lewis Chaucer; and in it the reader of poetry, if he wishes, can confirm an impression of Chaucer's attitude to *these astrologiens.* He may also mark a loyal salutation to the King, and to the King's English:

> . . . And preie God save the king, that is lord of this langage, and alle that him feith berith and obeieth, everich in his degre, the more and the lasse. But considre wel that I ne usurpe not to have founden this werk of my labour or of myn engyn. I n'am but a lewd compilator of the labour of olde astrologiens, and have it translatid in myn Englissh oonly for thy doctrine. And with this swerd shal I sleen envie.[3]

[1] *Boece* II pr.iii 8–12
[2] IV m. i 14–5
[3] *Astrolabe* prol. 64–74
*Engyn* skill
Chaucer expresses his opinion of the forecasting of human destiny in Part II 4, in which he speaks of *observaunces of judicial matere and rytes of payens, in whiche my spirit hath no feith . . .*

We expect an apology at least as well phrased from the author who had begun the *Canterbury Tales*, and it is no plea for general weakness in a man's prose to advance a single preface as the one extended passage in which he was not sticking to a text. The reader who looks no further must suppose that English, except in verse, had not only failed to achieve the maturity of Italian, but had come nowhere near a comparison. A condition in which it was much *easier* to write clear verse than clear prose is very difficult for our century to understand.

But that is not the whole story. If we are speaking of real achievement in English prose of the middle and later fourteenth century, the greatest English poet of the time is hardly placed. And we have very good reason, even in a book about an author who appears to inhabit another world, to say something of the *Cloud of Unknowing*, and Walter Hilton, and Julian of Norwich. Between the two worlds, if they are two, of comedian of Christendom and of mystic, there are strange similarities of language, and stranger relations of mind. In 'prose' of the *Cloud of Unknowing* is a grace given:

> What weri wrechid herte and sleping in sleuthe is that, the whiche is not waknid with the draught of this love and the voise of this cleping?

> He wil thou do bot loke on Hym and late Him alone

> And this is the eendles merveilous miracle of love, the whiche schal never take eende; for ever schal He do it, and never schal He seese for to do it

> This is sche, that same Marye, that whan sche sought Hym at the sepulchre with wepyng chere wolde not be counfortyd of aungele[1]

There are things more original and astonishing in this treatise, such as the composition of a paragraph of the fourth chapter of Dom Justin McCann's edition, the paragraph which concludes that in God's good time we are never expected to do more than one thing at once.[2] But I find nothing greater than the second sentence I have quoted, which is the simplification of a master.

---

[1] *The Cloud of Unknowing* edited by PHYLLIS HODGSON (Early English Text Society: Oxford, 1944) pp. 14, 15, 19, 55.
*Sleuthe* sloth   *With the drawing of this love and the voice of this calling* is the version of Dom Justin McCann's text (London: Burns Oates, 1924) and also of Mr. T. S. Eliot's *Little Gidding.*   *Late* let
[2] *The Cloud of Unknowing* ed. PHYLLIS HODGSON, p. 20

And this is very near to the peculiar ease of Walter Hilton coasting a marsh or scaling a mountain. 'Take it as it will come', he says to his reader, 'and not all at once': and there is his tone. The author of the *Scale of Perfection* is, supremely, the Well-Tempered Mystic. He is lucid, lucidly complete, and completely in tradition. And he can translate Holy Writ into an English which as Professor R. W. Chambers has shown[1] is superior to the Wicliffite. In the best of these translations he gives no literal rendering, but digests his text so that it is simplified or enriched as its essence turns into the mother tongue. When this happens, he may even set down something which is finer than the Authorized Version:

> Be ye rooted and grounded in charity, that ye may know . . . and feel with all hallows, which is the length of the endless being of God, the breadth of the wonderful charity and the goodness of God, the height of the almighty majesty of Him and the groundless deepness of the wisdom of God.

> These that God knew before should be made shapely to the image of His Son, these He called, these He righted, these He magnified, these He glorified.[2]

I do not apologize for this digression, for I believe that a modern who reads both Chaucer and Hilton will be surprised to find how much two men of very different calling can have in common. Walter Hilton is what Geoffrey Chaucer might have been, if he had been given to contemplation instead of literature and affairs; and having thought of Chaucer's poetry as an instrument advancing his King's English in Europe, I can only explain his prose as the penalty of a training for business. Chaucer shows, and Hilton says, that to love the man and hate the sin 'is a craft by itself, whoso could do it well'; and 'this is, as I under-

---

[1] 'The Continuity of English Prose from Alfred to More and His School', Preface to *Harpsfield's Life of More* (Early English Text Society, 1932) pp. cvii–iii
[2] *The Scale of Perfection* modernized from the first printed edition by an Oblate of Solesmes (Burns Oates, 1927), I ch. 93; I ch. 13; II ch. 28.
*Ephesians* iii 17–9: '. . . that ye, being rooted and grounded in love, may be able to comprehend with all saints what is the breadth, and length, and depth, and height: and to know the love of Christ, which passeth knowledge, that ye might be filled with all the fulness of God.'
*Romans* viii 29–30: 'For whom he did foreknow, he also did predestinate to be conformed to the image of his Son . . . Moreover whom he did predestinate, them he also called: and whom he called, them he also justified: and whom he justified, them he also glorified.'

stand, the teaching of Saint Austin.' And whether or not
Chaucer was conscious of writing, let us say, *as Austin bit,* this is
precisely the 'craft' of his portrait of the Monk. *Stryve not,*
Chaucer agrees; and Hilton writes of the soul exiled from heaven
it should have had 'if it had stood still'. Humility is 'endless
meekness', and with meekness and charity a man will do 'more
in a year than he should without this desire profit in seven, if
he strive with gluttony, lechery, and such other continually, and
beat himself with scourges each day from morning to evensong
time'.[1] What is true here is implied in Chaucer's understanding
of human desire: that appetite denied should be sublimated.
Julian of Norwich also understood: the great healer is the one
who makes the mind whole.

> God is nerer to us than our owen soule: for He is ground in
> whom our soul stondith, and He is mene that kepith the
> substance and the sensualite together so that thai shall never
> departyn.[2]

This is not easy to find in the *Parson's Tale,* and that is why I am
so long introducing it. Walter Hilton speaks of a 'stable mind,
clear sight, and clean burning love'; these he has, and good sense
raised to the power of divinity. His language can surprise—

> Fair is a man's soul, and foul is a man's soul . . . therefore
> we shall deem no man as evil for that thing that may be
> used both evil and well.[3]

But he is not dangerous. Mysticism, medieval religious well
knew, could be much too strong for the unprepared to stand;
possibly Chaucer had seen the warnings that contemplatives gave
of their charity. Today we are at a disadvantage. Even the false
mystic, or the pietist, is not so clearly exposed as in the age that
produced the *Theologia Germanica.* And when true mysticism
becomes material for verse, as in the finest poems of the first

---

[1] *Scale of Perfection* I ch. 64; ch. 70; ch. 38, etc.; II ch. 1; ch. 34; I ch. 76. I
quote again from the modernized edition, which is the only text in print at the time
of writing.
[2] *Revelations* of Julian of Norwich, British Museum MS Sloane 2499 f. 40  *Together,*
MS *to God*
    The *substance* is the 'image of God', our being as it was made and is in Him; the
*sensualite* is the power of perception and appetite, since the Fall lacking proper control
by human will unless the will is given grace. They are united and perfected in
Christ.
[3] *Scale of Perfection* II ch. 4; ch. 12

half of the twentieth century, we need to be careful. A poet cannot be expected to hide his best work in a poison-bottle; he would be accused of self-advertisement. But a reader should be sure that he is not prescribing for himself, without guidance, a course which the saints have taken only at an advanced stage of discipline.

The Lord has 'shown' to Julian, in the fourteenth of her *Revelations*,

> *I am ground of thi beseking: first it is my wille that thou have it; and sythen, I make thee to willen it; and sithen I make thee to besekyn it and thou besekyst it. How shuld it than be that thou shuld not have thyn besekyng?*[1]

This the reader may take or leave, as he will; the reader of Mr. Eliot's *Four Quartets* has taken a part of it already. Julian of Norwich, like Boethius, like Chaucer, was interested in the problem of evil. She was troubled by it, and was given a wisdom about it that is beyond the neat and not invariably consoling argument in the *Consolation of Philosophy*. The wisdom is no logic. It is her thirteenth present from her Lord: *synne is behovabil, but al shal be wel and al shal be wel and al manner of thyng shal be wele.*[2] It is a mystery not yet to be understood, but it shall be. It is dangerous, now to be kept for the contemplative. And this, like an echo of St. Thomas Aquinas: *whan synne hath no lenger leve to pursue, than shal the werkyng of mercy secyn . . .*[3] How near, from another direction, Chaucer had come—and, wise enough to know the danger of wisdom to fools, he proposed to end his pilgrimage with a scouring sermon and a retraction. To the retraction I shall return. The sermon would seem to suggest that evil is not merely deprivation of good, any more than *stinkynge ordure* is deprivation of incense. But we are to remember that this is an exhortation to the weak, including ourselves; and exhortation always tends towards dualism. By this I mean that exhortation, of the kind that works, must seem to grant more power to evil than evil can finally possess. The *Parson's Tale* is not a philosophical discussion of the problem of evil. It is an attempt to improve sinners. The Parson therefore does his utmost, in terms of things familiar to everyone, to make sin

---

[1] MS Sloane 2499 f.26ᵛ
*Besekyng* beseeching          *Sythen* then
[2] MS Sloane 2499 f.18ᵛ
*Scale of Perfection* I ch. 33: '. . . do as I have said, and all shall be well.'
[3] MS Sloane 2499 f.23ᵛ

repellent. But the last and profoundest sin is despair; and upon this he observes that *the feblesse of the devel may nothyng doon, but if men wol suffren hym*; and that the one who has lost hope of mercy *shal han strengthe of the help of God, and of al hooly chirche, and of the proteccioun of aungels, if hym list.*[1] To the literal-minded philosopher, I suppose, there must always appear a Manichean tinge even in the New Testament; and the exceptionally honest St. Augustine had a good deal of trouble with that which, intellectually, he concluded to be non-existent. The presence of the *Parson's Tale* is the homage of a great comedian of the intelligence to the spiritual life, to the call of penitence, to the resolution to become more worthy of the promises of Christ; it is to justify the medieval joy of Julian of Norwich and of the carol of *Adam lay ybounden*. This is the joy of *O felix culpa!*—the Fall brings a glorious Redeemer. And we deny the height if we deny the depth. The deprivation of air is merely vacuum; and a vacuum is suffocation. And the deprivation of light is blindness.

In her fifth revelation Julian knew evil conquered, and said

> I see three things: game, scorne, and arneste. I see game, that the fend is overcome; I see scorne, in that God scornith him, and he shall be scornyd. And I see arneste that he is overcome be the blissfull Passion and deth of our Lord Jesus Criste . . .[2]

Anyone acquainted with Chaucer could guess that this was written by a contemporary. And if the phrase 'merry England' has any meaning worth meaning for an age trying to recover from black death, then the meaning is this: that an England exists in which both a poet in the world and an enclosed anchoress can relax to laughter with the utmost seriousness of which they are capable. For the finest point of Chaucerian comedy is that which is both 'game' and 'earnest'. And when Mr. Kenneth Sisam, in an informed essay, contrasts thirteenth-century 'game' with the 'earnest' of fourteenth-century occasional satire, and adds of the fourteenth century that 'the greater writers—Rolle, Wiclif, Langland, Gower—were obsessed by the troubles of their

---

[1] I 1074
[2] MS Sloane 2499 f. 11ᵛ–12ʳ
My quotations from Julian can be found, in slightly modernized and altered form, in *Revelations* ed. GRACE WARRACK (Methuen, 1901, 1945) pp. 135, 84, 56, 72, 32. The version by Roger Hudleston (Burns Oates, 1927) may be preferred for general reading.

time',[1] there are two things which he fails to observe. One is that if his statement is true of those he selects as the 'greater' writers, it is certainly not true of the greatest. The other is that if anyone can grant it to be as true of Gower and even of Langland as it is of Wiclif, it is not true at all of Richard Hermit. If Rolle was obsessed by anything, it was by the love of Christ. He was absorbed, in contemplation, by the delights of his *calor, canor et dulcor*, by 'warmth, song and sweetness'. But Rolle, who lived when York westfront was building, at the beginning of the century, is before our period. A vital interest of Chaucer's 'anxious age',[2] for our own, is that according to the most influential assumptions of today it ought to have been, to the finest minds, an age of utter despair. Look, and see what it is.

And as I come to read through the present chapter, I receive unexpected and welcome confirmation of my rasher proceedings. It is in the form of a book by Dr. Joseph Dalby. Dr. Dalby does not in fact mention Chaucer at all, but the whole of his thesis has Chaucerian authority behind it, and should be read by anyone who has a more than superficial interest in our poet. Five sentences will show why.

> One of the most disastrous results of the break-up of the medieval synthesis has been the dissociation of the natural world from the spheres of morality and religion. It begins . . . with the notable discovery that man and his planet can no longer be regarded as the centre of a vast creation, but only as a rather insignificant incident in a colossal drama. . . . There is [in the modern world] . . . danger to the integration of the whole of man's life in a spiritual order which arises when the natural order, the background of the life of man as a creature, has been withdrawn from the scene, as irrelevant to the life of the spirit of man in the Divine order. Hence arises an impoverishment of the religious spirit which at its worst operates in a meaningless vacuum and at its best exhibits the characteristics of a hot-house pietism . . .

> There is in the mystics in their attitude to nature a perpetual rhythm, a *systole* and *diastole* of affirmation and denial, affirmation of the goodness of the natural as flowing from the primal goodness of God, and denial of nature because

---

[1] KENNETH SISAM, *Fourteenth Century Verse and Prose* (Oxford, 1921) p. xxvii. I may add that Mr. Sisam's introduction, p. xlii, contains a criticism of the state of Middle English studies that has not received the attention it deserves.
[2] The phrase is Mr. Sisam's, p. xxxviii.

in the actual world as tainted by sin the natural, which is the lower element, is always tending to dominate the higher spiritual element and therefore must be denied, with violence if need be.[1]

And this, represented in art, in an unfinished work of art, is also the perpetual rhythm of *Canterbury Tales*: movement from and towards, *systole* and *diastole*, the pattern of the Human Comedy in relation to the Divine. It is the pattern of the individual life striving for perfection, as of the life of the Body of Christ; to which every single pilgrim, when all the seven sins have been revealed, may yet belong. The mystic remains the *acies mentis* of the age, in solitude or in the *cenacolo* of St. Catherine of Siena, but the marvel of the human comedian is that through his eyes you can see so much of the age so clearly. I have re-written Dr. Dalby's words for Chaucer, not because they have to do with the pilgrim's progress of a particular person or group of persons, but because they express the highest wisdom of a whole community. It was a community that could accept as part of *Canterbury Tales* the uncompromising lecture to which we now turn.

The Parson's is not the first sermon in the tales: it is the reality after the illusion, and the comedy of the pilgrimage returns to the level of ordinary life with the Church pulpit above it. The *povre persoun* is doing his best to wash the dirty linen that has accumulated. Now, in our time, only the linen and the laundry have changed, not the dirt. The Parson could get at every one of his parishioners: there they were, and here were the pilgrims, and he was not expected to soothe them or ask them to come again. It was for him to speak out. The twentieth century was hardly his business. Our time could do with warnings upon deadly sin, but the kind of warning that would now be most effective is not likely to impress the year 2510. The preacher in every age has to try to reach the age's own Wife of Bath, and for the Parson that was not difficult. She could at least learn some theology. Now the Wife of Bath will always remain, but not always robust, or even instructed: at present she attends the nightclub at home, and abroad reads *Vogue*. So we

[1] JOSEPH DALBY, *Christian Mysticism and the Natural World* (London: James Clarke, 1950) pp. 53–4, 143

turn with the greatest respect to the *Parson's Tale*. After all, it
followed, at a distance, the most respectable thirteenth-century
Dominicans; even if St. Raymund of Pennaforte and Guilielmus
Peraldus do not necessarily fit together, and the Parson's schema
breaks down in redundancy at the end of a chapter upon confession. And his message is still active in a manuscript illustration
of *invidia* and *charite*.[1] Pictures can help, but so can straight
speech: and I quote some of it without ceremony. Sharp
snibbing needs no gloss.

> Where been thanne the gaye robes, and the soft shetes, and
> the smale shertes?

> . . . and eek the buttokes of hem faren as it were the hyndre
> part of a she-ape in the fulle of the moone

> . . . thanne wole he be angry . . . and defenden or excusen
> his synne by unstedefastnesse of his flessh; or elles he dide
> it for to holde compaignye with his felawes; or elles, he
> seith, the feend enticed hym; or elles he dide it for his
> youthe; or elles his compleccioun is so corageous that he
> may nat forbere; or elles it is his destinee, as he seith, unto
> a certein age; or elles, he seith, it cometh hym of gentillesse
> of his auncestres

> A man that is in a droppynge hous in manye places, though
> he eschewe the droppynge in o place, it droppeth on hym
> in another place. So fareth it by a chydynge wyf; but she
> chide hym in o place, she wol chide hym in another

> . . . swiche scorneres faren lyk the foule tode, that may nat
> endure to smelle the soote savour of the vyne whanne it
> florissheth

> . . . but though that hooly writ speke of horrible synne,
> certes hooly writ may nat been defouled, namoore than the
> sonne that shyneth on the mixen[2]

So much for the *language* of the 'tale': I do not think it could be
more generously displayed, without further impropriety, in a
publisher's advertisement. The dream of the earnest student is
that Mr. Coghill will translate the *Parson's Tale* into modern
idiom, that the censor will ban it, and that thousands will read
it for penance. But the student, to save his own soul, should

---

[1] MS Gg 4.27, f. 389ʳ: Cambridge University Library
[2] I 197 (of hell), 424 (of the immodestly dressed), 584–5, 632, 636, 911

beware of flattery.  He may say that the sermons which survive as literature are not necessarily the most successful in their own time; he must not pretend that either the Parson, or even Richard Wimbledon, can be admitted to the company of the Venerable Bede and Lancelot Andrewes and Newman, except in the mystical body of Christ.  The author of the *Cloud of Unknowing* was conscious of a vice of his age when he wrote that *somtyme men thought it meeknes to sey nought of theire owne hedes, bot yif thei afermid it by Scripture and doctours wordes; and now it is turnid into curioustee and schewyng of kunnyng.*[1]  Bede begins, let us say, 'the Holy Gospel which has been read to you, my brethren, is worthy of your utmost attention'; and proceeds to expound his text with the greatest care, and without a trace of gratuitous elaboration.  By the fourteenth century 'glosing' was a disease, with which the two preachers I mentioned are by no means the most afflicted.  And between the useful and the great there is a difference of intention.  An act which displays the invisible is permanent; pruning is never quite the same in succeeding years.   I take the figure from Richard Wimbledon, who is applying Christ's parable of the labourers in the vineyard to the society of his own time.[2]  Different offices, he says, are needed for the vine—the Labourer to dung, the Knight to protect, the Priest to prune.   And that office of the Priest we cannot deny.  But the highest ministry, if we accept Wimbledon's application, is to give the vine blood.

This is another reason to place the mystics before the preacher: they have a gift of grace which is bound to be hidden in a circumstantial criticism, however excellent, of immoralities.   Grace is more than a congregation of sinners can reasonably expect to be manifest in a sermon; and when they live at the right time for it, they are highly favoured.  We do not realize what we have been given in one moment, until it is taken away the next.   This is true, also, of the Canterbury comedy, which for many people is not complete, even if we imagine it all written, until the retraction of the tales *that sownen into synne*.  The *Parson's Tale* contains the morality that Chaucer wholly respected, but was not forced to mix with music: and those who do not know what was required for the reformation of the Pardoner and the Summoner and the Wife of Bath and the Man of Law and the Miller

[1] *Cloud of Unknowing* ed. PHYLLIS HODGSON, p. 125
[2] Richard Wimbledon's sermon of 1388 is preserved in Foxe's *Acts and Monuments*, and the first part reprinted in a slightly modernized form in *Famous English Sermons* edited by ASHLEY SAMPSON (London: Nelson, 1940).

and the Merchant may find out by reading it. They are thereby assured that Chaucer knew the dangers, as well as the arts, of irony, and the use of a man to whom sin stinks. His tale is of war and courtly love, marriage and birth-control, extortion and bad priests; and of mortification without excess, and the right way to Jerusalem Celestial. For on this side of the grave there is always a way of penitence open. So Chaucer ends, in obedience and humility, with his literary confession; which I confess I can never read without delight. If we try to imagine the whole pattern of which this last fragment is a part, it is like looking backward or forward, in a fallen and redeemed world, to the natural law *in his right poynt in paradys.*

And it seems that poetic freedom is possible only under such authority. The poet of the fourteenth century with a genius for comedy could know that his was not the last word; he could get on with his job in peace. Each liberal art within an order could claim its proper independence. Theology was still, at least to the conservative, supreme; but philosophy was not theology, and poetry was neither. Since that day, some portions of the material of the *Parson's Tale* have reappeared, in a different form, in Shakespearian tragedy; and others are related to poetry between our wars. There are sentences which may be printed in contemporary verse—as if Chaucer, under the mask of his Parson, knew very well what was coming, and that it 'always will be':

> But lat us go now
> To thilke horrible sweryng of adjuracioun and
>  conjuracioun,
> As doon thise false enchauntours
> Or nigromanciens in bacyns ful
> Of water, or in a bright swerd, in a cercle,
> Or in a fyr, or in a shulderboon of a sheep . . .
> What seye we of hem that bileeven on divynailes,
> As by flight or by noyse of briddes, or of beestes,
> Or by sort, by geomancie, by dremes, by chirkynge
> Of dores, or crakkynge of houses, by gnawynge
> Of rattes and
> Swich manere wrecchednesse?[1]

You may call this pure accident. The essential is that the great medieval tradition could still, in Chaucer's day, be taken for

---

[1] I 603ff.
Upon this passage it is not for me to comment. For *geomancie* Manly and Rickert prefer *nygromancye*: some MSS deal in *egromancy*, *egrimoynsie*, and even *griomancye*.

granted; and only too easily.  Now, in our time, the lay poet is left to convey, to very many who in our nominally Christian society would otherwise be unaware of it, the power that has been lost.  And the *Parson's Tale* is there to imply what I hope I have already suggested: that a dominant pulpit can relieve much distracting tension in the mind of a writer of comedy, and can even make great comedy possible.  Chaucer, here, could not be easily gay; and, as a distinguished layman, he might very well find himself preaching a disguised sermon, or broadcasting a Sunday evening postscript, for those who never listen to the clergy.  If he then returned to his own century, he would at first be troubled before growing used to the lighter air.  'To reflect that from one point of view religion is culture', he might begin, 'and from another point of view culture is religion'— recalling something he had recently read—'can be very disturbing.  To ask whether the people have not a religion already, in which the tournament and the ram for wrestling play their parts, is embarrassing; so is the suggestion that part of the religion of the higher monastic is purfled sleeves and a Canterbury holiday'—

> When we consider the quality of the integration required for the full cultivation of the spiritual life, we must keep in mind the possibility of grace and the exemplars of sanctity in order not to sink into despair . . . To reflect that from one point of view religion is culture, and from another point of view culture is religion, can be very disturbing.  To ask whether the people have not a religion already, in which Derby Day and the dog track play their parts, is embarrassing; so is the suggestion that part of the religion of the higher ecclesiastic is gaiters and the Athenæum.  It is inconvenient for Christians to find that as Christians they do not believe enough, and that on the other hand they, with everybody else, believe in too many things . . .[1]

So Mr. Eliot, whom Chaucer would have the intelligence to understand and the wit to remember.  But under his own sky Chaucer had reflected on all these things, with very little inconvenience, and no embarrassment.

Chaucer's 'retraction', whose authenticity has been so frequently and fruitlessly questioned, is almost the *quod erat demonstrandum* of his work: like the dyer meekly asking forgiveness

---

[1] T. S. ELIOT, *Notes Towards the Definition of Culture* (London: Faber, 1948) p. 32

before the Lord for the colour of his hands. It would be impertinent for anyone but Dan Geoffrey's confessor to make any more of it. And if Dan Geoffrey in the end desired the kind of perfection that Walter Hilton could so well describe, who are we to express surprise? Only one thing is left for this chapter: and that is to state a conclusion which I have hinted more than once, which I believe will be reached by all those who look at the *Parson's Tale* both in its immediate context and in the context of religious prose of fourteenth-century England, but which will shock the casual reader and the amateur analyst, and may produce between them a little harmless Kentish fire. It is the refreshing *psychological health* that is to be found in the period. Mr. Sidney Hayes Cox, in an article to which I have referred, makes the interesting statement that the Parson

> . . . warns husbands not to love their wives too much, and bids them ignore their sex except for breeding purposes.

I call this sentence interesting, because it is a very good test of the unconscious assumption of the Wife of Bath, and of her husbands, in our time. Mr. Cox admits more than they may see at a glance. Husbands are not *prevented* from loving their wives: they are warned not to love them *too much*. This means, presumably, that they are to love God first. They are not all commanded to chastity: they are bidden to ignore sex *except for breeding purposes*. And if that is how Mr. Cox wishes to refer to the act of human generation, let him do so. It is not how the Parson refers to it. I add only a memory of two customs. Readers of Chaucer will have heard of the first, and viewers of the twentieth century have remarked the second. One is the blessing of the marriage-bed; the other is divorce.

This is not, of course, a judgement of the middle age *versus* the modern. History is never so simple. But as I look back upon what I have been reading for the past several years, I am impressed by a single conviction: that the poetry and prose of Chaucer's time, before the fifteenth-century erosion, shows a way, and the end of the way, out of the 'age of anxiety'. And as we ponder the fourteenth century, we are at a turn of time when the end of the way out is also the way in.

# EPILOGUE

*No man shall ever make me believe that those who reared the cathedral of Ely . . . were rude, either in their manners, or in their minds and words . . . Nor shall any man persuade me that that was a rude and beggarly state of things, in which (reign of Edward the Third) an Act was passed regulating the wages of labour, and ordering that a woman for weeding in the corn should receive a penny a day, while a quart of red wine was sold for a penny, and a pair of men's shoes for two-pence.*

WILLIAM COBBETT: *Advice to Young Men and (incidentally) to Young Women* § 235

*The bay trees in our country are all withered.*

SHAKESPEARE: *Richard II, II iv*

*But what is Paradise? All things that are . . . save one tree and the fruits thereof . . .*

*Theologia Germanica L*

ELY LANTERN
*Photograph by Starr and Rignall*

I TAKE A LAST GLANCE, BEFORE THE 550TH ANNIVERSARY OF
his passing, at Chaucer in that time, and in this: not for a
summary but a fresh look at the same view, which has a
slightly different light every time we really regard it. Turn
towards the later fourteenth century, and you see building of
smooth surface but extraordinary complication, and a delta of
thought that is equally intricate. The initiative both in the
architecture and in the philosophy of Europe had passed to
England. It was an era of critical intelligence and vitality of
invention. And in spite of all its evils, it had not yet lost the
theological virtues. Then the intellect hardens; stone solidifies.
In verse, all but the anonymous lose a sense of movement, and
Lydgate suffers from muscular rheumatism. Skelton's brilliant
and desperate entertainment is a final flicker of the tail of medieval
England. And Shakespeare, looking back to the reign of Henry
IV, saw not so very much more of fraud or riot or opportunism
than was visible to Chaucer, but a spiritual disease of a whole
people. All things are possible except to despair.

But return to the architecture, in which the continuity of the
middle ages will be here and now as long as our cathedrals
remain. Chaucer still saw himself within an order of Catholic
Europe, in a Europe broken and divided, an England diseased
and heretical. 'To lead the things which are lower to the things
which are higher through the things which are intermediate':
that is the great principle of Catholic order: which needs more
than a few generations of division or disease or heresy to destroy
it. Chaucer was no regressive, but a most conscious mind of his
age: opposing to disorder not the tense, single-minded elevation
of High Gothic, of the *Divine Comedy*, but the Decorated of his
own humour, that is a humour of England and of Europe as well.
In an exact sense he is a more philosophical poet than Dante,
though Matthew Arnold was right to imply that if we had to
lose the one or the other we had better hold on to Dante. Chaucer
was constantly aware of the problems of evil and of the freedom
of human will; he knew the work of philosophers, and without

being a philosopher himself, had the philosophical habit of mind, the capacity to delay conclusion. Perhaps this is one reason why he left so much incomplete. But the Gothic builder was always telling his stories, and what remained unfinished was not therefore fragmentary, for it˅was never within a closed system. Nor are the *Canterbury Tales*. And for the patterns of these 'fragments' there is analogy in other arts: the medieval motet in which praise of the pious clergy, and satire of the hypocritical, could both be sung together with a scriptural text in musical counterpoint: or the beautiful early fourteenth-century decoration of Queen Mary's Psalter, in which a religious set-piece shares a page with an informal hawking party.

There is more to be said about the philosophers, and much more than I can say here. The reader of fourteenth-century English literature has too much of the superficies of social history forced upon his attention by commentators, and too little of the history of ideas. He turns away from the faggots and hides and pitchers, wanting a 'background' of the kind that Professor Basil Willey has assembled for later times. Chaucer lived in an age that had been enlightened by St. Thomas Aquinas: who described man not merely as a spirit imprisoned in flesh, but as a compositum of body and soul. Now the *logical probability* of the Resurrection of the Body, as well as the revelation, is a doctrine one would almost be inclined to invent for our poet, if it were not already so authoritatively behind him. Sense-experience, taught Aquinas, was to be respected; for through it we could attain, by analogy, to a concept of the infinite First Cause. *Nihil in intellectu quod prius non fuerit in sensu.* The greatest thinker of the past several centuries allowed an intelligent man to be in some sense at home in the world, so long as he was not too preoccupied with it. Thus, in the end, Troilus laughs, and the Parson has his turn. Chaucer was at ease with the balanced minds. He sensed the futility of medieval logic in decline, and, referring to Bradwardine, surely knew also of the Augustinian reaction against unfruitful argument in his day. He understood so much of complexity in human nature, and of our place in the universe, that we can see him a respected comedian in company with the best scholastics. And scholasticism can introduce us, in a new way, to comedy. Let us attend, for instance, to the developing thought of Aquinas and, later, of Scotus the Subtle Doctor, on the problem of individuation.

What we at first appreciate in Chaucer's pilgrims is what Scotus would call the *hæcceitas* of each particular person, which is a notion very much newer to the fourteenth century than to us, who have suffered from exaggerating the separate reality of the individual. What we do not readily understand in Chaucer is the *generalizing* power which Blake so finely admired. We could too easily pursue a parallel, once it is pointed out, between the critical development of fourteenth-century thought and the development of Chaucer's own work. When Durandus of Saint-Pourçain replied to the problem of individuation by saying that the individual is given in experience, and that knowledge of particulars is a higher knowledge than the abstract; and when in William of Ockham the knower comes face to face with the known without the Thomist apparatus of knowing in between— something is happening that is related to an abandonment of allegory in literature. But fortunately the old ways are not suddenly forgotten, even when they are changed; and our comedian remains in charity with the angelic doctor.[1] However receptive, he was unshaken by the dangerous tendencies of science or psychology, to which I shall return in a moment. If we eliminate the senses in which all of his work was not religious, there remains a sense in which it is. It could afford, in spite of 'everything', to take immense reserves of conviction, of assurance, for granted. It could occur only in a certain civilization, when that civilization had reached its highest point—and the higher the civilization, the steeper the downward gradient that the civilized think they can stand. So the historian might say, and not without reason; but forgetting that Chaucer is still alive in the mind, and still (Arnold was just again) central. Call this the epitaph of Cambiuskan, but Chaucer's true testimonial: *of his corage as any centre stable.* Chaucer surveyed the world from a centre apparently different from that to which Dante penetrated through and beyond the world; but the centre is the same, of the sphere that Aquinas describes, whose centre is everywhere and circumference nowhere intelligible; and Dante was permitted

---

[1] There is, as I have said, no *Fourteenth-Century Background*; but two recent English publications, with bibliographies, introduce the professional thinkers of the period. These are *A Sketch of Medieval Philosophy* by D. J. B. HAWKINS (Sheed and Ward, 1946), and *A Short History of Western Philosophy in the Middle Ages* by S. J. CURTIS (Macdonald, 1950). Frederick Copleston's *History of Philosophy* Volume II (Burns Oates, 1950) is a fuller survey from Augustine to Scotus, and Volume III will begin with Ockham and the fourteenth century.

to see the whole sphere. In another way Chaucer is central. His mind was at the centre of his humility; and humility, agree Walter Hilton and T. S. Eliot, is endless. In a third way Chaucer is central, between the extremes of life and character which he balanced for comedy. And we have to struggle to the centre he could always find.

Chaucer is living, but we cannot get back to Chaucer. In comparison with America, Lord Russell has assured us, Europe has not entirely lost the medieval tradition; and that may be why scholars inquire more actively in America than in England about the greatest medieval English poet. The belief in the force of human will and energy, which was sown a little before his time, has left him uncorrupted. We should not speak of 'Chaucer's world', for Chaucer is the poet of men humble and happy in God's world. And a study of the changes of fortune of the word *will* can be very improving. It has now degenerated, except in technical usage, to the sense of *drive*—the power that keeps a nose to the grindstone or a nation behind a leader. The violence of modern science, and cinema, is its disease: the present weakness of will. In the fourteenth century it still meant the power of choosing, loving, resting in, the good: and Chaucer's is the last great poetry that accepts this medieval peace. Villon leaves his testament, and the next event is a war of separate wills on the renaissance stage. Later English literature is either comparatively limited in vision, or Manichean in tendency. That is to say, it is inclined either to ignore or to dramatize the black and evil god; and when it dramatizes, to be closer to an over-excited reading of the *Parson's Tale* than to Chaucer. Nobody in his senses will go back five hundred and fifty years as to a golden age, or insist that Shakespeare arrived too late. Shakespeare stands: the middle age had its poet of intensity in Dante. And in Dante the separate human will is subsumed in an endless sounding of *terza rima*. Chaucer is our medieval poet of serenity, a poet *qui fait rire dans l'âme*, and the only one of his stature, I suspect, in whom contentment is not an enemy of genius. I doubt whether anyone has come so near to disproving the view that no major work of art can be produced without the aid of the devil: for to him the devil is finally impotent, and there remain the *clere sterres*.

But the great ironist is too present to allow me to close on a large and distant sentence. Refinement of irony, in the end, depends upon a tone of the voice: and it is a curious fact, or else a very persuasive illusion, that after these five and a half centuries one can hear the tones of certain passages of his poetry as clearly as the tones of the most recent verse in the language. However subtle or complicated medieval art becomes, it is always near to the tongue or the hand or the eye. When we try to get back to original pronunciations of poetry, Shakespeare seems to me to suffer slight pain, as if stored too long in a damp barn; but Chaucer always smiles more. And Chaucer alighting today in London would probably be amused to recognize, in so much that is unrecognizable, a certain vowel sound in Cockney. This is the man who did something for English that Dante did for Italian; the man with the most *art* of any English poet, and the easiest naturalness. So the best 'introduction' to Chaucer is to listen to him, to the English he wrote.

*Now preye I to hem alle that herkne this litel tretys or rede, that if there be anything in it that liketh hem, that therof they thanken our Lord Jesu Christ, of whom procedeth al wit and al goodnesse. And if ther be any thyng that displese hem, I preye hem also that they arrette it to the defaut of my unconnynge, and nat to my wil, that wolde ful fayn have seyd bettre if I hadde had connynge . . .*

# INDEX

*DEO GRATIAS*